GINGERBREAD
and all the trimmings

A Cookbook

Waxahachie Junior Service League, Inc.

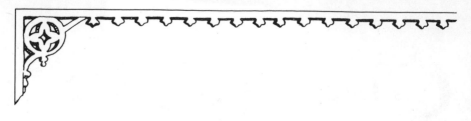

The Waxahachie Junior Service League was founded in 1952 as a non-profit organization whose purpose is to serve the community in a philanthropic manner. The proceeds from the sale of this book will be used to build a handicapped children's playground. We appreciate your support of our organization.

Library of Congress
Catalog Card Number
87-50927
ISBN: 0-9623576-0-X

Additional copies may be obtained at the cost of $13.95 per book, plus $2.00 postage and handling.
Send to:

Waxahachie Junior Service League, Inc.
P.O. Box 294
Waxahachie, Texas 75165

First Printing 1987, 5,000
Second Printing 1989, 5,000
Third Printing 1991, 7,000

Printed in the USA by
WIMMER BROTHERS
A Wimmer Company
Memphis • Dallas • San Antonio

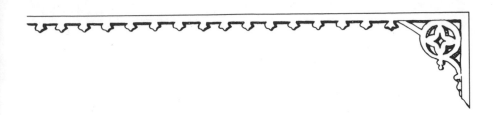

GINGERBREAD...and all the trimmings

Gingerbread is more than just a spicy dessert cake to the women of the Waxahachie Junior Service League. We live in the Gingerbread City—a city filled with large old homes trimmed with the intricate woodwork popular around the turn of the century. The lacey screens, carved finials, spindlework, fishscale shingles, cupolas, turrets, gables, and ornate towers are what is called gingerbread trim. In the Victorian Era, our little Texas town, just thirty miles south of Dallas, was a bustling cotton center that many people referred to as the Cotton Capital of the World. Waxahachie attracted the cotton industry's leading citizens—they brought their families to our town and indulged themselves with large, ornately trimmed homes. We have highlighted some of these homes in the pages of our cookbook.

Just as our fine old homes in Waxahachie have all the trimmings, so does our cookbook. We have included recipes which may be familiar to you as well as some which were passed down to us by our aunties or grannies. We hope that you will enjoy our book and that you will find in its pages a special recipe or two that will become your family's favorites.

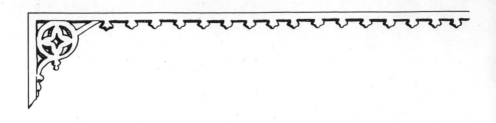

Cookbook Committee

Helen Mitchell, Chairman
Sharon Boone
Cindy Camp
Cathy Moore
Rikki Morrow
Sara Willis

Past Chairmen
Rikki Morrow
Susan Holey
Karen Ballard
Pam Jenkins
Delaina Wimpee

The Cookbook Committee would like to thank all the club members for their participation in testing and proofing the following recipes.

Artwork for the front and back covers as well as pen and ink drawings of homes in Waxahachie were drawn by Priscilla Parker, D.D.S. Dr. Parker grew up in Illinois, attended Illinois Wesleyan University and Baylor College of Dentistry. She received her Masters degree in Pediatric Dentistry from Baylor University. She practices in Waxahachie where she is an active member in the Waxahachie Junior Service League. She is married with two children.

Table of Contents

The Shackelford Home was built in 1894 at the cost of $1350.00. Mr. E. H. Griffin, a prominent local businessman and developer, chose to build his home on a site just two blocks from the trolley line that ran from downtown out to Marvin College. The modified L-plan home is in the Eastlake Victorian style and features a 5-bay porch and weatherboard siding. The irregularly shaped hip roof, delicate jig-sawn and turned bargeboards, cornice brackets, and porch posts are characteristic of this style.

APPETIZERS AND BEVERAGES

Blackeyed Pea Dip

4 cups blackeyed peas, drained
(2 cans)
3-5 jalapeño peppers, finely
chopped
1 tablespoon jalapeño juice
½ medium onion, chopped
1 (4-ounce) can green chilies,
chopped
1 clove garlic, crushed
½ pound Old English sharp
cheese, grated
½ pound butter

Mix all ingredients except cheese and butter in a saucepan. Heat slightly. In a double boiler melt cheese and butter. Add to pea mixture and serve in a chafing dish with large fritos or doritos.

Use mild peppers if you wish.

Mrs. Ron Johnson (Sharon)

Broccoli Dip Appetizer

2 packages chopped frozen
broccoli
¼ cup butter (I use margarine)
1 onion chopped
1 (4-ounce) can chopped
mushroom pieces
2 rolls Kraft garlic cheese
1 can condensed mushroom
soup

Cook broccoli according to directions. Drain completely. In top of double boiler, melt butter and sauté the onion and mushroom until the onion is soft. Add the broccoli, cheese, and mushroom soup. Mix together. Cook on low heat until the cheese is melted. Serve with your favorite chip. Serves 8-10.

Mrs. Cullen Eubank (Mary Pat)

Cheese Dip

1 stick Cracker Barrel
cheese—grated
2 (8-ounce) cream cheese
1 package bologna—chopped
2 cans chopped black olives
1 bottle green salad olives
1 can diced pimento
Mayonnaise

Mix well.

Delicious!

Mrs. Don Nelson (Judy)

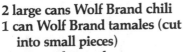

Chili Dip

2 large cans Wolf Brand chili
1 can Wolf Brand tamales (cut
    into small pieces)
1 onion, chopped
2 tablespoons butter
1 pound Velveeta cheese

In top of double boiler, cook onion in butter until soft. Add rest of the ingredients and cook on low heat until hot and the cheese melts. Serve with large size fritos or doritos.

Mrs. Cullen Eubank (Mary Pat)

Chili Con Queso Dip

1 can mushroom soup
1 can celery soup
1 roll garlic cheese
1 roll jalapeño cheese
1 pound ground beef
2 small cans green chili peppers
    (mild)
1 can Rotel tomatoes

Put soup and cheese in double boiler until melted. Brown hamburger meat until redness is gone. Add hamburger meat, green chilies and Rotel tomatoes. Serve with chips.

To make less hot, for instance for children to enjoy, omit half the green chilies and use only half the can of Rotel tomatoes. Add a roll of regular cheddar cheese.

Mrs. Mike Hayes (Eva)

Cucumber Dip

1 cucumber
½ cup sour cream
2 (8-ounce) cream cheese
Dash salt, pepper, tabasco,
    Worcestershire sauce,
    grated onion, lemon juice

Cut off ends of cucumber, scrub—then grate with peel on. Let drain, discard juice.

Soften cream cheese and beat in electric mixer, add sour cream gradually, then add cucumbers and seasonings. Can be prepared 24 hours ahead. Serve with potato chips or crackers.

Mrs. Robert M. Cox (Dee)

Guacamole

4-5 avocados
1 onion, diced
1 tomato, diced
1 clove garlic, crushed
1 tablespoon olive oil
1 tablespoon lemon juice
2-3 tablespoons picante sauce
Salt to taste

Mash avocados in a bowl. Add onion, tomato and garlic. Mash again. Stir in olive oil, lemon juice, picante sauce and salt. Serve with chips. Serves 6.

Mrs. F.A. Blankenbeckler III (Alice)

Hamburger Dip

1 pound ground beef
½ onion, diced
1 (8-ounce) cream cheese
1 (8-ounce) tomato sauce
Salt, pepper, garlic to taste
Mushrooms (small can, drained)

Brown the ground meat in a small amount of cooking oil along with the diced onion. Add the cream cheese and stir until melted. Add the remaining ingredients and simmer for 15 minutes. Serve warm with chips. Serves 4-6.

Mrs. Stan Parker (Priscilla)

Hot Crab Dip

6 tablespoons butter
6 tablespoons flour
1 onion, chopped
3 tablespoons chopped pimento or green pepper
1½ cups half and half
2 small cans button mushrooms, drained into 1 cup chicken broth to make 1½ cups with mushroom juice
⅓ pound (5 wedges) Gruyere cheese, grated
¼ pound parmesan cheese
Salt, cayenne pepper, tabasco, Worcestershire sauce, lemon juice to taste
2 (7-ounce) cans crab meat

Melt butter in large skillet. Stir in flour and cook 5 minutes. Add onion and pepper. Slowly stir in cream. Add broth. When smooth, add grated cheese. Season with salt, cayenne pepper, tabasco, Worchestershire sauce and lemon juice. Fold in crab meat.

Freezes well.

Mrs. Jeff Kosoris (Susan)

Sea Captain's Crab Dip
from Myrtle Beach, S.C.

1 can crabmeat, drained,
   cleaned and flaked
1¼ cups mayonnaise
½ cup sharp cheddar cheese,
   grated
4 tablespoons French dressing
2 teaspoons horseradish
Juice of ½ lemon

Mix all ingredients and chill. Great with Wheatbury crackers. Makes about 2 cups.

Mrs. Jim Jenkins (Pam)

Hot Creole Dip

1 pound ground beef
4 green onions, chopped
1 green bell pepper, chopped
1 stalk celery, chopped
2 tablespoons margarine
2 pounds Velveeta
4 ounces pimento, chopped
4 tablespoons chili powder
¼ teaspoon garlic powder
Tabasco, salt, pepper to taste

Brown meat. Sauté onion, pepper and celery in margarine. Melt cheese. Add all other ingredients to the cheese and pour into a large baking dish. Bake 300° for 2½ hours. Serve with fritos or melba toast.

Mrs. Pleasant Mitchell (Helen)

Delicious Dip for Fruit

2 cups marshmallow cream
1 (8-ounce) package soft cream
   cheese
1 tablespoon grated orange rind
Dash ginger

Combine marshmallow cream and cream cheese in bowl. Mix well. Add remaining ingredients, blending well. Serve with fresh fruit. Approximately 48 servings (dips).

Mrs. Lonell Wilson (Betty)

11

Deviled Dip

1 (5-ounce) jar pimento
cheese spread
1 (2-ounce) can deviled ham
½ cup salad dressing
2 tablespoons parsley
1 tablespoon onion
4 drops tabasco sauce

Mix cheese, deviled ham, and salad dressing. Chop parsley and onion and mix with cheese mixture. Add tabasco and mix well. Makes 1½ cups.

Mrs. Bill Price (Kay)

Mexican Hamburger Dip

1 pound ground beef
1 pound can whole peeled
tomatoes diced, plus juice
1 small onion, chopped
¾ cup pimento, chopped
1 (2½-ounce) package sliced
almonds
1 teaspoon salt
1 teaspoon pepper
¼ teaspoon garlic powder or
2 cloves garlic pressed
1 (6-ounce) can tomato paste
½ teaspoon oregano
1-2 jalapeño peppers, chopped
¾ cup water
½ cup water chestnuts,
chopped

Brown ground beef—pour off grease. Add all ingredients except almonds and water chestnuts and simmer. Just before serving, add almonds and chestnuts. Should be kept hot while serving.

Substitutions:
*½ pound sausage and ½ pound
ground beef*
*white seedless grapes in place of water
chestnuts — gives sweet and sour
effect.*

*This dip freezes well and can be made
ahead of time.*

Mrs. Erling Holey (Susan)

Nacho Cheese Dip

1 pound ground beef
1 small onion, chopped
1 pound sausage (Owens,
Jimmy Dean)
2 pounds Velveeta cheese (or
any easy melting cheese)
Dash Worcestershire sauce
1 small can chopped green
chilies *or* ½ cup chopped
jalapeños
1 teaspoon salt (optional)

Brown ground beef with onion. Drain and set aside. Brown sausage and drain. Combine beef and sausage with cheese, Worcestershire and chilies. Heat in double boiler or microwave until cheese is melted. Stir well. Serve warm with chips and vegetable slices.

Mrs. Roy Marchbanks (Pam)

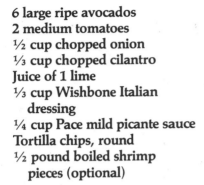

Pica De Gallo

6 large ripe avocados
2 medium tomatoes
½ cup chopped onion
⅓ cup chopped cilantro
Juice of 1 lime
⅓ cup Wishbone Italian
   dressing
¼ cup Pace mild picante sauce
Tortilla chips, round
½ pound boiled shrimp
   pieces (optional)

Cut tomatoes and avocados into bite size pieces. Reserve seeds. Dice onion, but not really fine. Chop cilantro using part of the stems. Combine all ingredients together; season to taste with salt and pepper. Set the reserved avocado seeds in the salad until ready to serve. This will help prevent browning of the avocados. Serve as a dip with preferably round tortilla chips because this is a chunky dip. If made too far ahead of time the avocados may brown.

Cilantro is a leafy vegetable that looks just like parsley, but has a different odor. Wonderful in Mexican dishes and ranch or pinto beans. When preparing, chop stems and all. Not available at all groceries.

Mrs. Dennis Horak (Barbara Sue)

 A warm lemon will yield much more juice than a cold one.

Sausage Cheese Dip

2 pounds hot bulk sausage
2 pounds Velveeta cheese
1 large can evaporated milk
1 package dry garlic salad
   dressing mix
Tabasco sauce to taste

Crumble and fry sausage until done. Drain on paper towel. Melt cheese in a double boiler to avoid scorching. Combine cheese and sausage in a large crock pot. Stir in evaporated milk and blend well. Add remaining ingredients. Dip with doritos.

Mrs. Ron Johnson (Sharon)

Shrimp Dip

4 tablespoons milk
1 cup mayonnaise
1 tablespoon Worcestershire
   sauce
Dash garlic salt
1 small onion
1 (5-ounce) can shrimp, drained
½ pound cheddar cheese,
   cubed
3 drops tabasco sauce

Put ingredients in blender in order given. Cover and run at high speed until well blended. Chill. Serve as dip for crackers or potato chips. This is "better the 2nd day."

Mrs. Steve Kelley (Cindy)

Tuna Dip

2 (6½-ounce) cans tuna
2 cups sour cream
1 package dry onion soup mix
1 teaspoon hot pepper sauce

Combine all ingredients and chill.

Mrs. Bill Price (Kay)

Vegetable Dip

1 package onion soup mix
1 pint sour cream
¼ cup finely chopped, pared
   cucumber
¼ cup finely chopped green
   pepper
¼ cup finely diced pimento

Combine all ingredients. Chill at least an hour to blend flavor.

Mrs. Erling Holey (Susan)

 To freshen up old unpopped popcorn, add a few drops of water and shake. Then pop. Then extra moisture helps you get bigger, fluffier kernels.

Wendy's Taco Layered Dip

2 cans jalapeño bean dip
3 avocados, mashed
2 teaspoons lemon juice
½ teaspoon salt
Dash pepper
1 cup sour cream
½ cup mayonnaise
1 package taco seasoning
1 large bunch green onions,
  chopped
1 (7-ounce) can black olives,
  sliced
8 tomatoes, chopped
1 (8-ounce) shredded sharp
  cheese

1st layer—jalapeño bean dip

2nd layer—avocados, lemon juice, salt and pepper

3rd layer—sour cream, mayonnaise, taco seasoning

4th layer—green onions, black olives, tomatoes

5th layer—cheese

Layer in a round or rectangular pan.

Mrs. Gary Morrow (Rikki)

Bacon Roll-Ups

2 (3-ounce) cream cheese with
  chives, softened
1 tablespoon milk or
  mayonnaise
25 slices bacon, cut in half
25 slices whole grain sandwich
  bread, crust removed and
  cut in half
Parsley sprigs to garnish
Toothpicks

Combine cream cheese and mayonnaise until spreading consistency. Spread 1 scant teaspoon of cream cheese mixture on each slice of bread and roll up tightly. Wrap each with bacon, securing with toothpick. Place roll ups on a broiler pan. Bake 350° for 30 minutes, turning as necessary to prevent over browning.

Note: *May be assembled and frozen. Thaw out overnight in refrigerator. Bake 350° for 30-40 minutes.*

Mrs. Lonell Wilson (Betty)

Beef Log

2 (8-ounce) packages cream
cheese
2 jars dried beef, chopped
2 teaspoons Worcestershire
2 teaspoons Accent
½ cup green tops of onions

Mix all ingredients, except ⅓ cup beef. Form into a log. Top with remaining beef.

Mrs. Jim Jenkins (Pam)

Sweet and Sour Chicken Wings

5 pounds chicken wings or
drumettes
4 eggs, beaten
2 cups cornstarch
½ cup vegetable oil
2 teaspoons garlic salt
1 teaspoon freshly ground
pepper
1 teaspoon salt

Sauce:
½ cup chicken stock
1 cup sugar
1 cup cider vinegar
6 tablespoons catsup
2 tablespoons soy sauce
2 teaspoons salt

Preheat oven to 350°. Cut each chicken wing into 3 sections. Reserve the wing tips to make stock. Dip the other chicken pieces in beaten eggs. Roll each piece in cornstarch and fry until golden brown. Transfer chicken to baking dishes. Mix garlic salt, pepper and salt together and sprinkle evenly over chicken. Serves 12.

Sauce: Combine the ingredients and pour over chicken. Bake for 30 minutes.

Note: *This can be made up to 3 days ahead. Reheat before serving.*

Mrs. William H. Atkinson (Pam)

Crab Canapé

1 (7-ounce) can crab meat
1 tablespoon chopped green
onion
1 cup shredded Swiss cheese
½ cup mayonnaise
¼ teaspoon curry powder
½ teaspoon salt
1 teaspoon lemon juice
1 (8-ounce) can sliced water
chestnuts
2 cans tenderflake biscuits

Preheat overn to 400°. Grease baking sheet. Combine ingredients and mix well. Separate biscuits and spoon small amount of mixture on top. Bake 12 minutes or until puffed and brown.

Mrs. Roy Worthington (Beverly)

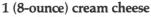

Crab and Crackers

1 (8-ounce) cream cheese
1 bottle Kraft pimento spread
1 bottle cocktail sauce (divided)
2 tablespoons minced onion
1 can crab meat

Mix cream cheese, pimento spread, 2 tablespoons cocktail sauce and onions. Spread on a plate to thickness of about ½-¾ inch. Spread all but 3 tablespoons of remaining cocktail sauce over cheese mixture. Top with crab meat and drizzle remaining sauce over the crab. May be decorated with parsley. Serve with crackers.

Mrs. Homer Denning (Linda)

Oyster Appetizer

½ cup butter
1 cup chopped parsley
1½ cups chopped green onions
2 cups oysters (about 1½ pints)
1 cup Italian bread crumbs
1 teaspoon mild hot sauce

Melt butter. Sauté parlsey and onions. Drain oysters. Add to onion mixture and cook about 3 minutes, or until oysters curl. Add bread crumbs and hot sauce and toss to cover. Serve on Triscuits. Serves 8-10.

Mrs. Pleasant Mitchell (Helen)

Alice Zackry's Shrimp Mousse

1 can Campbell's tomato soup
1 package Knox gelatin
¼ cup cold water
1 (8-ounce) package cream
    cheese
1 cup mayonnaise
½ cup chopped celery
½ cup chopped green pepper
½ cup chopped Bermuda
    onion
1 small can shrimp

In sauce pan heat tomato soup, undiluted. To hot soup, add gelatin which has been softened in cold water. Cool. Beat cream cheese until smooth. Add mayonnaise, celery, green pepper, onion and shrimp. Turn into 4-cup mold. Prepare the day before. Surround with crackers.

Mrs. Pat Gardenhire (Susan)

Cracker Snack

1 cup oil
4 tablespoons dill weed
1 package Hidden Valley salad
   dressing mix (milk—not
   buttermilk)
1 (24-ounce) box oyster
   crackers, (without salt)

Mix all together, drain on paper towels, and store in covered container.

Mrs. Griggs DeHay (Gay)

Cheese Olives

2 cups grated cheddar cheese
½ cup butter, softened
1 cup flour
½ teaspoon salt
1 teaspoon paprika
Dash cayenne
48 pimento-stuffed olives,
   drained on paper towel

Cream cheese with butter. Mix cayenne, paprika and salt with flour; add to cheese mixture. Mix well. Roll 1 teaspoon cheese dough around each olive, covering completely. Freeze. (Can be frozen up to 2 weeks.) When ready to serve, place on cookie sheet and bake 15 minutes at 400°.

Mrs. Jack Curlin (Nelda)

Melted Cheese Pastry Appetizer

1 can Pillsbury crescent rolls
1 (8-ounce) round of Gouda
   cheese (room temperature)
Butter
Mustard

Divide sheet of rolls into 2 sheets of 4. Flatten and smooth out perforations. Place cheese in middle of 1 sheet. Fold corners over top of cheese and invert over other sheet of rolls. Again bring corners over cheese. Smooth pastry around cheese. Bake at 375-400° until brown. Top with a few pats of butter. Serve with your favorite mustard and crackers.

This is an extremely simple appetizer that appears elegant (and much more difficult to prepare!!)

Mrs. Ben Boone (Sharon)

Mrs. Cook's Cheddar Cheese Wafers

1 stick soft margarine
2 cups grated sharp cheese
1 cup flour
½ teaspoon salt
½ teaspoon baking powder
½ teaspoon red pepper
½ teaspoon chili pepper
2 cups rice crispies

Mix together with fork and form into small fat cookies. Bake on ungreased cookie sheet 10-15 minutes at 350°. Makes 2 dozen.

Mrs. Robert M. Cox (Dee)

Jezebel Sauce

1 (10-ounce) jar apple jelly
1 (10-ounce) jar pineapple
  preserves
1 small jar creamed horseradish
Cream cheese
Assorted crackers

Mix in blender or processor until smooth. Make a day ahead so flavors can blend. Store in refrigerator up to 2 months. Serve over cream cheese with crackers.

Mrs. Lonell Wilson (Betty)

Festive Meatballs

1 pound lean ground beef
½ cup finely crushed bread
  crumbs
1 clove garlic, crushed
2 tablespoons finely chopped
  parsley
¼ cup evaporated milk
1 egg, slightly beaten
½ teaspoon salt
Flour
2 tablespoons oil
1 (7-ounce) can green chili salsa
1 cup beef bouillon

Mix beef with crumbs, garlic, parsley, milk, egg and salt. Form into about 30 small balls; roll in flour. Brown in hot oil; pour off any excess fat. Pour salsa and boullion over meat balls; cover and simmer 10 minutes. Serve on toothpicks or thicken sauce and serve as a main dish.

Mrs. Clovis Mitchell (Omajeanne)

Sweet 'N Sour Meatballs

Meatballs:
1 pound lean ground beef
¾ cup minced celery
¼ cup chopped almonds
1 clove garlic, minced
1 teaspoon salt
½ cup soft bread crumbs
1 teaspoon soy sauce
2 eggs, slightly beaten
½ teaspoon pepper

Sauce:
1 cup chicken bouillon
½ cup sugar
3 tablespoons cornstarch
½ cup pineapple juice (reserved
   from pineapple chunks)
½ cup vinegar
2 tablespoons soy sauce
1 green pepper, chopped
1 (8-ounce) can pineapple
   chunks

Meatballs: In large bowl thoroughly mix all ingredients. Form into small meatballs. Brown meatballs and drain on paper towels.

Sauce: In saucepan, add bouillon, sugar, cornstarch, pineapple juice, vinegar, and soy sauce. Over medium heat, stir for 3 minutes or until thickened. Add green pepper, pineapple chunks and meatballs. Simmer for 15 minutes. Serves 10.

Mrs. William H. Atkinson (Pam)

Pickled Mushrooms

2 (6-ounce) jars button
   mushrooms
½ cup mushroom broth
½ cup tarragon vinegar
½ cup dark brown sugar
¼ teaspoon salt
½ teaspoon whole pepper
   corns
1 bay leaf
1 sliced garlic clove

Combine all ingredients except mushrooms and bring to a boil. Pour over mushrooms. Cover and refrigerate 24 hours.

Mrs. Jack Curlin (Nelda)

Fried Mushrooms

1 package whole mushrooms,
   washed and drained
½ cup flour
1 beaten egg
2 teaspoons lemon juice
1 cup regular canned bread
   crumbs

Coat mushrooms in flour. Mix beaten egg and lemon juice together. Dip mushrooms in egg-lemon and coat in bread crumbs. Deep fry till golden brown.

Horseradish Dip

1 cup sour cream
2 teaspoons lemon juice
Horseradish to taste

Mix above ingredients. Serve with hot fried mushrooms.

Mrs. Mike Hayes (Eva)

Stuffed Mushrooms

3 strips bacon
½ cup finely chopped celery
½ cup finely chopped green
   onion
¼ cup salted sunflower seeds
½ can (4½-ounce) ripe olives,
   chopped
½ teaspoon Lawry's seasoned
   salt
Dash pepper
1 teaspoon parsley flakes
Velveeta cheese, cut into
   1 inch cubes
2½ dozen large mushrooms
   (silver dollar, cleaned and
   drained, stems removed
   and set aside)

Fry bacon. Drain. Set aside. Reserve 2 teaspoons drippings. Add to drippings: celery, onions, sunflower seeds, olives, salt, pepper, and parsley. Add bacon and chopped mushroom stems. Sauté until tender. Place in each mushroom cap a small chunk of cheese, then stuff with the sautéed vegetables. Place in oven till hot and mushrooms begin to get tender. Makes 2 dozen.

Mrs. Dennis Horak (Barbara Sue)

Stuffed Mushrooms

36 large mushrooms
3 tablespoons butter
6 tablespoons chopped dry
　parsley
6 teaspoons grated onion
1 package frozen spinach
　soufflé, baked

Wash mushrooms—pat dry. Remove and chop stems. Sauté mushrooms, including stems, in butter. Remove mushrooms. Leave stems and add parsley and onion. Cook 3 minutes. Mix with frozen spinach soufflé that is almost done. Fill caps. Broil for 5 minutes before serving. May be prepared hours ahead and broiled at last minute.

Mrs. Jack Curlin (Nelda)

Rolled Tortillas

3 (8-ounce) packages cream
　cheese, softened
1 pint sour cream
1 small onion, grated
5 jalapeño peppers, finely
　chopped
Juice of ½ lime
20 flour tortillas
Bottled hot sauce

Mix all ingredients except tortillas and hot sauce. Steam tortillas or place in microwave to soften; 3 tortillas, 25 seconds. (I find it much easier to have package of flour tortillas at room temperature than to steam or heat.) Spread cheese mixture on tortillas. Roll and chill. Cut into bite-sized pieces. Serve with toothpicks. Dip in picante sauce.

Mrs. Roy Worthington (Beverly)

Sausage Pinwheels

2 cups flour
½ teaspoon salt
3 teaspoons baking powder
⅔ cup milk
4 tablespoons shortening
1 pound sausage (room
  temperature)

Mix all ingredients but sausage. Divide dough in half and roll to ⅛ inch thickness. Spread ½ of sausage on to dough. After covering dough begin at one end and roll up tightly. Wrap in wax paper. Freeze 2 hours. Slice about ½ inch thick and bake at 400° for 20-25 minutes. Repeat these steps for second roll.

Mrs. Bobby Oliver (Emily)

Spinach Balls

2 (10-ounce) packages frozen
  spinach
2 cups herb-seasoned stuffing
  mix
2 medium onions, finely
  chopped
½ cup parmesan cheese, grated
2 teaspoons garlic salt
1 teaspoon thyme
1 teaspoon black pepper
¾ cup butter or oleo
5 large eggs

Cook spinach according to package directions, omitting salt. Drain thoroughly. Pat dry with paper towels. Add next 6 ingredients. Mix with fork until thoroughly mixed. Add butter and then beaten eggs. Blend with fork. Form into balls the size of a walnut. Bake on greased, shallow pan 18-20 minutes at 350°.

Mrs. Lonell Wilson (Betty)

Stuffed Jalapeños

3 (2-ounce) jars pickled
  jalapeño peppers
2 cups grated cheese
1 (8-ounce) Philadelphia cream
  cheese
2 green onions, chopped with
  tops

Slice jalapeños lengthwise in half. Mix cheese, cream cheese and onions. Stuff halves. Bake at 350° for 5-10 minutes or until bubbly.

Mrs. Ken Box (Dietra)

Cheese Ball

1 pound cheddar cheese
1 pound cream cheese
1 tablespoon mustard
1 tablespoon onion salt
1 tablespoon Worcestershire
  sauce
¼ teaspoon garlic salt
Dash of tabasco sauce
½ cup pecans, chopped
  finely
Parsley

Grate cheddar cheese and blend with cream cheese by hand. Add mustard, onion salt, Worcestershire, garlic salt, and a dash of tabasco sauce. Mix well and form into ball. Roll ball in pecans and parsley, if desired.

Mrs. Bobby Oliver (Emily)

Johnnie Lee's Cheese Ball

3 small packages Old English
  cheese
3 small packages cream
  cheese
½ pound Roch or blue
  cheese
1 large onion
1 pound pecans
Parsley

Soften cheeses and mix together. Grind pecans and onions twice and add to cheese mixture. Roll into ball. Roll in chopped fresh or dried parsley. Roll in wax paper and keep in refrigerator until you are ready to serve. Can be frozen for future use.

Mrs. Clovis Mitchell (Omajeanne)

Swiss Almond Cheese Ball

1 (6-8 ounces) Swiss cheese
1 (8-ounce) softened cream
  cheese
3 tablespoons butter
½ teaspoon almond extract
2 tablespoons Amaretto
  liqueur
1 (1½-ounce) package sliced
  almonds
Crackers

Use steel blade of food processor. Start with Swiss cheese and process ingredients in order listed. Form into ball or oval shape and chill before serving with crackers.

Mrs. Donald Locke (Marilyn)

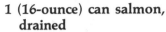

Smoky Salmon Ball

1 (16-ounce) can salmon,
  drained
1 (8-ounce) cream cheese,
  softened
1 medium onion, chopped
1 teaspoon pickle relish
1 teaspoon liquid smoke
½ teaspoon lemon juice
½ cup chopped nuts

Combine first 6 ingredients. Place mixture on plastic wrap and form into a ball. Chill overnight. Several hours before serving, roll in chopped nuts.

Mrs. Bill Price (Kay)

Avocado Spread

1 (8-ounce) package cream
  cheese
1 (8-ounce) bottle hot or
  mild taco sauce
1 avocado; seeded, peeled,
  and chopped
1-2 tablespoons lemon juice
Tortilla chips

Whip cream cheese with 3 table-spoons taco sauce; spread in a circle on a large platter. Sprinkle chopped avocado generously with lemon juice to prevent browning; place on top of cream cheese. Drizzle with additional taco sauce and serve with tortilla chips. Serves 6.

Mrs. Pete Cunningham (Martha)

Bacon Almond Spread

4 strips crisp bacon,
  crumbled
¼ cup slivered almonds,
  browned in bacon grease
1 cup grated cheddar cheese
3 green onions, chopped
½ cup mayonnaise
¼ teaspoon salt
¼ teaspoon pepper

Mix well and chill. Spread on Ritz crackers and either microwave on high one minute or bake 3-4 minutes at 350° to melt the cheese. Yields 1¼ cups.

Mrs. Pleasant Mitchell (Helen)

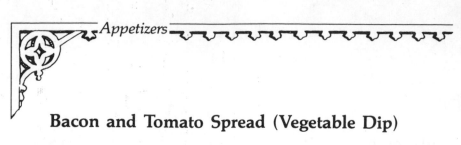

Bacon and Tomato Spread (Vegetable Dip)

1 (8-ounce) package cream cheese, softened
2 teaspoons prepared mustard
½ teaspoon celery salt
6 slices crisp bacon, crumbled
1 medium tomato, peeled, seeded, and finely chopped
¼ cup finely chopped green pepper
Vegetables such as celery, carrots, cucumbers, and green onion to dip

Stir together cream cheese, mustard, and celery salt. Stir in bacon, tomato, and green pepper. Cover and chill. Serve with vegetables. Makes 2 cups.

Mrs. Randy Owens (Liz)

Hot Beef Spread

1 (8-ounce) cream cheese
2 tablespoons milk
1 (2½-ounce) package dried beef, chopped
¼ cup finely chopped green pepper
2 tablespoons dried onion flakes
½ teaspoon garlic salt
¼ teaspoon pepper
½ cup sour cream
½ cup coarsley chopped pecans
2 tablespoons butter
½ teaspoon salt

Combine cheese, milk, beef, green pepper, onion flakes and seasoning. Fold in sour cream. Spoon into 8-inch pie plate or small baking dish. Heat and crisp pecans in butter. Salt them. Spread pecans on top of cheese mixture. Bake at 350° for 20 minutes. Serve with crackers.

Mrs. Randall Klein (Louise)

Cream Cheese Spread

1 tablespoon Lawry's garlic
   spread
1 (8-ounce) package cream
   cheese
1 tablespoon milk
1/8 teaspoon tabasco sauce

Melt garlic spread. Set aside. Whip together cream cheese, milk, and tabasco sauce. Blend in garlic spread.

Mrs. Bill Getzendaner (Betty)

Sandwich Spread

2 (8-ounce) packages
   cream cheese
Milk
1 jar maraschino cherries,
   (reserve juice)

Soften 2 (8-ounce) packages cream cheese with milk and cherry juice. Add chopped marachino cherries to taste. Spread on thin sliced wheat bread.

Note: *Good to use on decorator cut-out shaped sandwiches.*

Mrs. B.D. Cope (Charlene)

Shrimp Spread

2 cans small shrimp
Bottle French dressing
1 teaspoon grated onions
3 boiled eggs, chopped
Mayonnaise

Marinate shrimp overnight in French dressing. Next day, drain and mash shrimp. Add chopped eggs and onion. Add mayonnaise to spread for consistency desired. Keeps up to 5 days in refrigerator.

Mrs. Lonell Wilson (Betty)

Banana Punch

2 large bananas
2 cups sugar
2 packages unsweetened
  Kool-aid (any flavor)
1 (46-ounce) can pineapple
  juice
½ gallon water

Crush bananas in blender. Add all ingredients together. Freeze overnight. Thaw and serve as slush. Makes 1 gallon. Serves 12-15.

Note: *Wild Berry flavor Kool-aid is excellent in this.*

Mrs. Griggs DeHay (Gay)

Banana Slush Punch

6 cups water
4 cups sugar
1 (48-ounce) can pineapple
  juice
1 (48-ounce) can orange juice
Juice of 4 lemons
5 bananas (put through
  blender)
2-3 liter bottles of ginger ale

Heat water and sugar until dissolved. Cool. Mix with other ingredients. Freeze in rings until needed. Allow to thaw 2 or 3 hours before using. Place in punch bowl and add 2 bottles of ginger ale. Stir until "slushy." Serves 20-30.

Mrs. Alvis Bynum (Jimmie Faye)

Bug Juice

(Equal amount of)
Grape Juice
Lemonade
Orange Juice

Mix together and chill. A good way to get rid of that little juice left over. Very refreshing.

Mrs. Dwight Esselman (Ann)

Diet Punch

1 (48-ounce) can pineapple
   juice (unsweetened)
1 quart diet 7-up
1 large can frozen orange juice
   (undiluted)

Combine all ingredients. Serve with ice ring. Serves 10-12.

Mrs. Gary Morrow (Rikki)

Fruit Punch

1 (32-ounce) bottle Cranberry
   juice cocktail
1½ cup sugar
1 (32-ounce) can pineapple
   grapefruit juice
2 quarts ginger ale

Mix first 3 ingredients. Put in punch bowl. Add chilled ginger ale. Serves 32.

Mrs. Ken Box (Dietra)

Kool-Aid Slush Punch

1 quart pineapple juice
1 (12-ounce) can frozen
   orange juice
1 large package Kool-Aid
   (whatever color you desire)
½ cup sugar
2 quarts ginger ale

Mix together the pineapple juice, orange juice, and Kool-Aid. Add sugar and enough water to fill a gallon jug. Shake and freeze. Take out of freezer a couple of hours before ready to use. Put in punch bowl and mash with a potato masher to make slush. Add ginger ale. Serves 12-15.

An easy, do-ahead recipe. A nice break from colas.

Mrs. Lonell Wilson (Betty)

Party Punch

3 pints boiling water
5 pounds sugar
2 ounces citric acid (drug store)
1 ounce tartaric acid
1 tablespoon epsom salt
6 lemons - squeeze juice and grate peel
3 oranges - squeeze juice and grate peel
Pineapple juice
Ginger ale

Boil water. Add sugar, citric acid, tartaric acid, epsom salt, lemons and oranges, and cook until dissolved. This makes a syrup. Finish with pineapple juice and ginger ale. (Makes 15 to 16 cups of syrup.) 1 cup syrup = 24 cups punch.

(For 100 cups punch, add 8 large cans pineapple juice and 4 large ginger ales to 4 cups syrup.) Serves 100+.

Mrs. Bill Major (Patsy)

Slush Punch

3 small packages jello (any flavor)
4 cups sugar
1 ounce almond extract
1 (8-ounce) lemon juice
2 (48-ounce) cans pineapple juice
2 quarts chilled ginger ale

Mix 3 packages jello in 9 cups boiling water - set aside. Make a syrup using 4 cups sugar, 4 cups boiling water and 1 ounce almond flavoring. Mix together the 2 batches above. Add 8 ounces lemon juice and 2 large cans pineapple juice. Freeze until solid. 2 hours before serving, take out the slush mix. (You may want to use a fork and break up the mix.) Add chilled ginger ale at the time of serving. Serves 50.

Mrs. Dennis Horak (Barbara Sue)

Sparkling Pink Punch

3 tablespoons red hot
  cinnamon candies
¼ cup sugar
½ cup warm water
1 (46-ounce) can pineapple
  juice, chilled
1 quart ginger ale, chilled

Cook candies, sugar and water together over low heat, stirring constantly until candies are dissolved. Cool. Combine with pineapple juice and ginger ale. Serves 10-12.

Mrs. Robert M. Cox (Dee)

Hot Chocolate Mix

1 (8-quart) package powdered
  milk
1 (8-ounce) jar Cremora
1 pound box powdered sugar
1 pound can Hershey's instant
  cocoa mix

Mix all ingredients and store in large container. Use ⅓ to ½ cup mixture and add hot water to make a cup of hot chocolate. This recipe makes a lot—enough to share with a friend.

Mrs. Griggs DeHay (Gay)

Spiced Cider

1 gallon apple cider
1 quart ginger ale
5 cinnamon sticks
24 whole cloves
1 cup red hots

Put apple cider and ginger ale in large perculator. Put cinnamon sticks, cloves, and red hots in the perculator basket. Perk like coffee. Divide in half for smaller coffee pot. Serve warm. Serves 20. Can be served over ice in warm weather.

Mrs. Gary Morrow (Rikki)

Hot Spiced Apple Cider

2 quarts apple cider
½ cup brown sugar
¼ teaspoon salt
1 teaspoon whole allspice
1 teaspoon whole cloves
1 (3-inch) cinnamon stick
   Dash of nutmeg

Mix all in medium saucepan. Simmer 20 minutes. Remove spices and serve. Serves 10.

Mrs. Jim Beller (Linda)

Wassail

1 gallon apple cider
2 cups pineapple juice
2 cups orange juice
Juice of 2 lemons
1½ cups sugar
8 whole cloves
2 sticks of cinnamon

Combine all juices and sugar in a 2 gallon pan. Put cloves and cinnamon sticks into a small mesh bag and add to juice mixture. Heat slowly over a low burner until steamy hot. Serve in cups. Serves 10-12.

Great for holidays!

Mrs. Kirk Brown (Ellen)

Hot Spiced Drink

1 (48-ounce) can cranapple
   juice
1 (48-ounce) can pineapple
   juice
½ teaspoon whole cloves
4 cinnamon sticks (2-inch)

Simmer about 5 minutes. Serve in cups with (fresh) new tall cinnamon sticks. Serves 12-15.

Mrs. Jim Jenkins (Pam)

Christmas Spiced Tea

16 cups hot water
7 small tea bags
1 (48-ounce) can pineapple
    juice
2 (6-ounce) cans undiluted
    frozen orange juice
Juice of 2 lemons
2 cups sugar
12 cloves
6 cinnamon sticks

Divide water and make tea. Combine all ingredients in a large pot. Boil slightly. Serve hot. (Makes 5 quarts). Serves 20. Festive!

Mrs. Gary Morrow (Rikki)

Mint Tea

3 cups boiling water
4 regular size tea bags
6-8 sprigs mint
3 cups boiling water
1 cup sugar
¾ cup lemon juice
¼ cup orange juice

Pour 3 cups boiling water over 4 tea bags and mint. Cover and steep 15 minutes. Strain. Next, mix 3 cups boiling water with sugar, lemon juice, and orange juice. Pour two mixtures together and add water to make ½ gallon. Pour over ice to serve. Serves 8-10.

Mrs. James Fanning (Valanne)

Spiced Tea

1 cup dry Tang mix
½ cup instant tea mix (with
    lemon)
¼ cup sugar
1 teaspoon cinnamon
½ teaspoon ground cloves

Mix all ingredients. Use equal amounts of hot water and spice mix. Stir and serve. Serves 4-5.

You may use instant sweetened tea mix and omit the sugar.

Mrs. Dwight Esselman (Ann)

Orange Drink

⅓ cup frozen orange juice
½ cup milk
½ cup water
¼ cup sugar
½ teaspoon vanilla
10 ice cubes

Combine everything in a blender. Cover and blend 30 seconds till smooth. Serve immediately. Makes 3 cups. Serves 6.

Easy and refreshing.

Mrs. Ricky Pitts (Becky)

Texas Cooler

2 fifths white port
8 ounces light rum
4 lemons, juiced
12-16 fresh strawberries

Chill port. Add rum and lemon juice, mix well. Pour into a glass container and refrigerate. When ready to serve, put a strawberry in each wine glass. Serve cold and stir well. Serves 12-16.

Mrs. Jack Price (Betty)

Tomato Juice Cocktail

7 cups tomato juice
3 tablespoons lemon juice
2 tablespoons sugar
¼ teaspoon tabasco
2 teaspoons Italian salad
 dressing

Mix together and chill. You can freeze part of this in ice cube trays and use with cocktail so regular ice won't dilute it. Serves 8.

Mrs. Griggs DeHay (Gay)

Tomato Juice Cocktail

1 small onion, finely
  chopped
2 tablespoons butter
1 (46-ounce) can tomato
juice
Garlic salt
Worcestershire sauce
1 bay leaf

Soften onion in butter, add juice and spices to taste and simmer 1 hour. Remove bay leaf. Serve hot. Serves 8.

Mrs. Robert M. Cox (Dee)

Vodka Slush

1 family size tea bag
1 (6-ounce) frozen orange
  juice
1 (6-ounce) frozen lemonade
  mix
1½ cups water
1 cup vodka
¼ cup sugar
7-Up

Steep tea bag in ½ cup boiling water for 3 minutes. Cool. Mix all ingredients and freeze, stirring occasionally. Mix 3 tablespoons in a glass with 7-Up to serve. Serves 10-12.

Mrs. Randy Owens (Liz)

 If you run out of cocoa for chocolate milk, use two teaspoons of chocolate pudding per glass of milk instead.

The Alderdice-Hennig Home was built on the edge of town at the end of Main Street in 1895. The first owner, Mr. J. M. Alderdice, was a well-known educator and former superintendent of the Ellis County schools. Near the turn of the century, Mr. Alderdice began a long and distinguished career in the Texas legislature, serving ten terms in the House and four terms in the Senate before retiring back to this home. The upper gallery balustrade with the wooden spindle "spiderwebs" brackets on the projecting bay windows of this beautiful house is typical of Victorian Era architecture. Also featured are wood sash, double-hung windows, a recessed second story porch, gabled roof, and a 10-bay front porch.

SOUPS, SALADS AND DRESSINGS

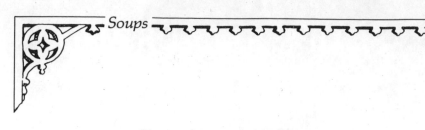

Easy Asparagus Soup

1 can cream of asparagus
  soup
1 cup sour cream
3 dashes Tabasco
½ teaspoon celery salt
1 cup milk
Asparagus tips (optional)
4 teaspoons finely chopped
  green onions

Combine first 5 ingredients. Add chopped asparagus tips, if desired. Chill for at least 4 hours before serving. Garnish each serving with 1 teaspoon of finely chopped green onions.

Mrs. Erling Holey (Susan)

Cheese Soup

¼ cup butter
½ cup diced onion
½ cup grated carrots
½ cup diced celery
2 cans cream of potato soup
1 can chicken broth
1 teaspoon Worcestershire
Salt & pepper to taste
¼ cup milk
8 ounces American cheese
1 cup sour cream
Parsley flakes to garnish

Sauté onion, carrots and celery in butter until very tender. Add potato soup, chicken broth, worchestershire and salt and pepper. Add milk and bring to slight boil. Add cheese and sour cream. Cook until thick and hot. Garnish with parsley flakes. Serves 10-12.

Mrs. Mike Hayes (Eva)

Canadian Cheese Soup

1 stick of butter
½ cup grated carrot
½ cup finely chopped celery
½ cup grated onion
¼ cup flour
1½ tablespoons cornstarch
2 cans Swanson chicken
  broth
3 cups whole milk
1 cup half and half
1/8 teaspoon soda
1 cup Cheese Whiz
Salt & pepper
2 tablespoons parsley flakes

Sauté carrot, celery and onion in one stick of butter. Add flour and cornstarch and cook until bubbly. Then add chicken broth, milk and half and half. Cook this until smooth. Then add soda, Cheese Whiz and salt and pepper to taste. Just before serving add 2 tablespoons of parsley flakes. Serves 6.

Mrs. Kirk Brown (Ellen)

Cheese Soup

10 tablespoons butter,
  divided
½ cup chopped celery
½ cup chopped green pepper
½ cup chopped onion
½ cup grated carrot
2 cups chicken broth
6 tablespoons flour
1 quart milk
2 cups grated American
  cheese (1 pound box)
Salt to taste

Melt 4 tablespoons butter and sauté celery, green pepper, onion and carrots. Add chicken broth to vegetables and set aside. Melt 6 tablespoons butter and stir in flour until smooth. Pour milk in gradually, stirring constantly. Bring to a boil and thicken on medium heat. Add cheese very slowly and stir until melted. Combine the cheese mixture with vegetable mixture and simmer 10 minutes or until hot.

Mrs. Pete Cunningham (Martha)

Cheddar Cheese Soup

6 cans cheddar cheese soup
3 soup cans of milk
5-6 slices of bacon
⅓ cup chopped black olives
⅓ cup chopped fresh parsley
½ cup finely chopped onion
  (fresh green onions and
  stems)
1 cup finely chopped carrots

In small skillet fry the bacon. Remove bacon and let drain, reserve bacon drippings. Sauté carrots and onions in bacon drippings till a little tender. In Dutch oven combine the 6 cans of soup and 3 cans full of milk. Heat over low temperature level. After soup and milk are combined add all the other ingredients and mix. Crumble bacon and add to soup mixture. It can be eaten as soon as it is hot but is best if cooked for a couple of hours. Makes a full Dutch oven full of soup. Serves 12.

Mrs. Dennis Horak (Barbara)

Cheese Soup

¼ cup butter
½ cup diced celery
½ cup diced onion
½ cup grated carrots
¼ cup flour
1½ tablespoons cornstarch
4 cups milk
4 cups chicken broth
½ teaspoon baking soda
1 pound Old English cheese
1 teaspoon salt
Dash white pepper
1 tablespoon dried parsley

Sauté celery, onion and carrots in butter. Stir in ¼ cup flour and cornstarch. Gradually add milk (room temperature). Blend into a smooth sauce. Add chicken broth and stir. Add baking soda and cheese (cut into small pieces). Stir until thickened. Season with salt, pepper, and parsley.

Mrs. Jim Beller (Linda)

Chicken Soup

4 chicken breasts
2 chicken bouillon cubes
2 carrots, chopped
2 stalks celery, chopped
1 onion, chopped
1 cup raw rice
3 cups water
1 small can evaporated milk
1 cup white wine
½ stick butter

Cover chicken and bouillon cubes with water and boil until tender. Remove chicken, bone, and chop. In broth, add chicken, vegetables, rice, and water. Simmer for 45 minutes. Add milk, wine, and butter and simmer 15 minutes. Serves a bunch.

Mrs. David Ballard (Karen)

South of the Border Soup

2 (10¾-ounce) cans
  condensed chicken broth
2 soup cans water
2 envelopes chicken flavor
  broth mix
1 can tomatoes (broken up)
2 tablespoons instant minced
  onion
¼ teaspoon garlic powder
3 chicken breasts, cut
  in chunks
1½ cups thinly sliced carrots
¾ teaspoon salt
½ teaspoon chili powder
½ teaspoon ground cumin
⅛ teaspoon red pepper
1 cup peas
1 cup sliced zucchini
1 large avocado (chunked)

In large saucepot combine broth, water, broth mix, tomatoes, onion and garlic. Bring to a boil. Stir in chicken, carrots, and all spices. Return to boiling. Reduce heat and simmer, covered, until carrots and chicken are tender (about 20-25 minutes). Stir in peas and zucchini. Cover and simmer 3 minutes. Serve garnished with avocado chunks. Serves 4-6.

Mrs. Jeff Kosoris (Susan)

Corn & Tomato Soup

1 cup cream corn
6 tomatoes
1 cup spring green onions
½ cup water
2 tablespoons cream
Salt & pepper to taste

Blend tomatoes and corn. Combine with the other ingredients. Simmer 5 minutes.

Mrs. Erling Holey (Susan)

Gazpacho

3 pounds ripe tomatoes,
  (seeded and peeled)
1 onion cut in chunks
½ cup green pepper chunks
1½ cups cucumber chunks
1 garlic clove minced
1 can tomato paste
½ teaspoon ground cumin
1 teaspoon salt
½ teaspoon ground black
  pepper
Dash of tabasco
¼ cup olive oil or salad oil
¼ cup white vinegar
Garnish as desired

Seed tomatoes over strainer to preserve juice. Puree all ingredients in blender. Add tomato paste to add color and consistency. Add cumin, salt and pepper and tabasco. Stir together and chill. Before serving add ¼ cup olive oil and ¼ cup white vinegar. Garnishes: croutons, chives, chopped green peppers, peeled chopped tomatoes.

Mrs. Bill Major (Patsy)

Gazpacho (Cold Tomato Soup)

1 large can Campbell's
  tomato soup
2 cups cold water
1 tablespoon olive oil
2 tablespoons Heinz wine
  vinegar
1 cup finely chopped
  cucumber
½ cup finely chopped green
  pepper
¼ cup minced onion

Mix all ingredients together and chill. Serve cold as a punch or soup with sandwiches. Serves 4-8.

Mrs. Dennis Horak (Barbara Sue)

Mulligatawny - From Ceylon

2 tablespoons butter
½ cup finely chopped onion
1 small clove of garlic,
   crushed or the equivalent
   in garlic powder
2 tablespoons flour
1 tablespoon curry powder
1 pint half and half milk
1 quart chicken stock, or
   1 can Swanson's chicken
   broth
1 tablespoon salt (or less,
   to taste)
Dash of pepper
1 raw apple, peeled and
   finely chopped

Melt the butter in the double boiler you are going to use for the soup. Cook the onion and the crushed garlic (or garlic powder) over low heat just until the onion is soft. Add the flour and curry powder and cook 2 minutes. Add the half and half milk and chicken stock and cook slowly until smooth. Add salt and pepper. Add the apple 10 minutes before serving so that it is still a little crisp.

Mrs. David Williams (Shirley)

Mushroom Vegetable Soup

1 pound fresh mushrooms
2 tablespoons margarine
1 cup finely chopped carrots
1 cup finely chopped celery
1 cup chopped onions
1 clove garlic, minced
1 can (13¾-ounce)
   condensed beef broth
2 cups water
½ cup tomato paste
2 tablespoons parsley flakes
1 bay leaf
½ teaspoon salt
¼ teaspoon pepper
2 tablespoons dry sherry

Wash mushrooms. Slice half of them and set aside. Chop remaining mushrooms and sauté in 1 tablespoon margarine in a large pot. Add remaining ingredients (except the set aside mushrooms, remaining margarine and sherry). Simmer with pot covered for 1 hour. Puree soup in a blender. Saute the mushrooms in remaining 1 tablespoon margarine. Return pureed soup to pot. Add sauteed mushrooms and sherry. Reheat. Serves 6 (1 cup servings).

Mrs. Steve Kelley (Cindy)

Navy Bean Soup

1 cup Great Northern beans
1-1½ cups ham pieces
1 tablespoon Worcestershire
    sauce
½ teaspoon salt
¼ teaspoon pepper
1 cup celery, chopped
1 cup onion, chopped
1 can whole peeled tomatoes
    with juice
1 can chicken broth

Cook beans with ham, Worcestershire, salt and pepper. Add vegetables about one hour before serving. Cook soup until beans are tender.

Mrs. Erling Holey (Susan)

Onion Soup Au Gratin

6 tablespoons butter
12 medium onions, thinly
    sliced
2 quarts chicken broth or
    beef broth
Salt
Pepper
4 hard rolls cut into 4 slices
    (or 16 slices French bread),
    toasted
8 tablespoons grated
    Parmesan cheese

Melt butter in a soup kettle, add onions, and cook slowly until brown. Add broth, boil a few minutes, and season with salt and pepper. Pour into a large casserole or 8 individual ones which can be put under a broiler or into a hot oven. Float toasted slices of rolls (or bread) on top, sprinkle each with cheese, and brown under broiler heat or in a very hot oven (450°). Water may be substituted for broth, in which case the slices of rolls or bread should be buttered before sprinkling the cheese on. Serves 8.

Mrs. William H. Atkinson (Pam)

French Onion Soup

1½ pounds onions, thinly
sliced
½ cup butter or margarine
3 (10½-ounce) condensed
beef broth
1 teaspoon Worcestershire
sauce
6-8 slices French bread
toasted
Shredded Swiss cheese

In large saucepan cook onions, covered in butter about 20 minutes or until tender. Add beef broth, Worcestershire sauce, ½ teaspoon salt and dash pepper. Bring to boiling point. Sprinkle toasted bread with cheese, place under broiler till cheese is slightly browned. Ladle soup into bowls and float bread atop. Serves 6-8.

Mrs. Ken Box (Dietra)

Big Pot O'Soup

5 pounds stew meat
2 cans French onion soup
4 cans stewed tomatoes
3 packages "Swift
Homemade" beef stew
starter
1 stalk of celery, sliced
3 carrots, sliced
2 bags frozen vegetable
soup mix

Sear stew meat in skillet. Put meat into 12 quart soup pot with 2 quarts of water. Add 2 cans French onion soup and 2 cans water. Add 4 cans stewed tomatoes. Simmer 2 hours. Add 3 packages (7.6 ounces) of beef stew starter. Add celery, carrots, and frozen vegetables. Simmer 3 hours. Serves about 20 people. Freezes well.

Mrs. Robert C. Fuller (Madelon)

Pioneer Potato Soup

1 large onion chopped
1 clove garlic minced
1 carrot diced
1 quart chicken broth
3 tablespoons flour
Salt and pepper to taste
2 tablespoons margarine or butter
3 cups potatoes, pared and diced
1 stalk celery diced
¼ cup parsley chopped
1 cup half and half
1 chicken bouillon cube

In 4 quart casserole cook onion and garlic with butter for 4 minutes uncovered on high stirring every 2 minutes. Add potatoes, carrots, and chicken broth. Cover tightly and cook high about 15 minutes stirring occasionally. Add parsley. Mix flour with ½ cup half and half to make a smooth paste. Add flour mixture and remaining half and half to soup. Cook covered 5-7 minutes on medium high stirring several times until soup is hot and thickened. Salt and pepper taste.

Mrs. Roy Marchbanks (Pam)

Vegetable Soup

1 pound ground meat, browned
2 teaspoons garlic salt
2 tablespoons chili powder
Dash of pepper
1 onion, chopped
1 can tomato soup
1 (16-ounce) can tomatoes
3 cans water (soup cans)
4-5 medium potatoes (cubed)
½ cup marcaroni
½ cup corn
½ cup green beans
3-4 carrots (sliced)

Set aside browned ground meat. Bring to a boil first seven items. Add macaroni, potatoes, and vegetables. Bring to a boil again. Stir. Reduce heat and simmer until vegetables are tender. Stir occasionally.

Mrs. Roy Marchbanks (Pam)

Fresh Zucchini Soup

1½ pound zucchini (3 cups)
2 slices bacon, cooked and
  crumbled
1 small onion, chopped
⅔ cup condensed consomme
1⅓ cups water
½ teaspoon basil
1 small clove garlic
2 tablespoons parsley flakes
1 teaspoon salt
⅛ teaspoon pepper
½ teaspoon seasoned salt
Parmesan cheese, to taste

Cut zucchini into 1 inch chunks. Place in 2-3 qt. glass casserole. Add remaining ingredients except cheese. Cover and cook on full power in microwave for 15 minutes or till zucchini is just tender. Cool slightly. Blend in blender till smooth. Heat to serving temperature and top with parmesan cheese. Serves 5.

Mrs. Erling Holey (Susan)

Blueberry Salad

2 cups boiling water
1 (6-ounce) package
  blackberry jello
1 (8-ounce) can crushed
  pineapple, drained (reserve
  juice and add enough water
  to make 1 cup)
1 can blueberry pie filling

Topping:
1 (8-ounce) package cream
  cheese
½ cup sugar
1 cup sour cream
Chopped nuts

Dissolve jello in 2 cups boiling water. Add pineapple, juice & water and blueberry pie filling. Chill until firm.

Topping: Mix cream cheese and sugar. Fold in sour cream. Spread on jello. Garnish with chopped nuts.

Mrs. Don Nelson (Judy)

Grandma Lo's Blueberry Salad

1 large package raspberry jello
1 cup boiling water
1 can blueberries in heavy
  syrup
1 small can crushed pineapple
½ pint whipped cream
½ cup nuts

Mix boiling water with jello. Add blueberries and pineapple and allow mixture to gel. Stir well and add whipped cream and nuts. Mix thoroughly. Chill. Serves 8.

Mrs. Stan Parker (Priscilla)

Cherry Salad

2 (8-ounce) packages cream
 cheese
½ bottle maraschino cherries,
 with juice
1 large can crushed pineapple,
 drained
1 cup whipped cream
½ cup miniature
 marshmallows

Soften cream cheese with cherry juice. Mix until smooth. Then add other ingredients. Chill. Serves 6-8.

Mrs. Bill Price (Kay)

Cherry Salad

1 can cherry pie filling
1 (8-ounce) can crushed
 pineapple
1 small package
 marshmallows
3 sliced bananas
¼ cup chopped pecans

Mix all ingredients into a medium size bowl. Chill in refrigerator for 1 hour and serve. Serves 4 to 6.

Mrs. Kirk Brown (Ellen)

Cherry Coke Salad

2 (3-ounce) packages cherry
 jello
½ cup boiling water
1 cup sugar
Juice from 1 can pitted
 cherries
1 (10-ounce) bottle Coke
1 cup chopped pecans
1 can pitted cherries

Dissolve jello in boiling water, and pour into 9x9 pyrex dish. Boil sugar and juice from can of pitted cherries for 3 minutes. Add this to jello mixture. Pour in coke, chopped pecans and the can of pitted cherries. Chill at least 6 hours. Serves 9.

Note: *You may add 1 (8-ounce) package of cream cheese to vary recipe.*

Mrs. Jim Jenkins (Pam)

Grandmother Long's Frozen Cranberry Salad

2 cups ground fresh
    cranberries
2 cups sugar
2 cups finely diced celery
2 cups ground nuts
2 cups crushed pineapple and
    juice
2 packages lemon jello
    (3-ounce size)
12 teaspoons salad dressing
    or mayonnaise

Grind cranberries, mix with sugar, and let stand overnight in the refrigerator. Add celery, nuts and drained, crushed pineapple (reserve juice) the next morning. Dissolve 2 packages lemon jello in 2 cups of hot liquid-use the reserved pineapple juice as part of the liquid, adding water to bring to 2 cups. Bring mixture to a boil. Cool. When Jello is thickened, but not firm, add fruit and nut mixture and put in mold or pyrex rectangular pan, and freeze. When ready to serve, cut into squares and let stand a short while. Garnish with a teaspoon of salad dressing or mayonnaise. Serves 12.

Wonderful for Christmas dinner and so pretty molded in a Christmas tree.

Mrs. Dennis Horak (Barbara Sue)

Lime Gelatin Salad

1 (3-ounce) package lemon
    gelatin
1 (3-ounce) package lime
    gelatin
2 cups boiling water
1 (14-ounce) can sweetened
    condensed milk
1 pint large curd cottage
    cheese
1 cup mayonnaise or Miracle
    Whip salad dressing
1 (13½-ounce) can crushed
    pineapple in heavy syrup

Dissolve both packages of gelatin in two cups boiling water. Pour in milk, cottage cheese, mayonnaise and pineapple. Stir until smooth and pour into rectangualr dish. Refrigerate until firm. Cut into squares and serve on lettuce leaf. Serve 8-10.

May top each square with a cherry or pineapple section if desired.

Mrs. Steve Loftis (Nina)

Mango Salad

1 can Mangoes (drained, reserve juice)
3 boxes lime or lemon jello (3-ounce) size
3 cups water (use the reserved mango juice as part of the 3 cups, using water to bring it up to 3 full cups)
1 (8-ounce) package cream cheese

Let cream cheese stand until room temperature. Put mangoes and cheese in blender and blend. Dilute jello with the 3 cups of liquid. Pour the mango-cheese mixture in with the jello mixture and stir until well blended. Pour into a bowl or oiled mold to chill. When firm, cut into servings and serve on a bed of lettuce. You can garnish with a teaspoon of salad dressing or mayonnaise. Serves 8.

Mrs. Dennis Horak (Barbara Sue)

Frozen Raspberry Loaf

1½ cups miniature marshmallows
⅓ cup orange juice
1 (3-ounce) softened cream cheese
¼ cup mayonnaise
1 (10-ounce) frozen raspberries, thawed
½ cup whipping cream, whipped
¾ cup chopped pecans

Combine marshmallows and juice. Melt in a double boiler. Cool. Add cream cheese and mayonnaise. Beat smooth. Stir in remaining ingredients. Pour into a lightly oiled loafpan and freeze overnight. Remove pan from freezer 10-15 minutes before serving. Slice and serve. Serves 8.

Mrs. Joseph S. Smith (Margaret)

Fresh Strawberry Salad

1 pint fresh strawberries
   (sliced)
1 cup Angel Flake coconut
½ cup chopped pecans
1 can pineapple tidbits
2-4 cups miniature
   marshmallows
½ pint sour cream

Combine all ingredients in a large bowl. Refrigerate 24 hours before serving. Serves 8.

Mrs. Robert M. Cox (Dee)

Strawberry Gelatin Delight

2 (3-ounce) packages
   strawberry-banana gelatin
2 cups boiling water
2 (10-ounce) packages frozen
   sliced strawberries
1 (13-ounce) can crushed
   pineapple
2 large ripe bananas, peeled
   and diced
½ cup pecans (optional)

Dressing:
1 cup sour cream
1 teaspoon sugar
¼ teaspoon ground ginger
Dash of salt

Dissolve gelatin in boiling water. Add strawberries, stirring occasionally until thawed. Mix in pineapple and bananas. Add pecans if desired. Pour into retangular dish and refrigerate until firm. In small bowl combine sour cream, sugar, ginger and salt. Chill well. Spread over firm gelatin delight. Slice and serve. Serves 12.

Mrs. Steve Loftis (Nina)

Your jello will come out of your mold easier if you grease the mold with a little bit of mayonnaise before you fill it.

Strawberry Jello Salad

3 large bananas, mashed
1 lemon
2 cups boiling water
2 (3-ounce) packages
  strawberry jello
1 (8-ounce) can crushed
  pineapple
1 (16-ounce) package frozen
  strawberries
1 (3-ounce) package cream
  cheese
1 (8-ounce) carton sour
  cream

Mash bananas in small bowl and pour juice of lemon over bananas. Set aside. Pour boiling water over strawberry jello in large bowl. Add pineapple, bananas, and frozen strawberries. Pour half of mixture into 11x9-inch pyrex dish. Leave remaining half at room temperature. Set pyrex dish into refrigerator until firm. Blend cream cheese and sour cream in blender or with electric mixer. Pour over congealed jello. Place in refrigerator and let set until firm. Pour remaining jello mixture on top and chill til firm. Serves 10.

May use jello with nutrasweet for less calories.

Mrs. Kirk Brown (Ellen)

24 Hour Fruit Salad

2 large cans fruit cocktail,
  drained
1 large can pineapple chunks,
  drained
1 jar maraschino cherries
½ package slivered almonds
Small marshmallows
  (if desired)
3 tablespoons mayonnaise
1½ teaspoons vinegar
Dash of salt
½ to ¾ container of Cool
  Whip (12-ounce)

Mix, chill 24 hours, and serve. Serves 8-10.

Mrs. Bobby Oliver (Emily)

Creamy Fruit Salad

1 (3-ounce) package orange
  flavored gelatin
1 (12-ounce) container
  Cool Whip
1 (11-ounce) can mandarin
  oranges, drained
1 (15-ounce) can crushed
  pineapple and juice
2 tablespoons frozen orange
  juice concentrate
1 cup miniature
  marshmallows
½ cup chopped nuts

Stir undissolved gelatin into container of whipped topping until smooth. Add drained oranges, undrained crushed pineapple, orange juice concentrate, marshmallows, and nuts, if desired. Stir. Cover with plastic wrap and refrigerate until serving time. Serves 8.

Mrs. Pete Cunningham (Martha)

Frozen Fruit Salad

1 quart Cool Whip
1 pint sour cream
½ cup sugar
1½ cups chopped pecans
½ cup maraschino cherries
4 tablespoons lemon juice
1 large can crushed pineapple,
  (drained)
5 mashed bananas

Mix all ingredients together. Freeze in muffin tins, using bake cup linings. Makes about 26.

Mrs. Mike Hayes (Eva)

Under the Sea Salad

1 large package orange
  gelatin
2 cups boiling water
½ pound marshmallows, cut
  fine
1 (3-ounce) package cream
  cheese, softened and
  whipped
1 cup whipped cream
1 cup mayonnaise
1 cup crushed pineapple
1 large package lime gelatin
2 cups boiling water

Mix boiling water and orange gelatin. Cool to lukewarm. Add marshmallows, cream cheese (whipped), whipped cream, mayonnaise, and pineapple. Mix well. Place in refrigerator and let gel. When gelled, mix the lime gelatin with boiling water, cool. Pour over top of first layer. Chill. Serve in squares. Serves 12.

Mrs. Michael Leath (Kay)

Hot Fruit Salad

1 can pears, cut in chunks
1 can pineapple (chunks)
1 can peaches, sliced
1 can blue plums or pitted black cherries
2 bananas, cut up
1 bottle maraschino cherries (red)
½ cup butter
¾ cup brown sugar
1 can applesauce
1 cup chopped pecans

Drain fruit well and let stand. Add bananas and cherries. Combine butter, brown sugar (reserve 3 teaspoons), and apple sauce and heat. Place drained fruit in dish and pour hot sauce over; mix. Sprinkle with 3 teaspoons brown sugar. Add chopped pecans. Bake 1 hour at 300°. Serves 10.

Mrs. Rick Pitts (Becky)

Chicken Salad

4 cups cooked cubed chicken
1 cup chopped celery
1 cup halved seedless grapes
1 (2½-ounce) package slivered toasted almonds
1 teaspoon salt
¼ teaspoon pepper
¾ cup mayonnaise
¼ cup sour cream

Mix all ingredients in the order listed. Chill well. Serve on lettuce leaf. Serves 4.

Mrs. Pete Cunningham (Martha)

Chicken Salad

1 boiled, diced chicken
½ stalk celery
1 medium onion
1 small jar pimento
½ cup relish
6 boiled eggs
Miracle Whip to taste
Salt and pepper to taste

Chop all ingredients and mix together. Add Miracle Whip, salt and pepper to taste. Serves 6.

Mrs. Ken Box (Dietra)

Fruited Chicken Salad

1 cup chopped cooked
   chicken
½ cup finely chopped apple
½ cup finely chopped celery
⅓ cup crushed pineapple,
   well drained
3 tablespoons mayonnaise
   (Not salad dressing)
¼ teaspoon salt
⅛ teaspoon white pepper
1 teaspoon lemon juice

Combine all ingredients and chill overnight. Good on Pita bread. Serves 4.

Mrs. Donald Locke (Marilyn)

Chicken and Fruit Salad

2 (5-ounce) cans chunk or
   chunk white chicken, and
   broth
2 cups grapes, seeded, if
   necessary
1 cup strawberries, cut in half
1 large banana, sliced
½ cup mayonnaise
1 tablespoon lime juice
½ teaspoon honey

Drain chicken, reserving broth. Toss chicken with grapes, strawberries, and banana. Combine reserved broth, mayonnaise, lime juice, and honey. Serve over chicken mixture. Serves 4.

Mrs. Rick Pitts (Becky)

Chicken Salad with a Twist

1 (8-ounce) package corkscrew
  macaroni
½ cup mayonnaise
½ cup commercial Italian
  salad dressing
3 tablespoons lemon juice
1 tablespoon prepared
  mustard
1 teaspoon pepper
3 cups chopped cooked
  chicken
1 cup chopped cucumber
1 cup chopped celery
¾ cup sliced ripe olives
1 medium onion, chopped
Leafy lettuce (optional)

Cook macaroni according to package directions, drain and cool. Combine next 5 ingredients; stir until blended. Add macaroni, stirring well. Stir in chicken, cucumber, celery, olives and onion. Chill 2 hours. Serve salad in a lettuce-lined bowl if desired. Serves 8.

Mrs. Jeff Bertsch (Diane)

Tossed Chicken Salad

4 cups diced chicken (turkey
  or tuna)
1 pint mayonnaise
2 teaspoons prepared Dijon
  mustard
¼ cup dried minced onion
  (or fresh grated)
1 cup chopped celery
½ cup stuffed green olives,
  halved (optional)
1 small can drained mandarin
  oranges
1 small can drained pineapple
  tidbits
½ cup chopped pecans
1 can Chinese noodles

Combine all ingredients except noodles. Add canned Chinese noodles on top of each serving. Will stay fresh in refrigerator several days. Serves 8.

Mrs. M. S. Weedon (Kay)

Chicken-Mushroom Salad

½ cup pecan halves
4 cups diced, cooked chicken
4 slices cooked bacon,
   crumbled
2 cups sliced celery
¾ cup sliced, fresh
   mushrooms

Dressing:
½ cup mayonnaise
½ cup sour cream
2 tablespoons lemon juice
1 teaspoon salt

Toast pecans at 350° for 15 minutes in shallow pan. Mix all ingredients together and cover with dressing. Chill before serving. Serves 8.

Mrs. Erling Holey (Susan)

Hot Chicken Salad

4 cups cooked, diced chicken
2 cups celery, diced
2 tablespoons lemon juice
4 hard boiled eggs, cut up
¾ cup almonds
2 pimentos, cut fine
1½ cups mayonnaise
1 teaspoon salt
1 tablespoon onion, cut fine
1 cup grated cheese
1½ cups crushed potato chips

Combine all except cheese and potato chips. Toss gently. Top with cheese and crushed potato chips. Bake at 350° for 35 minutes. Serves 8.

Mrs. Brett Thacker (Joyce)

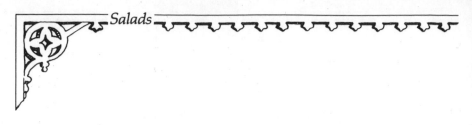

Crunchy Hot Chicken Salad

3 cups diced cooked chicken
1 cup finely chopped celery
2 teaspoons chopped onion
½ cup sliced almonds
1 can cream of chicken soup,
  undiluted
1½ cups cooked rice
1 tablespoon lemon juice
½ teaspoon salt
¼ teaspoon pepper
¾ cup mayonnaise
¼ cup water
3 hard-cooked eggs, diced
2 cups crushed potato chips
¾ cup shredded cheddar
  cheese

Combine first 9 ingredients; toss gently and set aside. Combine mayonnaise and water and beat with wire whisk until smooth. Pour over chicken mixture; stir well. Add eggs, and toss gently. Spoon into a greased 2-quart shallow baking dish; cover and refrigerate 8 hours or overnight. Bake 450° for 10 minutes or until thoroughly heated. Sprinkle with potato chips and cheese; bake an additional 5 minutes. Serves 6-8.

Mrs. Rick Pitts (Becky)

Macaroni Salad

1 medium package elbow
  macaroni
3 chopped boiled eggs
¾ cup diced sweet pickles or
  pickle relish
¾ cup chopped onion
½ cup chopped pimento
1 cup mayonnaise
2 cups whole cooked shrimp

Cook macaroni according to package directions. Drain and cool slightly. Pour in large bowl and add remaining ingredients in order given. Mix well and refrigerate. Serve chilled. Serves 8.

Mrs. Gary Morrow (Rikki)

Mexican Salad

1 pound ground beef
1 large onion
1 (16-ounce) can red kidney
    beans, rinsed & drained
1½ teaspoons cumin seeds
½ teaspoon garlic salt
1 head iceberg lettuce, torn
    in bite size pieces
2 tomatoes
1 avocado, diced
3 green onions, chopped
1 (3-ounce) can sliced ripe
    olives
1 (2-ounce) jar chopped
    pimentos
2 cups shredded cheddar
    cheese
1 (8-ounce) bag tortilla chips,
    crushed
1 cup Green Goddess salad
    dressing

In a skillet, sauté beef and onions until onion is transparent. Drain. Add beans and spices and simmer for 10 minutes. In large serving bowl, combine lettuce, tomatoes, avocados, onions, olives and pimento. Add warm beef mixture, chips and dressing. Top with cheese. Serves 6-8.

Mrs. William H. Atkinson (Pam)

If you must make a green salad for a large group, cut up your lettuce and drop it into a clean pillow case. Then put the pillow case of lettuce in your washing machine on the final spin cycle. After just a few minutes, your lettuce will be dry and ready to go into the salad without diluting the dressing.

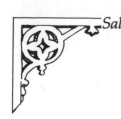

Mexi-Pea Salad

¾ cup dried black-eyed peas
2½ cups water
1 pound ground meat
½ cup chopped onion
½ cup chopped green pepper
1 tablespoon chili powder
½ teaspoon salt
⅛ teaspoon pepper
1 head lettuce (½ iceberg,
    torn, ½ leaf)
2 tomatoes, peeled & chopped
1 cup shredded cheddar
    cheese
½ cup chopped onion
1 (8-ounce) can kernel corn,
    drained
1 (7-ounce) package tortilla
    chips, crushed
½ cup Thousand Island
    dressing
½ cup creamy Italian dressing

Sort and wash peas. Place in saucepan, cover with water and boil. Cook 2 minutes. Remove from heat. Cover and let soak 1 hour. Drain. Combine peas with 2½ cups water. Bring to boil. Reduce heat, cover and simmer 1½ hours or until tender. Drain. Cool and set aside. Cook ground meat, ½ cup onion, and green pepper until tender. Drain well. Stir in chili powder, salt, and pepper. Let cool. Combine peas, meat mixture, and remaining ingredients. Toss with dressing and serve immediately. Serves 15.

Mrs. Jeff Kosoris (Susan)

Molded Salmon Salad

1 envelope gelatin
¼ cup cold water
¼ cup lemon juice
2 cups mayonnaise
3 tablespoons minced onion
1 pound can salmon, drained
    and flaked
2 hard cooked eggs, chopped
½ cup chopped stuffed
    olives

Sprinkle gelatin into the water and let stand 5 minutes. Place over hot water, stirring until dissolved. Mix in the lemon juice and mayonnaise until smooth. Add remaining ingredients. Pour into oiled 1½ quart mold and chill until firm. Serves 6.

Mrs. Bill Price (Kay)

Shrimp Salad

1 tablespoon French dressing
1 cup mayonnaise
½ teaspoon prepared mustard
1 teaspoon lemon juice
1 teaspoon salt
⅛ teaspoon cayenne pepper
⅛ teaspoon pepper
1 small onion, chopped
½ cup minced green olives
1 cup chopped celery
¼ cup chopped green pepper
¼ cup chopped sweet pickles
2 pounds shrimp, cooked
   & peeled

Combine first 7 ingredients. Mix well. Stir in remaining ingredients except shrimp. Mix well. Pour over shrimp and toss well. Chill a minimum of 4 hours. Serve on lettuce individually or in large clear glass serving dish. Serves 6-8.

Mrs. Pete Cunningham (Martha)

Shrimp-Vermicelli Salad

5 ounces vermicelli
1 green pepper, chopped
½ medium red onion,
   chopped
1 small jar pimentos
3 tablespoons sweet pickle
   relish
2 cans medium shrimp or
   2 cans crab meat or
   1 of each
¼ cup mayonnaise
Salt to taste
Pepper to taste

Cook vermicelli according to directions on the package and drain well. Add remaining ingredients. Chill at least 1 to 2 hours before serving. Serves 6.

Mrs. Craig Curry (Karen)

Tuna Macaroni Salad

2 cups cooked shell macaroni
1 cup drained tuna, flaked
1 cup ripe olives, quartered
2 eggs, boiled and chopped
½ cup Miracle Whip
2 teaspoons prepared mustard
1 tablespoon vinegar
1 teaspoon salt

Combine first four ingredients after preparing as specified. Blend the next four ingredients and toss with first mixture. Chill entire mixture before serving. Serves 6.

Mrs. James Alderdice (Rosemary)

Three Bean Salad

1 (15-ounce) can kidney beans
1 (16-ounce) can all green lima beans
1 (16-ounce) can cut green beans
½ cup chopped green pepper
½ cup chopped onion
¾ cup sugar
½ cup oil
½ cup vinegar
1 teaspoon salt
½ teaspoon black pepper
½ teaspoon dill weed

Rinse beans in cold water. Drain. Place in 13x9-inch glass dish and add green pepper and onion. Stir together remaining ingredients until sugar is dissolved. Pour over beans. Mix lightly so that beans are covered in the liquid. Cover and chill overnight. Serves 10.

Mrs. Erling Holey (Susan)

Garlic Bean Salad

3 cans French style green
  beans, drained
2 cups oil
1 cup vinegar
7 cloves garlic, minced
Salt and pepper to taste

Combine oil, vinegar, garlic, salt and pepper and pour over beans. Refrigerate for 24 hours. Drain. (Oil can be saved and used again.) Serve cold. Serves 10-12.

Mrs. Stan Parker (Priscilla)

Four Bean Salad

1 can golden wax beans,
  drained
1 can green beans, drained
1 can lima beans, drained
1 can red kidney beans,
  drained
1 large green pepper, cut into
  1-inch strips
1 medium onion, thinly
  sliced and separated into
  rings
1 pint cherry tomatoes, cut
  in half
1 medium cucumber, thinly
  sliced
½ cup red wine vinegar
½ cup vegetable oil
½ cup sugar
2 tablespoons chopped fresh
  tarragon or ½ teaspoon
  dried whole tarragon
2 tablespoons chopped fresh
  basil or ½ teaspoon dried
  whole basil
2 tablespoons chopped fresh
  parsley
½ teaspoon salt
½ teaspoon dried mustard
Lettuce leaves

Combine first 8 ingredients in a large bowl; toss gently. Combine next 8 ingredients in a jar. Cover tightly, and shake vigorously; pour marinade over vegetables, tossing gently. Cover vegetables, and chill at least 4 hours. Serve in a lettuce lined bowl, if desired. Serves 12-15.

Mrs. Rick Pitts (Becky)

Marinated Salad

1 (17-ounce) can French-style green beans
1 (17-ounce) can English peas
1 (2-ounce) jar pimentos
1 medium bell pepper, chopped
1 small onion, chopped
4 medium stalks celery, chopped
¾ cup sugar
½ cup vinegar
¼ cup salad oil
Salt and pepper to taste

Place vegetable in a large bowl. Mix the sugar, vinegar, and salad oil and pour over the vegetables. Do not crowd vegetables and marinate at least 8 hours, stirring occasionally. Drain the vegetables one hour before serving and save the oil mixture. If any salad is left, return to the oil and refrigerate. Serves 6-8.

Mrs. Stan Parker (Priscilla)

Cauliflower Salad

1 head cauliflower
8 radishes
3-5 stalks celery
2-3 green onions
½ cup sour cream
½ cup mayonnaise

Cut vegetables into bite size pieces. Mix sour cream and mayonnaise to make the dressing and toss with vegetables. Serves 6.

Mrs. Stan Parker (Priscilla)

Cauliflower-Broccoli Salad

1 head fresh cauliflower
1 bunch fresh broccoli
1 can ripe olives (pitted and drained)
1 basket cherry tomatoes
2 small cucumbers (sliced)
Dash salt
1 large bottle Wishbone Italian dressing

Wash and break the cauliflower and broccoli into flowerettes. Add the olives, tomatoes and cucumbers. Pour the dressing over the other ingredients and chill several hours before serving. Serves 10.

Mrs. Bill Major (Patsy)

Cauliflower-Broccoli Toss

1 bunch broccoli
1 head cauliflower
1 bunch green onions, chopped
1.4 ounce buttermilk salad dressing mix
2 tablespoons sugar
¾-1 cup mayonnaise
2 tablespoons vinegar

Combine broccoli, cauliflower and onion. Toss gently. Combine remaining ingredients, mixing well, and pour over vegetables. Toss, cover and chill overnight. Serves 8.

Mrs. Roy Marchbanks (Pam)

Copper Pennies

2 pounds fresh carrots sliced ¼ round
2 medium onions thinly sliced and separated
1 medium green pepper cut into thin strips
1 (10¾-ounce) can tomato soup
¾ cup vinegar
⅔ cup sugar
½ cup cooking oil
1 teaspoon Worcestershire sauce
1 teaspoon prepared mustard
½ teaspoon salt

Cook carrots in boiling salt water till just tender (8 to 10 minutes). Drain, combine with onion and green pepper in large bowl. Add remaining ingredients. Cover and marinate in refrigerator several hours or overnight.

Mrs. Rusty Graham (Nelda)

Le Seur Pea Relish Salad

1 can Le Seur Peas
1 can Le Seur white corn
1 can French cut green beans
1 small jar diced pimento

Drain the above ingredients

1 cup green pepper, diced
1 cup onion, diced
1 cup celery, diced

Marinade:
½ cup sugar
½ cup Wesson oil
¾ teaspoon salt
¾ cup vinegar
1 teaspoon pepper

Mix all ingredients together and add the marinade. Mix well and chill at least 24 hours before serving. Will keep in refrigerator for three weeks. Makes two quarts.

Mrs. Kirk Brown (Ellen)

Crunchy Pea Salad

1 (10-ounce) package frozen petite peas
1 cup chopped celery
¼ cup chopped green onion
1 cup cashews
¼ cup crisp bacon bits
1 cup sour cream
½ teaspoon salt

Garden Cafe Dressing:
½ teaspoon lemon juice
¼ cup red wine vinegar
1 teaspoon salt
¼ teaspoon pepper

Combine peas, celery, green onion, cashews, bacon bits, sour cream, and salt. Cover with Garden Cafe Dressing and fold together. Chill and serve on a bed of crisp lettuce. Serves 6.

Mrs. Roy Marchbanks (Pam)

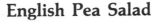

English Pea Salad

2 cans LeSeur sweet peas,
  drained
2 large ribs celery
¾ cup sharp cheddar
5 green onions
¼ teaspoon black pepper
Dash of garlic salt
½ teaspoon salt
½ teaspoon mustard
¾ cup tartar sauce

Finely chop celery and onion. Cube cheese. Mix all ingredients together. This can be served immediately but it is better if marinated overnight. Serves 6.

Mrs. Brett Thacker (Joyce)

Cool Carrots

1½ pounds carrots
1 large green pepper, diced
  fine
1 can condensed tomato soup
½ cup oil
¾ cup vinegar
1 cup sugar (or less as
  desired)
1 teaspoon dry mustard
1 small jar pickled onions
  sliced (optional)

Peel and slice carrots thin, cook in salted water approximately 10 minutes. Drain and cool. Mix remaining ingredients and cook for five minutes. Pour over carrots and refrigerate. Serve cold. It will keep in the refrigerator for 1 week. Serves 10.

Mrs. Tommy Nelson (Nancy)

Quick Old-Fashion Corn Relish

¼ cup sugar
½ cup vinegar
½ teaspoon salt
¼ teaspoon tabasco sauce
½ teaspoon celery seed
¼ teaspoon mustard seed
1 (12-ounce) can whole
  kernel corn
2 tablespoons chopped green
  pepper
1 tablespoon chopped
  pimento
1 tablespoon minced onion

Combine sugar, vinegar, salt, tabasco, celery seed, and mustard seed in a saucepan. Bring to a boil and simmer 2 minutes. Remove from heat. Combine with remaining ingredients. Chill. Flavor improves on standing. Yield: 1⅔ cups. Serves 4.

Mrs. Joseph S. Smith (Margaret)

Cucumbers in Sour Cream

1 cup sour cream
2 tablespoons cider vinegar
½ teaspoon salt
1 teaspoon dill weed
½ thinly sliced onion
Dash paprika
2 medium cucumbers

Combine all ingredients except cucumbers in a 1 quart or 1½ quart container. Mix well. Peel cucumbers, slice thinly and add to sour cream mixture. Refrigerate for 3-4 hours before serving. Serves 6.

Mrs. Craig Curry (Karen)

Molded Guacamole Salad

1 cup hot water
1 (3-ounce) package lemon
   gelatin
⅔ cup cold water
1 cup mashed avocado
2 teaspoons lemon juice
Dash tabasco
3 tablespoons onion, chopped
½ teaspoon sugar
½ cup canned tomatoes,
   drained & chopped
¼ cup sour cream
¼ cup mayonnaise

Pour boiling water over gelatin and stir until dissolved. Add cold water and chill until slightly thickened. Fold remaining ingredients except mayonnaise into thickened gelatin. Chill until firm. Top with mayonnaise. Serves 6.

Mrs. Bill Price (Kay)

 The next time you make jello, pour it into the cups of a twelve cup muffin tin. This way you have individual servings and each one can be different — add fruit to one or two, add ground up celery or carrots to some, etc.

Granny's Potato Salad

1 Dutch oven full of boiled
    potatoes (leave jackets on)
4 cooked diced eggs
2 chopped pickles
1 medium jar diced pimentos
Salt and pepper to taste
1 pint mayonnaise or Miracle
    Whip
3 heaping teaspoon French's
    mustard

Allow boiled potatoes to cool on flat surface. In a large bowl peel and dice potatoes. Add eggs, pickles, and pimentos. Salt and pepper to taste. Add mustard and mayonnaise and stir. Do not over-mix as the salad will be creamy instead of chunky. Is best when left to sit for a few minutes before serving to allow flavor to travel through the salad. Servings: The family.

Mrs. Rusty Graham (Nelda)

Fancy Potato Salad

6 pounds potatoes
1 cup salad dressing
1 cup French dressing
½ ounce salt
3½ tablespoons vinegar
6 eggs, boiled and diced
2 ounces chopped green
    pepper
3 ounces chopped pimentos
½ pound chopped celery
6 ounces diced onions
4 ounces chopped dill pickles

Cook potatoes in jackets until tender. Cool, peel, and cut up in pieces. Mix all ingredients together and serve chilled. Flavor is better if refrigerated overnight. Serves 12.

Mrs. Kirk Brown (Ellen)

Fresh Spinach Salad

½ pound fresh spinach
1 small head lettuce
3 green onions, chopped
3 hard-boiled eggs, sliced
1 cup frozen peas
½ cup chopped celery
1 cup grated cheddar cheese
½ pound bacon, crumbled

Dressing:
1 cup Hellman's mayonnaise
1 cup sour cream
1 package Hidden Valley
   Ranch dressing

Tear spinach and lettuce into bite-size pieces. Layer all in order given except bacon. Seal with dressing and let set several hours. Add crumbled bacon, toss and serve. Serves 6.

Mrs. Brett Thacker (Joyce)

Spinach Salad & Dressing

1 bag spinach
1 (8-ounce) can sliced water
   chestnuts
8 bacon strips, browned and
   crumbled
4 hard boiled eggs, sliced

Toss and refrigerate.

Dressing:
1 cup oil
¾ cup sugar
½ teaspoon salt
¼ cup vinegar
⅓ cup catsup
2 tablespoons
   Worcestershire
1 onion (or 3 tablespoons
   minced onion)

Mix in blender. Add dressing at serving time.

Mrs. Mackey Morgan (Margaret)

Mandarin Salad

¼ cup oil
2 tablespoons sugar
2 tablespoons vinegar
½ teaspoon salt
Dash red pepper sauce
¼ head lettuce (be sure to wash, dry, and chill well before using)
¼ bunch spinach (wash, dry, and chill)
¼ cup sliced almonds
2 green onions, sliced
1 (11-ounce) can mandarin oranges
2-3 slices crisp fried bacon, crumbled

Mix the oil, sugar, vinegar, salt, and pepper sauce together. Toss together lettuce, spinach, almonds, onions, mandarin oranges, and bacon. Pour dressing over lettuce mixture and mix well. Serves 4.

Mrs. Roy Marchbanks (Pam)

Spinach and Avocado Salad with Dressing

⅓ cup red wine vinegar
1 cup olive oil
½ teaspoon mustard
¼ cup chopped parsley
2 tablespoons sugar
1 teaspoon salt
2 cloves garlic, minced
⅓ cup sour cream
1¼ pounds fresh spinach
3 ripe avocados
8 slices crisp bacon
1½ cups croutons
⅓ cup sour cream
Sliced mushrooms (optional)
Sliced tomatoes (optional)
Red onions (optional)

Mix the vinegar, oil, mustard, parsley, sugar, salt, and garlic. Add the sour cream just before serving on salad. Trim spinach. Wash and let drain. Toss spinach with sliced avocados, diced bacon and croutons. Toss with dressing until spinach is well coated. Serves 6.

You may add sliced mushrooms, sliced tomatoes, and red onion if desired.

Mrs. F. A. Blankenbeckler, III (Alice)

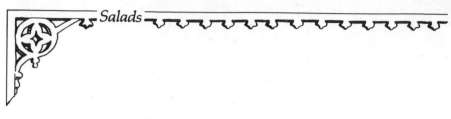

Tomato Soup Salad

1 can tomato juice
1 envelope plain gelatin
¼ cup cold water
½ cup chopped celery
½ cup chopped green pepper
Grated onion to taste
Lemon juice to taste
1 cup chopped pecans
1 cup mayonnaise
3 (3-ounce) packages
  Philadelphia cream cheese,
  softened
⅓ cup sliced green olives

Heat soup, gelatin and water. Cool and add remaining ingredients. Pour mixture into mold and let set overnight. Serves 8.

Mrs. Erling Holey (Susan)

Tomatoes Vinaigrette

4 large tomatoes
¼ cup plus 2 tablespoons
  parsley
1 clove garlic, crushed
¼ cup plus 2 tablespoons
  olive oil
2 tablespoons vinegar
1½ teaspoons basil
1 teaspoon salt
⅛ teaspoon pepper

Slice tomatoes and place in a serving bowl. Sprinkle with parsley. Combine next 6 ingredients in a jar, cover and shake, then pour over tomatoes. Chill 3 hours. Serves 8.

Mrs. John Stroope (Susan)

Creamy Garden Fiesta

1 cup mayonnaise
2 teaspoons chopped green
  onion
1 teaspoon lemon juice
½ teaspoon salt
¼ teaspoon pepper
1½ cups chopped cucumber
¼ pound cooked green
  beans, cut 1-inch pieces
1 cup sliced carrots
1 cup sliced zucchini
½ cup sliced radishes
4 ounces thin spaghetti,
  cooked
½ cup chopped green pepper

In large bowl combine and stir ingredients until smooth. Toss to coat well. Cover. Chill. Serves 6-8.

Mrs. Mike Hayes (Eva)

Vermicelli Salad

2 quarts water
2 tablespoons salt
1 package vermicelli
4 tablespoons Wesson oil
2 tablespoons fresh lemon
  juice
3 tablespoons Accent
2 bunches (or 1 cup) green
  onions
1 bell pepper
6 celery stalks
1 large can ripe olives
1 small jar pimentos
1 pint mayonnaise

Bring water and salt to a rapid boil. Drop in vermicelli, small amounts at a time, stirring gently. Boil rapidly for 10 minutes. Drain water but do not wash. Mix Wesson oil, lemon juice and Accent together and pour over vermicelli. Cover and place in the refrigerator. Chop the vegetables *very fine* and mix all ingredients in with vermicelli. Cover and refrigerate. Serves 12.

Note: *The longer in the refrigerator the better.*

Mrs. Bobby Oliver (Emily)

Vermicelli Salad

1 (12-ounce) package
   vermicelli
4 tablespoons vegetable oil
3 tablespoons lemon juice
1 tablespoon Accent (MSG)

Next day add:
1 jar (small) pimento
1 cup chopped celery
1 pint mayonnaise
½ cup chopped onion
1 cup chopped ripe olives
1 cup chopped green pepper

Break vermicelli into small pieces and cook according to directions-let cool and marinate overnight in oil, juice, and MSG.

Chill and serve.

Mrs. Ben Boone (Sharon)

Easy Caesar Salad

4 heads romaine, torn into
   bite size pieces and chilled
3-4 cups seasoned croutons

Garlic croutons:
6 slices white bread, dry or
   lightly toasted
½ cup clarified butter
2 cloves garlic, minced

Dressing:
1 (8-ounce) bottle Caesar
   salad dressing
1 cup sour cream
¼ cup dry mustard
1½ tablespoons
   Worcestershire sauce
1 cup grated Parmesan cheese
½ teaspoon anchovy paste
1 garlic clove, minced
1 teaspoon pepper

To prepare dressing, combine all of the ingredients and purée in a blender or food processor. Toss with the lettuce and top with the croutons. Garlic croutons: Remove crusts and cut bread into ½-inch squares. Sauté the garlic in butter for 2 minutes over medium heat. Add bread cubes and stir until crisp and golden. Drain on a paper towel. Makes 3-4 cups. Serves 8.

Mrs. William H. Atkinson (Pam)

Platter Salad

1 head lettuce
1 onion, sliced
2 stalks celery-sliced
½ pint sour cream
½ cup sugar
½ cup salad dressing
   (Miracle Whip)
2 tablespoon vinegar
Crisp bacon bits
Parmesan cheese

Tear head of lettuce on platter. Place sliced onion and celery on top. Mix sour cream and sugar. Drizzle over lettuce. Mix salad dressing and vinegar and drizzle over top of vegetables. Sprinkle with crisp bacon bits, then sprinkle generously with Parmesan cheese. Cover with Saran Wrap and refrigerate for 2 hours. Serves 8.

Mrs. Pete Cunningham (Martha)

Seven Layer Salad

1 head lettuce, chopped
1 cup celery, chopped
1 green pepper, chopped
1 small onion, chopped
1 (10-ounce) package frozen
   green peas, cooked

Topping:
1 pint mayonnaise
2 teaspoons sugar
1 cup Parmesan cheese
10-12 slices cooked bacon

Place chopped lettuce in bottom of clear glass serving bowl. Layer celery, green pepper, onion, and peas (cooked according to directions on package). Combine mayonnaise, sugar, Parmesan cheese. Top with crumbled bacon. Mix well and seal over layered ingredients. Cover with plastic wrap and refrigerate the day before. It will stay crisp up to 3 days in the refrigerator. Serves 8-10.

Mrs. Joseph S. Smith (Margaret)

Chinese Salad

1 can La Choy Chinese
vegetables, drained
1 can Del Monte seasoned
green beans, drained
1 can La Choy water
chestnuts, drained
1 medium onion, chopped
1 medium bell pepper,
chopped
1 package sliced almonds,
toasted
Salt and pepper
to taste
¾ cup sugar
1 cup vinegar
¼ cup oil

Drain first three ingredients and mix with all other vegetables and almonds. Bring sugar, vinegar and oil to a boil. Pour over vegetables and chill overnight. Keeps for a long time in the refrigerator. Serves 6.

Mrs. Elmer Nooner (Margaret)

Italian Salad

Italian Dressing:
½ cup salad oil
⅓ cup vinegar
2 tablespoons water
1 tablespoon sugar
1 small onion, thinly sliced
1 clove garlic, crushed
¼ teaspoon celery seed
½ teaspoon salt
Dash of pepper

1 (9-ounce) jar artichoke
hearts
1 (4-ounce) jar pimentos,
chopped
2 cups iceberg lettuce
2 cups romaine
2 cups spinach

In saucepan, bring Italian dressing to a boil; add artichoke hearts. Cook until tender - about 3-5 minutes. Cool. Stir in pimentos and chill dressing until serving time. Add mixture to greens and toss. Serves 4-6.

Mrs. Erling Holey (Susan)

Mexican Salad

1 head lettuce
3-4 chopped green onions
1 cup grated cheddar cheese
1 chopped tomato
1 can Ranch style beans
1 small package Fritos
1 bottle Kraft Catalina
  dressing

Combine lettuce, onions, cheese, and tomato. Drain beans and add to vegetables. Toss Fritos and Catalina dressing with salad ingredients just before serving. Serves 6.

Mrs. Homer Denning (Linda)

Creamy Blue Cheese Dressing

½ cup sour cream
2 tablespoons mayonnaise
Juice of ½ lemon
Tops of 2 green onions,
  chopped
1 (4 ounce) blue cheese,
  crumbled
½ tablespoon
  Worcestershire sauce
Pinch of salt (optional)
Pinch of sugar (optional)

Mix all ingredients together. Add a pinch of salt and a little sugar if desired. Yields 1 cup.

Mrs. Robert M. Cox (Dee)

Honey French Dressing

1 cup salad oil
½ cup catsup
½ cup vinegar
⅓ cup honey
1 teaspoon salt
½ onion, thinly sliced
¼ clove garlic

Blend and chill.

Mrs. Edward Burleson (Nan)

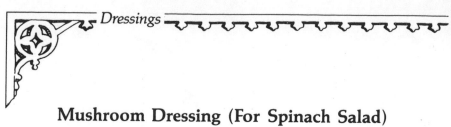

Mushroom Dressing (For Spinach Salad)

1 can cream of mushroom
  soup
¼ cup water
¼ cup tarragon vinegar
1½ tablespoons sugar
1 teaspoon dry mustard
¼ teaspoon celery seed
¼ teaspoon marjoram leaves,
  crushed
Dash Worcestershire

In saucepan, combine above ingredients. Heat, stirring occasionally. Chill or serve room temperture. Yield 1½ cups.

Mrs. Mike Hayes (Eva)

Orange Herb Dressing

1 cup orange marmalade
1 cup salad oil
½ cup lime juice
¼ cup lemon juice
1 small onion, minced
1 small garlic clove, minced
1 teaspoon tarragon,
  crumbled
1 tablespoon parsley, minced
½ teaspoon salt

Combine all ingredients and blend until thick and creamy. Chill until ready to serve. Makes 2½ cups.

Mrs. Griggs DeHay (Gay)

Poppy Seed Fruit Salad Dressing

¾ cup sugar
1½ teaspoons salt
1 teaspoon dry mustard
⅓ cup vinegar
1 cup Crisco oil
1 tablespoon poppy seeds

Combine sugar, salt, and dry mustard in small mixing bowl. Stir in vinegar. Beat at medium speed while adding oil. Beat for 5-10 minutes. Add poppy seeds. Pour into screw top jar and refrigerate. Serve over any fruit.

Mrs. James Beller (Linda)

Salad Dressing

1 cup salad oil
5 tablespoons red wine
   vinegar
4 tablespoons sour cream
1½ teaspoons salt
1½ teaspoons dry mustard
2 tablespoons sugar
Pepper to taste
2 teaspoons chopped parsley
2 cloves garlic, crushed
1-2 eggs, boiled and chopped
4-5 slices bacon, fried and
   crumbled

Flash blend first 9 ingredients. Stir in eggs and bacon.

Mrs. Ben Boone (Sharon)

Strawberry Bavarian Dressing

1½ cups strawberries
   (fresh or frozen)
1 teaspoon unflavored gelatin
¼ cup cream sherry
3 tablespoons sugar
1 egg
1 teaspoon vanilla
½ cup whipping cream
Fresh fruit

Crush ½ cup of berries. In small pan, soften gelatin in crushed berries and sherry. Cook and stir over low heat until gelatin is dissolved. Cool slightly. Place gelatin mixture in blender on high speed for 30-45 seconds. Add sugar, egg, vanilla and blend 5 seconds. Add remaining berries and blend 5 seconds more. With blender running, add whipping cream and continue blending 20-30 seconds more. Chill several hours. Serve with fresh fruit.

Mrs. Mike Hayes (Eva)

This 1½ story modified L-plan home with Queen Anne details was built in 1894 on Main Street, near the turn in to Getzendaner Park with its Chatauqua Auditorium. Mr. E. F. Owen, a reporter for the old Dallas News newspaper, was a longtime owner. One of the most striking features of this home is the 3-bay porch with the shed roof design. This porch is distinguished by its frieze and the unusual paired columns linked by Gothic-inspired lancet arches. The tower and stained glass transoms are typical Queen Anne details.

BREADS

Measurements

Dash	⅛ teaspoon
1 Tablespoon	3 teaspoons (½ ounce)
2 Tablespoons	⅛ cup (1 ounce)
4 Tablespoons	¼ cup (2 ounces)
5 Tablespoons + 1 teaspoon	⅓ cup
8 Tablespoons	½ cup (4 ounces)
16 Tablespoons	1 cup (8 ounces)
1 cup	½ pint (8 ounces)
2 cups	1 pint (16 ounces)
4 cups	1 quart (32 ounces)
1 quart	2 pints
2 quarts	½ gallon (4 pints)
4 quarts	1 gallon
16 ounces	1 pound
1 pound butter	2 cups or 4 sticks

Borden's Buttermilk Biscuits

2 cups flour
½ teaspoon salt
3 teaspoons baking powder
¼ teaspoon soda
5 tablespoons shortening
1 cup Bordens buttermilk

Combine dry ingredients. Add shortening and blend with pastry blender or 2 knives. Add buttermilk, all at once, and stir until dough follows fork around bowl. Turn out on well floured surface and knead ½ minute. Roll ⅜-inch thick, fold, cut and bake on ungreased pan at 450° for 12 to 15 minutes. (I learned to make these as a bride. They aren't as difficult as they sound!) 1 cup whole milk with 1½ tablespoons lemon juice may be substituted for buttermilk. Yields 12 muffins.

Mrs. Donald Locke (Marilyn)

Quick Drop Biscuits

1¼ cups self-rising flour
1 cup whipping cream (not whipped)

Combine flour and cream, and stir until well mixed. Drop dough by the teaspoon onto lightly greased baking sheet. Bake at 425° for 8-10 minutes. Makes 3-4 dozen bite size or 2-3 dozen 1½-inch diameter biscuits.

Mrs. Steve Loftis (Nina)

 To save time cooking your morning sausage, crumple up some tinfoil in a pie pan and arrange your sliced sausage on it. Then put it in the oven with your biscuits to cook. The grease will drain into the crumples of the foil.

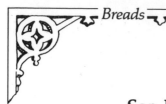

San Jacinto Inn Biscuits

4 cups flour
3 teaspoons baking powder
1 teaspoon salt
1 teaspoon sugar
¾ cup shortening
1¾ cups milk

Sift flour and dry ingredients in mixing bowl. Add shortening and milk and work with hands on lightly floured board. Roll out and cut with biscuit (cookie) cutter. Place on cookie sheet lightly sprayed with PAM. Bake at 425° for 15 minutes. Yields 20 large biscuits.

Mrs. Michael Leath (Kay)

Peggy's Beer Biscuits

4 cups Bisquick
1 (12-ounce) can beer (flat)
2 tablespoons sugar

Mix well. Pour into greased muffin tins or muffin cups. Bake at 425° for 10 minutes. To flatten beer, leave can opened for several hours or put in a container and shake vigorously until it quits foaming. Serves 12.

Mrs. Dennis Horak (Barbara Sue)

Coconut Praline Toast

6 slices of bread
2 tablespoons butter
4 tablespoons brown sugar
2 tablespoons cream
¼ teaspoon vanilla
¼ cup coconut

Remove crusts from six slices of bread. Broil toast on one side. Melt butter in a saucepan. Remove from heat and add brown sugar, cream, vanilla, and coconut. Spread mixture over the untoasted side of the bread. Return to broiler until it bubbles (approximately 1½ minutes) Serves 6.

Nice at breakfast, for a change.

Mrs. F. A. Blankenbeckler, III (Alice)

West Texas Cornbread

1 cup yellow cornmeal
1 tablespoon double acting
  baking powder
1 cup (4-ounce) cheddar
  cheese (sharp)
2 eggs
1 cup oil (salad)
1 cup sour cream
1 can (8-ounce) cream-style
  corn
1 can (4-ounce) chopped
  green chilies
1 small onion, chopped
1 small jar diced pimentos
1 pound *hot* sausage-cooked
  and crumbled

In large bowl, combine dry ingredients. Next add wet ingredients and stir. Pour into greased sheath cake pan. Cook uncovered 350° oven until lightly brown. Test for doneness with toothpick.

A meal in itself!

Mrs. Rusty Graham (Nelda)

Easy Cornbread

¾ cup white cornmeal with
  buttermilk
1¼ cups Bisquick
⅓ cup sugar
1 cup milk
1 egg
1 tablespoon melted butter

Mix all the dry ingredients. Combine all the wet ingredients. Mix together well. Pour into a buttered 8-inch square baking pan. Bake at 350° for 20 minutes. Serves 8.

Mrs. F. A. Blankenbeckler III (Alice)

Mexican Cornbread

1½ cups yellow corn meal
3 teaspoons baking powder
2 eggs
1 tablespoon salt
⅔ cup Wesson oil
1 cup sweet milk
1 cup grated cheese
 (Velveeta)
3-4 Jalapeño peppers, finely
 chopped
1 small can creamed corn

Mix all ingredients together well. Grease pan and pour in batter. Bake at 400° until nicely brown. (About 30-45 minutes.) Serves 6.

Good with pinto beans for a different meal.

Mrs. Dennis Horak (Barbara Sue)

Hot Water Cornbread

1 cup cornmeal
3 tablespoons flour
1 teaspoon salt
1 pod red pepper
½ teaspoon dried onion
Boiling water

Mix ingredients together and add boiling water gradually until mixture will stick together. Dampen hands in cold water and roll into sticks. Fry in hot grease. Serves 4-6.

Mrs. Randy Owens (Liz)

Hoe Cakes

1 cup self-rising flour
2 cups self-rising white corn
 meal
1½ cups chopped green
 onions (white & green)
 lightly packed
2 tablespoons sugar
2 ¼ cups cold milk

Mix dry ingredients; add cold milk to make a medium batter. Drop one tablespoon of batter at a time into hot oil ¼-inch deep. (A Fry Baby works great!) Turn only once. When brown all over, drain on paper towels. The finished cakes should be golden brown and about ½-inch thick. Serves 6.

These are perfect served with seafood or fresh vegetables.

Mrs. James Fanning (Valanne)

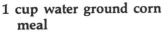

Kentucky Spoon Bread

1 cup water ground corn
  meal
1 teaspoon salt
1 teaspoon baking powder
2 cups milk, scalded
3 tablespoons butter
1 cup milk
3 egg yolks
3 egg whites, beaten stiff

Mix dry ingredients. Melt butter in hot milk, remove from heat and slowly pour into cornmeal, beating vigorously to avoid lumps. Return to heat and cook, stirring for a few seconds until quite thick. Beat in the extra milk and when slightly cooled, the yolks. Fold in the whites. Bake, uncovered, in a buttered casserole until firm. Bake at 350° for 50-60 minutes.

Mrs. Ben Boone (Sharon)

Golden Popovers

3 tablespoons unsalted butter
4 medium eggs
1 cup all-purpose flour
Pinch of salt (optional)
Freshly ground black pepper
  to taste
½ cup heavy cream
1 cup milk
¼ cup fresh chives, snipped
  fine or freeze-dried

Make them in muffin tins, in miniature or in your favorite shapes. Ad lib with your favorite herbs. Preheat oven to 400° . Butter muffin tins with one tablespoon butter. Melt remaining two tablespoons. In a food processor fitted with steel blade, process eggs, flour, salt and pepper for 10 seconds, or until well blended. With motor running, slowly pour in cream, milk and melted butter. Process until smooth. Remove to a bowl and gently fold in chives. Fill buttered muffin tins ⅔ full with batter. Place on middle rack of oven and bake for 35 minutes. DON'T OPEN OVEN OR POPOVERS WILL FALL! Serve warm. Makes 12.

Mrs. Rusty Graham (Nelda)

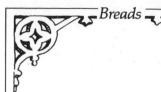

New York's Town and Country Popovers

2 eggs
1 cup milk
1 cup sifted flour
½ teaspoon salt

Beat ingredients till smooth. Fill pre-heated iron popover pans or iron muffin tins ¾ full. Bake in hot oven (450°) for 30 minutes. Then reduce heat to 375°. Bake until firm to the touch, 10-15 additional minutes. Serves 12.

Variation—add cut up green onions and tops to batter.

Mrs. Clovis Mitchell (Omajeanne)

Apple Flaps

1½ cups flour
2 tablespoons sugar
1 tablespoon baking powder
¼ teaspoon salt
⅛ teaspoon nutmeg
2 eggs, beaten
¾ cup milk
2 tablespoons melted butter
1 cup applesauce

Mix dry ingredients; add eggs, milk, melted butter and applesauce. Stir until moistened. Cook on hot griddle. Serves 4-6.

Mrs. Gary Morrow (Rikki)

Waffles

2 eggs, separated
1 cup milk
½ teaspoon vanilla
2 tablespoons vegetable oil
1¼ cups flour
1 tablespoon baking powder
1 teaspoon salt
2 tablespoons sugar

Beat egg whites until stiff. Set aside. Add egg yolks to other liquid ingredients. Add these to dry ingredients. Fold in egg whites. Pour on griddle and cook. Makes 8 waffles.

Mrs. Joe Grubbs (Jo Beth)

Stuffed Bread

4½ pounds margarine or butter
2 large onions, chopped finely
1 bottle dried parsley flakes
5 packages Swiss or mozzarella
   cheese slices
1½ pounds bacon
12 large loaves French bread

Melt buttter. Add chopped onion and parsley. Cut cheese slices in half, then again in triangular halves. Cut bread into 8 pieces (being sure not to cut all the way through). Put a slice of cheese into each cut. Pour butter, onion and parsley mixture into each cut and on top. Be generous. Lay two strips of uncooked bacon on top of bread. Wrap tightly in foil and heat. Just before serving, open foil and turn on broiler to crisp bacon. (If you prepare and freeze, do not heat or broil bacon until ready to use.) Makes 12 loaves.

This recipe may be cut down in order to prepare fewer loaves. Great served with Italian food or barbeque. Also, good served as an appetizer with or without soup.

Mrs. Dennis Horak (Barbara Sue)

Bread Sticks

1 loaf bread (crust removed and
   bread sliced in strips)
½-1 cup butter, melted
Cayenne pepper
Parmesan cheese

Quickly dip both sides of the crustless bread sticks in melted butter. Place on cookie sheet, sprinkle lightly with pepper and cheese. Cook 30 minutes at 250°. Serves many.

Mrs. Bill Price (Kay)

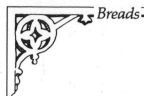

Garlic Bread Sticks

1 (9-inch) loaf unsliced bread
½ cup butter, softened
2 cloves garlic, minced
3-4 tablespoons sesame seeds,
  toasted.

Trim crust from bread. Cut loaf in half length-wise, then in 8 equal cross-wise slices. Combine butter and garlic, mixing well. Spread on all sides of bread slices. Arrange on baking sheet and sprinkle with sesame seeds. Bake at 400° for 10 minutes.

Mrs. Griggs DeHay (Gay)

Peanut Sticks

1 loaf bread (2 or 3 days old)
½ cup peanut butter
1½ cups Wesson oil

Take 2 or 3 day old sliced bread. Trim crusts off generously. Save to toast. Cut slices of bread into five strips. Place trimmings and slices in 250° oven for one hour. Dice or crush the crust into crumbs. Can use blender or food processor to do crumbs. Mix peanut butter and oil. Dip bread sticks into this mixture and then roll in bread crumbs. Store in air tight container on paper towels. Serves 20.

A different party snack.

Mrs. Lonell Wilson (Betty)

Apricot Bread

1 cup dried apricots
1 cup sugar
½ cup brown sugar
2 tablespoons butter
1 egg
¼ cup water
½ cup orange juice
2 cups flour
2 teaspoons baking powder
½ teaspoon soda
¾ teaspoon salt
½ cup nuts

Soak apricots 30 minutes. Drain and cut into pieces. Mix sugars, butter, egg, water, and juice. Sift dry ingredients and blend into sugar mixture. Stir in nuts and apricots. Let stand 30 minutes. Fill loaf pan(s) half full. Bake for 60 minutes at 350°. Yields 1 loaf.

"This recipe will make 2 small loaves, also. It can be doubled nicely."

Mrs. Kirk Brown (Ellen)

Banana Nut Bread

1½ sticks butter
1½ cups sugar
3 eggs, separated
4 large bananas mashed, about 1½ cups
½ cup milk
½ cup sour cream
3 cups flour
1½ teaspoons soda
¾ teaspoon salt
¾ cup pecans—pieces or finely chopped

Grease and flour 4 small loaf pans or two 9x5-inch loaf pans. Cream butter and sugar. Add egg yolks, mixing well. Mix in bananas. Measure ½ cup milk and add sour cream to make one cup. Sift together flour, soda, and salt. Add flour and milk mixture alternately to the banana mixture. Mix in pecans. Beat egg whites until stiff and fold into batter. Divide batter equally among loaf pans. Bake at 300° for 40 -50 minutes. Cool on a rack. Yields 2 loaves.

Mrs. Craig Curry (Karen)

Blender Banana Bread

1 egg
¼ cup margarine
1 cup mashed bananas
1 cup sugar
1 cup raisins
2 cups flour
1 teaspoon baking soda
1 teaspoon salt

Put first five ingredients into the blender. Whirl on low until smooth. Combine dry ingredients in large bowl. Add blender mixture, and stir until moistened. Turn into a greased loaf pan. Bake at 325° for 55-60 minutes. Yields 1 loaf.

Mrs. Kirk Brown (Ellen)

Fresh Blueberry Bread

1 cup all purpose flour
1 cup whole wheat flour
1 cup quick-cooking oats,
  uncooked
½ cup sugar
1 tablespoon baking powder
½ teaspoon salt
½ teaspoon soda
1 teaspoon cinnamon
¼ cup plus 2 tablespoons
  margarine, softened
2 eggs, slightly beaten
1 cup milk
¼ cup light corn syrup
1 cup fresh blueberries

Combine all dry ingredients in large mixing bowl. Cut in margarine until mixture resembles coarse meal. Combine eggs, milk, and corn syrup; mix well. Add to dry ingredients, just mixing until moistened. Fold in blueberries. Bake in a greased and floured 9x5x3-inch loaf pan at 350° for 1 hour or until a wooden pick comes out clean. Cool in pan 10 minutes, remove from pan and cool completely on wire rack. (You can also use smaller loaf pans and make several from this recipe. Freezes well.)

Mrs. David Ballard (Karen)

Cranberry-Nut Bread

2 cups flour
1 cup sugar
1 teaspoon salt
1½ teaspoons baking powder
½ teaspoon baking soda
1 tablespoon lemon or
    orange peel
2 tablespoons shortening
¾ cup orange juice
1 egg, well beaten
½ cup nuts, chopped
1 cup whole cranberries,
    finely chopped

Combine all ingredients. Mix well. Pour into greased loaf pan. Bake at 350° for 50 minutes or until wooden toothpick inserted in center comes out clean. Freezes well. Yields 1 loaf.

Mrs. Pat Sullivan (Gloria)

Hawaiian Bread

1 package yellow cake mix
2 packages yeast
½ teaspoon salt
2½ cups warm water
5 cups flour
4 tablespoons melted butter

Combine cake mix and yeast. Next, combine salt and water. Add cake mixture to water and salt mixture. Add flour last. Mix well and knead lightly. Let rise 1 hour. Knead lightly again, pat out and cut for rolls. Let rise until double. Bake at 375°. When brown, brush with melted butter and bake a little longer. Serves 24.

Mrs. B. D. Cope (Charlene)

Monkey Bread

1½ cups sugar
2 teaspoons vanilla
1 stick butter
2 teaspoons cinnamon
3 cans refrigerator biscuits
  cut into pieces.

Bring 1 cup sugar, vanilla, and butter to a boil. Remove from heat. Combine ½ cup sugar and cinnamon in large tupperware bowl with lid. Shake to mix well. Cut one can of biscuits at a time and drop into sugar-cinnamon mixture. Mix until well coated. Arrange in well greased tube pan. Drizzle 3 tablespoons syrup mixture over biscuits. Repeat with remaining biscuits, using all of syrup. Pecans may also be sprinkled over each layer, Bake at 350° for 30 minutes. Cool 10 minutes before inverting on serving dish. Serves 10-12.

Mrs. Lonell Wilson (Betty)

Poppy Seed Bread

3 eggs
1½ cups Wesson oil
2¼ cups sugar
3 cups flour
1½ teaspoons salt
1½ teaspoons baking
  powder
1½ cups milk
1½ teaspoons almond
  extract
1½ teaspoons butter extract
1½ teaspoons vanilla
1½ tablespoons poppy seed

Glaze:
¼ cup orange juice
¾ cup powdered sugar
½ teaspoon butter extract
½ teaspoon almond extract
½ teaspoon vanilla

Beat together eggs, oil, and sugar. Sift together flour, salt, and baking powder. Add to egg mixture alternately with milk. Stir in extracts and poppy seed. Pour into two greased and floured 9x5-inch loaf pans. Bake at 350° for 60 minutes or until toothpick comes out clean. Combine all glaze ingredients. Remove bread from oven and cool in pans slightly. Spoon glaze mixture over warm breads. When cool remove from pans. Makes 2 loaves.

Mrs. Bill Price (Kay)

Ma Ballard's Pumpkin Bread

1 cup Wesson oil
3 cups sugar
1 can pumpkin
4 eggs, beaten
3 cups flour
1 teaspoon salt
1 teaspoon baking powder
1½ teaspoons soda
1¼ teaspoons cinnamon
1 teaspoon cloves
1 cup walnuts, chopped
  (optional)

Mix all ingredients in order. If dry, add 1 tablespoon water. Grease and flour 3 (1-pound) coffee cans. Fill ⅔ full and bake at 350° for 1 hour. Freezes well. Just remove from cans and wrap well in plastic wrap. Yields 3 loaves.

Mrs. David Ballard (Karen)

Strawberry Bread

3 cups sifted flour
1 teaspoon soda
1 teaspoon salt
1 tablespoon cinnamon
2 cups sugar
4 eggs, beaten
1¼ cups vegetable oil
2 cups strawberries, sliced
1¼ cups chopped pecans

Preheat oven to 350°. Sift dry ingredients together. Mix eggs, vegetable oil, strawberries and nuts. Add to dry ingredients, stirring just enough to moisten. Pour into 2 greased, standard-size loaf pans. Bake for 1 hour. Let loaves cool 5 minutes before removing from pans. Finish cooling on wire rack. Makes 2 loaves.

Mrs. Jack Curlin (Nelda)

Zucchini Bread

3 eggs
1 cup oil
2 teaspoons vanilla
1½ teaspoons cinnamon
¾ teaspoon nutmeg
2 cups sugar
1 teaspoon salt
2 teaspoons baking soda
¼ teaspoon baking powder
3 cups sifted flour
1 (8-ounce) can crushed
   pineapple, drained
2 cups grated zucchini,
   peeled first
1 cup chopped nuts
1 cup raisins

Beat eggs. Add everything except nuts and raisins with eggs and mix well. Add nuts and raisins. Pour into 4 small greased and floured loaf pans. May be baked in a bundt cake pan. Bake at 350° for 50 minutes. Makes 4 loaves.

Mrs. Rick Pitts (Becky)

Aunt Ruby's Muffins

1 cup flour
1 cup oatmeal
2 teaspoons baking powder
1 teaspoon cinnamon
½ teaspoon salt
1 egg, beaten
⅔ cup milk
⅓ cup Wesson oil

Combine dry ingredients. Add liquids and mix just enough to wet dry ingredients. Bake at 400° until done. Good with soup, stew, etc. Yields 12 muffins.

Mrs. Donald Locke (Marilyn)

Arkansas Peach Muffins

1 egg
1 cup milk
¼ cup oil
⅔ cup sugar
½ teaspoon salt
¼ teaspoon cinnamon
1 teaspoon lemon juice
¼ teaspoon vanilla
2 cups flour
3 teaspoons baking powder
1 cup unpeeled chopped
   peaches

Beat together egg, milk, oil, sugar, salt, cinnamon, lemon juice, and vanilla. Sift together flour and baking powder. Stir mixtures together with 1 cup peaches until dry ingredients are moistened. Fill greased muffin tins ⅔ full and bake at 450° for 20 minutes. Serves 16.

A nice break from blueberry muffins.

Mrs. Mike Owens (Suzy)

Coffee Cake Muffins

1½ cups flour
½ cup sugar
2 teaspoons baking powder
¼ cup liquid shortening
1 well beaten egg
½ cup milk
½ cup brown sugar
½ cup chopped nuts
2 tablespoons flour
2 teaspoons cinnamon
2 tablespoons butter, melted

Mix first six ingredients to make a batter. Mix next five ingredients in a separate bowl to make the filling. Layer in greased muffin tins (1 tablespoon batter, 1 teaspoon filling, 1 tablespoon batter, 1 teaspoon filling) Bake 350° for 20 minutes. Yields 12.

Tastes great and they look pretty, too. You can add raisins to the filling for a change.

Mrs. Ken Box (Dietra)

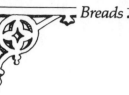

Date-Nut Muffins

1½ cups all-purpose flour
½ cup sugar
2 teaspoons baking powder
½ teaspoon salt
½ cup chopped dates
½ cup chopped pecans
1 egg, beaten
½ cup milk
¼ cup butter, melted

Combine first four ingredients in a bowl. Stir in dates and pecans. Make a well in center of mixture. Combine egg, milk and butter. Add to dry ingredients, stir just until moistened. Spoon into greased muffin pans filling ¾ full. Bake at 400° for 18 - 20 minutes. Yields 12.

Kids like these.

Mrs. Jeff Kosoris (Susan)

Megan's Muffins

2 cups flour
1 tablespoon baking powder
½ teaspoon salt
1 tablespoon cinnamon
½ teaspoon cloves
1 egg
⅓ cup honey
4 tablespoons melted butter
¾ cup milk
½ teaspoon vanilla
1 cup coarsely grated
   zucchini

Sift dry ingredients in meduim bowl. In another bowl, beat egg well. Add honey and butter and vanilla and beat well. Add milk and beat well again. Combine this with dry mixture and stir just till moistened. Gently stir in zucchini. Immediately spoon into well-greased tins. Bake 400° for 20-25 minutes. To make sweeter add 1/4 cup sugar. Yields 12.

Mrs. Pleasant Mitchell (Helen)

My Favorite Muffins

⅔ cup shortening
1 cup sugar
3 eggs
3 cups flour
2 heaping teaspoons baking powder
1 teaspoon salt
1 cup milk

Cream together shortening and sugar; add eggs one at a time. Sift flour, baking powder, and salt together. Add dry ingredients alternately with 1 cup milk. Bake at 375° until light brown (about 30 minutes). Yields 12.

Mrs. Jeff Kosoris (Susan)

Six Weeks Muffins

1 (15-ounce) box raisin bran
3 cups sugar
5 cups flour, sifted
2 teaspoons soda
2 teaspoons salt
4 eggs, beaten
1 cup Crisco oil
1 quart buttermilk

Mix dry ingredients in a very large bowl. Add eggs, oil, and buttermilk. Mix well. Fill muffin tins ⅔ full. Bake 15-20 minutes at 400°. Store, covered, in refrigerator for six weeks. Serves many.

You can subsitute 40% Bran Flakes if you don't care for raisins.

Mrs. Rick Pitts (Becky)

Sweet Muffins

1 egg
½ cup milk
¼ cup oil
1½ cups flour
½ cup sugar
2 teaspoons baking powder
½ teaspoon salt
1½ cups fruit (blueberries)

Preheat oven to 400°. Grease bottoms of 12 medium muffin cups. Beat egg, stir in milk and oil. Mix in rest of ingredients (except blueberries) just until flour is moistened. Batter should be lumpy. Fold in blueberries. Fill cups ⅔ full. Bake 20-25 minutes. Remove immediately from tins. Makes 12.

Mrs. Michael Leath (Kay)

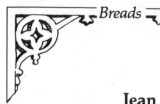

Jean Claire's Sweet Rolls

1 cake of Fleischmann's yeast
1 tablespoon sugar
¼ cup sugar
2 eggs lightly beaten
½ teaspoon salt
1 stick margarine, melted
1 cup lukewarm water
4 cups Gold Medal Wondra
   Flour
Butter
Brown sugar
Cinnamon
Pecans

Sprinkle 1 tablespoon sugar over yeast cake and let set 5-10 minutes. Sprinkle ¼ cup sugar over this and stir lightly. Add beaten eggs. Add salt, margarine, warm water and flour to yeast mixture. Knead until smooth and then divide dough in half for easier handling. Let rise 1-2 hours. Roll out dough into a rectangle, brush with butter, sprinkle generously with brown sugar and cinnamon. Roll up jelly roll fashion and slice. In bottom of shallow pan, melt 1 or 2 sticks of margarine, depending on pan size, and sprinkle with brown sugar, cinnamon and pecans. Place rolls on top of this mixture and press down lightly. Repeat with remaining dough. Let rise 1 to 2 hours in warm place. Bake at 375° for 8-10 minutes or until golden brown. Turn out onto serving plate while still hot. Yields approximately 3 dozen rolls.

**Submitted by Cathy Moore
in memory of her mother
Jean Claire McElroy**

To make something different for breakfast, cut canned biscuits in quarters and drop them in hot grease to fry till brown. Roll the warm biscuits in cinnamon-sugar and serve.

Grandma's Caramel Rolls

2 (1-pound) loaves frozen
   bread dough
1 stick butter (softened)
Cinnamon
2 cups brown sugar (packed)
1 cup half and half
Chopped pecans

Thaw dough and spread in 15x30-inch rectangle shape on floured board. Spread butter over dough. Sprinkle with cinnamon. Then cover with ¾ cup to 1 cup brown sugar. Sprinkle with chopped nuts and roll into a tight log. Cut into 24 slices with a string or very sharp knife. In a 9x13-inch greased pan, spread remaining brown sugar. Pour cream over sugar. Place slices of roll on top of sugar and cream. Let rise. Bake at 350° for 30-40 minutes. (You may have to cover top with foil to keep from browning too much. When done turn over into cookie sheet, remove pan and cool. Serves 24.

Mrs. Griggs DeHay (Gay)

Ice Box Rolls

1 cake compressed yeast
1 quart scalding hot milk
1 cup sugar
1 cup shortening
2 teaspoons baking powder
1 teaspoon soda
3 teaspoons salt
1 cup boiled potatoes
Flour (to mix in)

Scald milk; add shortening, sugar and mashed potatoes. Let cool before adding yeast which has been dissolved in water or cool milk. Mix in yeast thoroughly. Add enough flour to make soft dough and let rise. Add soda, baking powder and salt and work in sufficient flour to make stiff dough. Place in refrigerator until needed. When ready, knead dough, mold into rolls, place in well greased pans and let rise until double in size. Bake in hot oven (400°). Makes 100 small rolls.

Mrs. Randy Owens (Liz)

Ice Box Rolls

2 packages yeast
¼ cup warm water
½ cup sugar
1 teaspoon salt
2 cups warm water
2 tablespoons oil
5 cups flour

In a small bowl mix the yeast and warm water. In another bowl mix the next 4 ingredients. Then mix contents of both bowls together. Add the flour. Put in large bowl with flour around the edges. Let rise once outside the refrigerator. Mash down and put in refrigerator. Lasts a couple of weeks. Let rise 2 hours before baking at 400° for approximately 20 minutes. Serves many.

Mrs. Steve Kelley (Cindy)

Quick Bread

2 cups warm water
1 package dry yeast
¼ cup sugar (or less)
¾ cup cooking oil
1 beaten egg
4 cups self-rising flour

Mix all ingredients and store in refrigerator. Grease muffin tins and fill each tin almost full. Bake at 400° until brown. These may be baked and frozen and reheated in the microwave. Makes 24.

Mrs. Bobby Oliver (Emily)

Sally Lund Bread

1 package active dry yeast
¼ cup warm water
2 tablespoons Crisco
½ cup sugar
2 eggs
1 teaspoon salt
3½ cups all purpose flour
1 cup warm milk

Soften yeast in warm water. In mixing bowl, cream Crisco and sugar. Beat in eggs and salt. Stir in 1½ cups of flour. Beat vigorously. Stir in milk and softened yeast. Mix well. Add remaining flour. Beat vigorously. Cover. Let rise in warm place until double, about 1 hour. Stir down batter and spoon evenly into greased 10-inch fluted tube pan. Cover. Let rise again until double, 30-45 minutes. Bake in 325° oven for 10 minutes. Increase oven temperature to 375° and bake 20 minutes more. Remove from pan. Serve warm or cool. Serves 10-12.

Mrs. Roy Marchbanks (Pam)

Whole Wheat Bread

2 packages dry yeast
2 cups warm water
3½ cups whole wheat flour
3 cups white flour
¼ cup Crisco oil
1 egg
¾ cup brown sugar
1 teaspoon salt
2 tablespoons honey

Add yeast to warm water. Beat. Measure flours into a bowl and set aside. In another bowl, beat Crisco oil and egg. Add brown sugar, salt, and honey. Beat well. Add 2 cups of flour mixture and yeast and beat well. Add egg mixture and remaining flour. Beat well. Grease dough with oil, cover with a damp cloth, and let rise several hours. Divide into 3 parts. Place dough into greased loaf pans and let rise till double. Cook at 400° for 45 minutes to 1 hour. Makes 3 loaves.

Mrs. Mackey Morgan (Margaret)

The Ellis County Courthouse is one of the finest examples of noted architect J. Gordon Reilly's work. The cornerstone of this red sandstone and granite building was laid on July 4, 1895, when Ellis County, Texas, was the Queen Cotton County of the World. Italian artisans were brought in to fashion the intricate sculptures around the first floor windows and doors. Legend has it that one of the Italian young men fell in love with a local young lady and carved her beautiful features into the Courthouse. As the months went by, the young lady tired of her Italian suitor. The sculptor, betrayed by his love, gradually changed the face of his carvings till they no longer resembled the beautiful young lady. In fact, as you walk around the building, you can see how the face on the Courthouse becomes an ugly gargoyle!

MAIN DISHES

D.PARKER 1987

Substitutions

For These	Use These
1 square unsweetened chocolate	3 Tablespoons cocoa plus 1 Tablespoon butter or margarine
1 whole egg	2 egg yolks plus 1 Tablespoon water
2 large eggs	3 small eggs
1 cup buttermilk or sour milk	1 Tablespoon white vinegar or lemon juice plus milk to fill cup (let stand 5 minutes)
1 cup commercial sour cream	1 Tablespoon lemon juice plus evaporated milk to equal 1 cup
1 cup yogurt	1 cup buttermilk or sour cream
½ cup butter or margarine	7 Tablespoons vegetable shortening
1 Tablespoon cornstarch	2 Tablespoons all purpose flour
1 teaspoon baking powder	½ teaspoon cream of tartar plus ¼ teaspoon baking soda
1 cup cake flour	1 cup all purpose flour minus 2 Tablespoons
1 cup self rising flour	1 cup all purpose flour plus 1 teaspoon baking powder and ½ teaspoon salt
1 clove fresh garlic	1 teaspoon garlic salt or ⅛ teaspoon garlic powder
⅓ cup chopped raw onion	2 Tablespoons instant minced onion
1 Tablespoon fresh herbs	1 teaspoon ground or crushed dry herbs
2 teaspoons fresh minced herbs	½ teaspoon dried herbs
1 pound fresh mushrooms	6 ounces canned mushrooms
1 cup diced cooked chicken	1 can (5 ounces) boned chicken
Juice of 1 lemon	3 Tablespoons bottled juice
Juice of 1 orange	⅓-½ cup canned juice
1 cup barbeque sauce	1 cup ketchup plus 2 teaspoons Worcestershire sauce
1 Tablespoon dry sherry	1 Tablespoon dry vermouth
15 ounce can tomato sauce	6 ounce can tomato paste plus 1 cup water

Barbe Cups

¾ pound ground beef
½ cup barbeque sauce
1 tablespoon minced onion
2 tablespoons brown sugar
1 (8-ounce) can Pillsbury Tenderflake Biscuits
¾ cup shredded sharp Cheddar cheese

Brown the ground beef and drain. Add barbeque sauce, onion, and brown sugar. Take each biscuit and press into an ungreased muffin cup, making sure dough goes up to edge of cup. Spoon meat mixture into cups and sprinkle with cheese. Bake at 400° for 10 to 12 minutes. Serves 10.

Mrs. Kirk Brown (Ellen)

Beef and Rice Casserole

1½ pounds ground meat
1 teaspoon garlic salt
3 cups cooked rice
1 can cream of mushroom soup
½ can Ro-tel tomatoes
½ cup beef broth
1 cup finely chopped onion
2 cups shredded cheddar cheese
3 cups small corn chips

Brown meat with garlic salt in lightly greased skillet. Drain off excess fat. Combine meat and rice. Blend together soup, tomatoes, and beef broth. Stir into meat mixture. In a buttered 2 quart casserole layer half the meat mixture, onions, cheese, and corn chips. Repeat, ending with corn chips. Bake uncovered at 350° for 30 minutes until hot and bubbly.

Mrs. Jeff Kosoris (Susan)

Black-Eyed Casserole

1½ pounds ground beef
1 large onion, chopped
2 garlic cloves, chopped
1 (15-ounce) can Jalapeño
 black-eyed peas, drained
1 (10-ounce) can tomatoes
 with green chilies
1 (10-ounce) can cream of
 chicken soup
1 (10-ounce) can cream of
 mushroom soup
1 (10-ounce) can enchilada
 sauce
¼ teaspoon liquid hot
 pepper seasoning
16 corn tortillas, cut
 in eighths
2 cups sharp Cheddar cheese,
 grated

Sauté ground beef, onion and garlic until lightly browned, stirring to crumble the meat. Stir in remaining ingredients except tortillas and cheese. Alternately layer the mixture of meat and tortillas, beginning and ending with meat mixture in a greased 13x9x2-inch pan. Sprinkle with cheese. Bake at 350° for 30 minutes or until bubbly. Also freezes well.

Mrs. Griggs DeHay (Gay)

Blackeyed Pea Casserole

1 cup white cornmeal
½ cup flour
1 teaspoon salt
½ teaspoon soda
1 cup buttermilk
2 eggs
½ cup oil
1 cup chopped onion
1 cup cooked blackeyed peas
¾ cup creamed corn
1 pound browned ground
 meat
½ pound grated cheddar
 cheese

Mix all ingredients except cheese. Pour into a greased 2 quart casserole dish. Add the cheese last by pressing down into top of casserole. Bake at 350° for 45 minutes.

Mrs. Craig Curry (Karen)

B B Q Brisket

Brisket
Salt
Pepper
Garlic salt
Worcestershire sauce

Sauce:
Water
1 cup catsup
½ cup worcestershire sauce
⅔ cup brown sugar
1 tablespoon lemon juice

Season brisket with salt, pepper, and garlic to individual taste. Sprinkle well with worcestershire sauce. Wrap tightly with two sheets of foil. Bake 30 minutes at 450° then reduce heat to 225° for 7 or 8 hours.

Sauce:
Pour off liquid from brisket and add water to make 1 cup. Add catsup, worcestershire sauce, brown sugar, and lemon juice. Bring to boil and serve over brisket.

Mrs. Randy Owens (Liz)

Brisket

Brisket
Seasoning salt
Garlic salt
Celery salt
Unseasoned tenderizer
4 tablespoons Worcestershire
  sauce
½ bottle liquid smoke

Sprinkle both sides of brisket with the ingredients. Marinate for 24 hours in a covered dish. Wrap brisket in foil and cook in a 225° oven for 6 to 8 hours. Baste with marinade. Refrigerate when the brisket is done. Slice the meat cold and reheat.

Mrs. Rick Pitts (Becky)

 Add two cups of tea (instant is fine) to your juices when cooking cheaper cuts of beef to tenderize them.

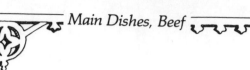

Easy Ground Meat Dish

1 pound ground meat
1 medium onion, chopped
Salt, pepper, garlic (to taste)
1 cup rice
2½ cups water
½ teaspoon salt
1 (1-pound) can bean
  sprouts, drained
⅓ cup soy sauce
1 can mushroom soup
  (undiluted)

Brown meat and onion; season with salt, pepper and garlic salt and drain well. Put uncooked rice in bottom of 3 quart casserole and add 2½ cups water; add salt. Spoon meat over rice and spread bean sprouts over meat. Sprinkle on soy sauce and then spoon on the undiluted mushroom soup. Cover and bake at 350° for 45 minutes to 1 hour. Serves 4-6.

Mrs. Bill Price (Kay)

Easy Oven Meatloaf

1½ pounds ground beef
3 tablespoons Worcestershire
1 egg
1 onion, chopped
½ teaspoon garlic powder
1 teaspoon salt
Pepper, to taste
1 cup quick cooking oatmeal
1 (16-ounce) can tomatoes

Mix all ingredients, using only the juice of the tomatoes (set tomatoes aside). Line rectangular pan with foil and place loaf shaped mixture into pan. Place tomatoes on top of loaf. Bake for one hour at 350°. Serves 4-6

Mrs. Steve Loftis (Nina)

Italian Beef

5 pounds rump roast
1 onion, chopped
2 celery stalks, chopped
4 bay leaves
1 teaspoon thyme
1 bottle red wine
1½ cups rum
3 garlic buttons
Salt
Pepper

Place all ingredients in Dutch oven, cover and bake at 300°, 4 hours. Remove bay leaves; slice or shred meat into bowl. Pour liquid over meat and serve on rolls or buns.

Better the next day.

Mrs. David Ballard (Karen)

Italian Beef Pie

1 pound ground meat
1 (8-ounce) can mushrooms,
    drained
1 tablespoon salad oil
2 packages frozen chopped
    spinach or chopped
    broccoli
1 cup sour cream
1 can cream of celery soup
1 teaspoon garlic salt
½ teaspoon pepper
5 teaspoons minced onion
1 (6-ounce) package sliced
    mozzarella cheese

Preheat oven to 350°. Brown meat and mushrooms in salad oil. Spoon into 2 quart casserole. Stir in spinach, lightly cooked and drained. Add sour cream, soup, garlic salt, pepper, and minced onion. Cut cheese into strips. Put cheese on top of casserole. Do not cover. Bake at 350° for 35-45 minutes. Serves. 4-6.

Mrs. Pat Gardenhire (Susan)

Meal In One For A Crowd

1 tablespoon cooking oil
2 onions, chopped
1 green pepper, chopped
3 buttons garlic, sliced
1 pound ground beef
1 #2 can tomatoes
3 tablespoons chili powder
1 cup water
1 (10-ounce) package frozen
    English peas
1 (16-ounce) can corn
Salt and pepper
1 small can mushroom pieces
8-12 ounces spaghetti
    noodles
2 cups grated sharp cheese

Melt oil and cook onions, pepper, and garlic, but do not brown. Add meat and cook until brown. Add tomatoes, chili powder, and water. Cover and cook over low heat for 30 minutes. Add cooked peas, corn, salt, pepper, and mushrooms. Add cooked spaghetti and blend well. Fill 2 baking pyrex dishes (11x7-inch) or 1 large (13x9-inch) baking pyrex dish with half the mixture and cover with half the cheese. Add rest of mixture and cover with remainder of cheese. Bake 20-30 minutes in preheated 350° oven. Serves 12.

Mrs. Roy Marchbanks (Pam)

Pepper Steak and Vegetables

1 pound round steak
6 tablespoons salad oil, divided
2 tablespoons soy sauce
1 tablespoon cooking sherry
4 tablespoons cornstarch
½ teaspoon sugar
½ teaspoon ginger
1 teaspoon salt
2 green peppers, cut in strips
2 onions, quartered
1 (16-ounce) can stewed tomatoes
1 cup rice, cooked

Cut steak into bite size pieces. Combine with 1 tablespoon salad oil, soy sauce, sherry, cornstarch, sugar, and ginger and set aside. In a large skillet, heat 2 tablespoons salad oil. Sprinkle salt over peppers and onions and cook until tender and crisp. Remove. Add 3 tablespoons salad oil. Cook steak until done. Stir in vegetables and tomatoes and simmer until tomatoes are heated, about 5 minutes. Serve over cooked rice.

Mrs. Roy Marchbanks (Pam)

Roast Tenderloin Diane

¼ cup dry white wine
¼ cup brandy
3 tablespoons lemon juice
2 tablespoons snipped chives
1½ teaspoons salt
1 teaspoon Worcestershire sauce
¼ teaspoon freshly ground pepper
1 (2-pound) beef tenderloin
2 tablespoons water
2 tablespoons butter or margarine

Combine wine, brandy, lemon juice, chives, salt, Worcestershire, and pepper. Place meat in plastic bag, set in loaf dish. Pour marinade over meat and tie bag closed. Let stand no longer than 2 hours at room temperature or overnight in refrigerator, occasionally pressing bag against meat to distribute marinade. Remove meat, reserving marinade. Pat meat dry with paper toweling. Place tenderloin on rack in shallow roasting pan. Bake at 425° for 45-55 minutes, basting meat occasionally with about half of the marinade. In small saucepan heat remaining marinade, the water, and butter till mixture bubbles. Slice meat and arrange on platter. Spoon sauce over meat. Garnish with cooked mushrooms. Serves 6.

Mrs. Jeff Bertsch (Diane)

Prime Rib

5 pounds standing rib roast
  (thawed)
Tenderizer
Garlic
Salt
Pepper

Wash roast and trim fat. Pierce with fork. Rub tenderizer, garlic, salt, and pepper over roast. Cook slowly (325°) for 3 hours on rack. Slice and serve.

Mrs. Rusty Graham (Nelda)

Standing Rib in Rock Salt

Standing Rib or Prime Rib
2 tablespoons Worcestershire
Salt
Pepper
Paprika
Rock salt

Preheat oven to 500°. Rub a standing rib or prime rib roast with Worcestershire. Sprinkle with salt and pepper and dust with paprika. Use the bottom of a large roasting pan such as a turkey roaster without the cover. Completely cover the bottom of the roasting pan with a layer of rock salt. Sprinkle with water until moist but not overly wet. Place the roast, ribs down, on the bed of salt. Cover the roast on all sides in rock salt. It must be totally encased in salt. Sprinkle the salt lightly with water. Do not cover. Place the roast in the oven and bake 12 minutes a pound. Remove the roast. The salt will have hardened. Break it with a wooden mallet or hammer. It will crack. Pull off the hardened salt and carve in the usual fashion.

Mrs. Roy Worthington (Beverly)

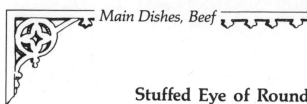

Stuffed Eye of Round

3 pounds eye of round
2 tablespoons salt
1 strip salt pork
3 Spanish sausages
½ pound uncooked ham
4 tablespoons shortening
1 large onion, quartered
1 large green pepper,
  quartered
3 cloves garlic, minced
2 tablespoons oregano
4 tablespoons paprika
4 bay leaves
3 cups water

Pierce a hole through the length of the eye of round. Season inside with salt. Stuff with salt pork, sausage, and ham. Heat 1 tablespoon of shortening in a heavy skillet and brown meat on all sides. Transfer meat to roasting pan. Add onions, green peppers, garlic, oregano, paprika, and bay leaves. Rub remaining shortening into seasoning with hands and press around and on top of the meat. Pour in water and place overnight to marinate. Roast at 325° in uncovered pan for 1 hour. Then cover pan and cook 2 and ½ hours more, basting occasionally.

Mrs. Erling Holey (Susan)

Michael's Beef Stew

1 large onion
¼ cup oil
Salt
Pepper
Flour
6 cups boiling water
2 pounds chuck roast
  (cut up)
1 (10-ounce) can whole
  tomatoes
1 (6-ounce) can tomato paste
1½ teaspoons chili powder
2 beef bouillon cubes
5-6 drops Tabasco
1 teaspoon Worcestershire
  sauce
4 large carrots
2 medium potatoes

Sauté 1 large onion chopped in ¼ cup oil in large stew pot. Salt, pepper and coat with flour 2 pounds well trimmed stew meat. (I buy a small chuck roast and cut up my own meat. There's less waste and it's more tender.) Brown meat in oil with onion. When well browned add 6 cups boiling water, the whole tomatoes broken up, and the can of tomato paste. Bring to boil and simmer 1 and ½ to 2 hours or until meat is tender. While simmering add chili powder, beef, bouillon cubes, Tabasco, carrots cut in small chunks, and potatoes cut into bite size pieces. Add salt and pepper to taste.

Mrs. Mike Owens (Suzy)

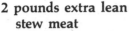 
No Peep Stew

2 pounds extra lean
  stew meat
1 can cream mushroom soup
  (undiluted)
1 (4-ounce) can (plus juice)
  mushroom pieces
1 package Lipton dry onion
  soup mix (regular)
¾ cup dry red wine
¼ cup water
Coarse black pepper to taste

Place ingredients listed in order in Dutch oven. Mix. Cover tightly with foil. Bake at 325° for 3 hours without opening. Serves 6. Serve over rice or noodles.

Mrs. Bill Major (Patsy)

Mushroom Meatballs

1 pound ground beef
1 small onion
1 small green pepper
  (optional)
1 egg
1½ cups cracker crumbs
1 can cream of mushroom
  soup

Mix ingredients well using ½ can soup and make into 7 or 8 nice size meat balls. Place in greased pyrex dish. Cover with foil. Bake at 350° about 35-40 minutes. Remove foil, drain off excess grease. Spoon balance of mushroom soup over each meat ball and return uncovered to oven for 10 minutes. Serves 7-8.

Mrs. Roy Marchbanks (Pam)

 To keep meatloaf from cracking on top as it cooks, rub the loaf with your palm dipped in cold water until it is smooth-then put it in the oven.

Swedish Meatballs

1 (10½-ounce) can cream of celery soup
½ cup water
2 tablespoons chopped dill pickles
1 pound ground beef
⅔ cup dry bread crumbs
1 egg
2 tablespoons minced onion

Mix cream of celery soup, water and chopped dill pickles. Set aside. Combine next 4 ingredients with 1½ cups of soup mixture. Shape into balls and brown in 1 tablespoon shortening. Add remaining soup mixture over balls. Cover and cook 20 minutes.

Mrs. Roy Marchbanks (Pam)

Swedish Meatballs

¾ pound lean ground beef
½ pound ground veal
½ pound ground pork
1½ cups soft bread crumbs
1 cup light cream (half and half)
½ cup chopped onion
1 tablespoon butter
1 egg
¼ cup finely chopped parsley
1½ teaspoons salt
¼ teaspoon ginger
Dash of pepper & nutmeg
2 tablespoons flour
¾ cup canned beef broth
¼ cup cold water
½ teaspoon instant coffee

Grind meat together. Soak bread in cream about 5 minutes. Cook onions in 1 tablespoon butter until tender but not brown. Combine meats, crumb mixture, egg, onion, parsley, and seasonings. Beat and form into 1½-inch balls. Brown in 2 tablespoons butter in skillet, shaking pan to keep balls round. When browned, remove from skillet. Stir into drippings 2 tablespoons flour, beef broth, cold water and instant coffee. Heat and stir until gravy thickens. Return balls to gravy. Cover and cook slowly about 30 minutes.

Mrs. Robert M. Cox (Dee)

Denise's Deep Dish Pizza

1 package active dry yeast
1 cup warm water
2 tablespoons oil
1 teaspoon salt
1 teaspoon sugar
2½ cups flour
1 pound ground beef or
   sausage
1 small can tomato sauce
1 (4-ounce) mozzarella cheese

Dissolve yeast in water. Stir in oil, salt, sugar, and flour. Beat twenty strokes. Let rise 5 minutes. Cook 1 pound ground beef or sausage. Drain. Press dough into lightly greased oblong pan. Add tomato sauce, meat mixture, and any extras you desire (olives, mushrooms, peppers, onions, etc). Bake 15 minutes at 400°. Add cheese and bake another 5 minutes.

Mrs. Lonell Wilson (Betty)

Homemade Lasagna

2 pounds ground beef
2 cups chopped onion
2 cloves chopped garlic
2 teaspoons Accent seasoning
2 teaspoons salt
⅓ cup oil
2 (2-pound) cans tomatoes
2 (4-ounce) cans tomato
   paste
3 teaspoons ground oregano
2 teaspoons onion salt
½ teaspoon black pepper
1 (12-ounce) lasagna noodles,
   cooked
1 (12-ounce) mozzarella
   cheese
1 (14-ounce) ricotta cheese or
   dry cottage cheese
Parmesan cheese, grated

Sauté first 5 ingredients in oil until meat is cooked and onions are tender. Add remaining ingredients (except cheeses and noodles) and simmer for 2½ hours. Cook lasagna noodles according to directions on package. Grease an 11x9-inch casserole dish. Layer noodles, beef, mozzarella cheese, ricotta cheese, and repeat. Top with grated parmesan cheese. Bake at 325° for 45 minutes.

Mrs. Steve Loftis (Nina)

Pizza Patio Burgers

1 (6-ounce) can tomato paste
½ teaspoon each tarragon,
   oregano, & sweet basil
¼ cup grated parmesan
   cheese
2 pounds ground beef
1 cup rolled oats, uncooked
1 egg
¼ cup milk
Mozzarella cheese

Combine tomato paste, tarragon, oregano, sweet basil, and parmesan cheese in small bowl. Combine ground beef, oats, egg, and milk in large bowl. Add 3 tablespoons of tomato mixture to beef mixture. Blend well. Shape to form 16 thin patties. Spread a heaping tablespoon of tomato mixture on 8 of the patties. Cut cheese into 8 squares and put on top of patty. Cover with remaining patties; pinch edges together to seal. Place on broiler rack or over hot coals about 3 inches from source of heat. Cook about 7 minutes. Turn and cook 5 additional minutes for medium doneness. Serve on toasted hamburger buns with sesame seeds on top.

Mrs. Pat Gardenhire (Susan)

Chili

1 pound ground beef
1 (8-ounce) can tomato sauce
2 cups water
2 tablespoons chili powder
1 teaspoon cumin
½ teaspoon garlic powder
Pinch of salt
1 (23-ounce) can Ranch Style
   beans
3 tablespoons dry onion
   soup mix

Brown ground beef. Drain grease. Add tomato sauce and water. Stir in chili powder, cumin, garlic powder, salt, onion soup mix, and beans. Bring to a boil. Thicken with flour and water. Simmer for 30 minutes. Serves 4.

Mrs. Ken Box (Dietra)

Beef and Sausage Chili Con Carne

1½ pounds ground beef
½ pound bulk pork sausage
2 cups chopped onion
2 cloves garlic, minced
2 (16-ounce) cans tomatoes,
   undrained & chopped
1 (6-ounce) can tomato paste
1 (4-ounce) can chopped
   green chilies, undrained
¼ cup chopped fresh parsley
2 tablespoons chili powder
1½ teaspoons brown sugar
1 tablespoon vinegar
1 teaspoon cumin seeds
1 teaspoon salt
1 teaspoon pepper
3 whole cloves
1 bay leaf
1 (16-ounce) can kidney or
   pinto beans, undrained

Combine beef, sausage, onion, and garlic in Dutch oven. Cook over medium heat until brown. Drain off drippings. Stir in next 10 ingredients. Tie cloves and bay leaf in cheese cloth-add to mixture. Cover, reduce heat, and simmer 1½ hours, stirring occasionally. Add beans and simmer an additional 30 minutes. Remove spice bag to serve.

Mrs. Jeff Kosoris (Susan)

Cornbread Meat Dish

1 cup yellow corn meal
2 eggs, well beaten
1 cup milk
½ teaspoon soda
¾ teaspoon salt
1 can cream style corn
1 pound ground meat
1 onion, chopped
½ pound grated cheddar
   cheese
4 jalapeño peppers, chopped

Mix corn meal, eggs, milk, soda, salt, and corn and set aside. Brown ground meat. Add onion, cheese, and peppers to meat. Pour ½ of batter into hot greased 9-inch skillet or large casserole dish. Add meat, onion, cheese, and peppers—then add remaining batter. Bake uncovered at 350° for 45-50 minutes.

Mrs. Jim Jenkins (Pam)

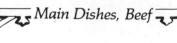

Crescent Taco Pie

1 can crescent rolls
1 pound ground meat
⅓ cup stuffed olives
½ cup picante sauce (hot)
1½ cups corn chips-divided
1 cup sour cream
1 cup grated cheddar cheese

Press crescent rolls in 9-inch pie plate. Brown ground meat. Add olives and picante sauce. Cook 5 minutes. Sprinkle ¾ cup crushed corn chips over rolls. Add ground meat mixture. Spread sour cream over meat. Sprinkle with grated cheddar cheese. Sprinkle with ¾ cup corn chip crumbs. Bake 350° for 25-30 minutes.

Mrs. Mackey Morgan (Margaret)

Crock Pot Green Enchiladas

1 or 2 pounds ground beef
2 small cans diced green chilies
2 cans cream of mushroom soup
1 large package corn tortillas
1 large onion, chopped
1 pound cheese, grated

Brown ground meat. Mix together diced green chilies and cream of mushroom soup. Layer crock pot on bottom and sides with corn tortillas. Next layer meat, sauce, onion, and cheese; relayer until crock pot is full. Cook 3 hours on low heat.

Mrs. Thomas Nelson (Nancy)

 Put a little cooking oil on your cheese grater before using it to make clean-up easier.

El Dorado Casserole

1 pound ground meat
1 onion, chopped
½ teaspoon garlic salt
2 (8-ounce) cans tomato
  sauce
1 cup sliced ripe olives
1 (8-ounce) carton sour
  cream
1 cup small curd cottage
  cheese
¾ cup chopped green chilies
1 (7-ounce) package tortilla
  corn chips, crushed
2 cups Monterey Jack cheese,
  grated

Brown meat, drain. Add next four ingredients. Cook over low heat until onion is transparent. Combine sour cream, cottage cheese, and chilies. Layer half the chips, meat mixture, sour cream mixture, and cheese in a greased 2½ quart casserole. Repeat the layers. Top with cheese. Bake at 350° for 30 minutes. Serves 6.

Mrs. Bill Price (Kay)

Mexican Chuck Roast

3 pounds chuck roast
1½ teaspoons MSG
1 teaspoon salt
Pepper to taste
3 tablespoons salad oil
½ cup chopped onion
2 tablespoons canned green
  chilies, chopped
1 (16-ounce) can red kidney
  beans
1 (16-ounce) can tomato
  sauce
1 (16-ounce) can tomatoes
2 tablespoons vinegar
1 (10-ounce) package frozen
  whole kernel corn
1 cup grated Monterey Jack
  cheese

Sprinkle roast on both sides with MSG, salt and pepper. Heat oil in Dutch oven or large skillet. Add roast and brown on both sides. Add onion, chilies, beans, tomato sauce, tomatoes, and vinegar. Cover and simmer 2½ hours. Add corn, cover and simmer ½ to 1 hour longer, until meat is tender. Serve sprinkled with cheese. Serves 6.

Mrs. Roy Marchbanks (Pam)

Picadillo

2 tablespoons olive oil
1 medium onion, finely
  chopped
4 small cloves garlic, crushed
1½ pounds lean ground beef
3 large tomatoes, peeled &
  chopped
1 medium green pepper,
  chopped
¾ cup raisins
½ cup sliced pimento stuffed
  olives
1 teaspoon salt
2 teaspoons vinegar
¼ teaspoon ground cloves
20 (6-inch) flour tortillas
Vegetable oil
Commercial taco sauce

Heat oil in large skillet; add onions and garlic cloves and sauté until tender. Add ground beef; cook over medium heat until browned, stirring to crumble. Drain off pan drippings. Add next 7 ingredients; stir well. Simmer uncovered 20 to 25 minutes, stirring until most of the liquid is gone. Fry tortillas, one at a time, in ¼-inch hot oil (375°) for 5 seconds each side or till softened. Drain tortillas on paper towels. Spoon 2 or 3 tablespoons beef mixture on each tortilla; roll up tightly. Place on serving dish. Serve with taco sauce. Serves 10.

Mrs. Rick Pitts (Becky)

Souper Mexican Casserole

1 pound ground beef
1 can cream of mushroom
  soup
1 can cream of chicken soup
1 can cheddar cheese soup
1 can Ro-tel tomatoes
1 teaspoon salt
1 package (10-12) corn
  tortillas
1 cup cheddar cheese, grated

Brown meat in skillet. Add soups, tomatoes, and salt; stir well. Layer meat mixture and tortillas in a 13x9-inch baking dish. Top with cheese. Bake at 350° for 25-30 minutes. Serves 6.

Mrs. Steve Loftis (Nina)

Taco Pie

1 (8-ounce) can crescent rolls
2 cups crushed Doritos
1 pound ground beef
1 cup taco sauce
1 cup sour cream
1 cup shredded cheese
  (cheddar or mozzarella)
Lettuce & tomato (optional)

Press crescent rolls into a 9-inch pie pan. Sprinkle half the chips on the pie crust. Brown meat and drain and add taco sauce. Spoon meat mixture over chips. Spoon sour cream on top. Add cheese and top with remaining chips. Bake 20 minutes at 350°. Garnish with lettuce and tomato.

Mrs. Pat Gardenhire (Susan)

Ham, Asparagus, and Noodle Casserole

2 cups cooked noodles
1 tablespoon parsley flakes
2 tablespoons butter or
  margarine
2 tablespoons flour
1 cup milk
½ teaspoon salt
¼ teaspoon pepper
1 (3-ounce) package cream
  cheese, cut up
6 slices boiled ham
3 teaspoons prepared
  mustard
1 (14½-ounce) can aparagus
  spears or 18 fresh
  asparagus spears, cooked
  and drained
Paprika

Combine cooked noodles with parsley, mix lightly, then set aside. In sauce pan, melt butter. Stir in flour, blend well. When bubbly, stir in milk, salt and pepper. Bring to a boil. Stir in cream cheese until melted. Pour half of sauce over noodles to coat. Spread noodles in shallow 1½ quart round or oval dish. Spread ½ teaspoon mustard on each ham slice. Roll up 3 asparagus spears in each ham slice. Place ham rolls over noodles. Pour remaining sauce over ham. Sprinkle with paprika. Cook in microwave until heated through, 5-7 minutes.

Mrs. Mike Hayes (Eva)

Golden Ham Pie

3 tablespoons chopped onion
¼ cup chopped green pepper
¼ cup fat or oil
3 tablespoons flour
2 cups milk
1 can cream of chicken soup
2 cups diced cooked ham
1 tablespoon lemon juice

Sauté onion and green pepper in fat. Remove from heat and blend in flour, then stir in milk and soup. Bring to boil and boil 1 minute. Stir in ham and lemon juice. Pour into greased baking dish and place in hot oven at 450° while making cheese biscuits. (This portion can be made ahead of time and left in skillet until later and reheated or put into ice box overnight and reheated the next day before putting in oven.) Serves 6.

Mrs. Pete Cunningham (Martha)

Cheese Biscuits

1 cup sifted flour
1½ teaspoons baking powder
½ teaspoon salt
2½ tablespoons Crisco or shortening
¾ cup grated sharp cheese
1 chopped pimento
½ cup milk

Sift together flour, baking powder, and salt. Cut in shortening and cheese until mixture looks like meal. Stir in pimento and milk. Knead very lightly just to smooth. Roll out ¼-inch thick, cut into small biscuits and quickly place biscuits on hot mixture. Bake 15-20 minutes at 450°. Yields 12 biscuits.

Mrs. Pete Cunningham (Martha)

Mexican Pockets

2 cups shredded
   Monterey Jack or
   mozzarella cheese
1 (4-ounce) can sweet green
   chilies, drained and diced
2 cups chopped smoked ham
1 package small pita
   bread (8)

In a bowl, mix cheese, chilies, and ham. Cut pita bread in half crosswise, and open. Fill with cheese and ham mixture and place on a cookie sheet. Bake at 400° until cheese melts. Makes 8 servings.

Mrs. Stan Parker (Priscilla)

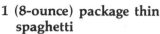

Ham Tetrazzini

1 (8-ounce) package thin
  spaghetti
1 (6-ounce) jar sliced
  mushrooms, undrained
1 small onion, chopped
¼ cup butter or margarine
¼ cup all-purpose flour
½ teaspoon dry mustard
1½ cups milk
1 teaspoon chicken-flavored
  bouillon granules
1 teaspoon Worcestershire
  Sauce
2 cups diced cooked ham
½ cup grated Parmesan
  cheese

Cook spaghetti according to package, drain and set aside. Drain mushrooms, reserving liquid. Add enough water to mushroom liquid to equal 1 cup, set aside. Sauté onion in butter in a medium sauce pan until tender. Add flour and mustard, stirring constantly. Gradually add 1 cup mushroom liquid, milk, bouillon granules, and Worcestershire sauce; cook, stirring constantly until thickened and bubbly. Combine spaghetti, mushrooms, onion sauce and ham; mix well. Spoon mixture into greased, shallow 2 quart baking dish; cover and refrigerate several hours or overnight. Remove from refrigerator and bake covered at 350° for 30 minutes. Uncover and bake 5 minutes; sprinkle with cheese and bake 10 minutes.

Mrs. Jeff Bertsch (Diane)

 Buy a ham but let the grocer slice it on his electric slicer. Make some slices thin, some thick and leave a butt. Tie together with a string when you get home and cook as usual. When time comes to eat...place on a platter and garnish, untie string and let those perfect slices fall into place like a pro. No more chunks!

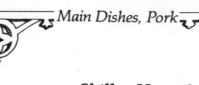
Skillet Ham & Vegetables

½ pound cooked ham—
 ½-inch strips
½ pound fresh mushrooms
4 small green onions,
 chopped
2 medium carrots, thinly
 sliced
2 medium tomatoes, chopped
2 medium potatoes, sliced
2 stalks celery, chopped
1 medium green pepper,
 chopped
1 (8-ounce) tomato sauce
¼ cup Italian dressing
1 tablespoon lemon juice
Dash salt
Dash pepper
Hot cooked rice

Combine all ingredients except rice in electric skillet. Cook covered 350° for 15-20 minutes. Stir occasionally. Serve over rice. Serves 6-8.

Mrs. Joe Grubbs (Jo Beth)

Cornbread and Sausage Dressing

½ pound bulk pork sausage
¼ cup chopped onion
4 cups coarsely crumbled
 cornbread
1 cup coarsely crumbled day-
 old bread
2 eggs
2-3 cups chicken or turkey
 broth
1 cup chopped parsley
½ teaspoon poultry
 seasoning
¼ teaspoon salt

Combine sausage and onion in a skillet. Cook until sausage is browned, stirring to crumble. Drain fat. Combine sausage and remaining ingredients. Spoon into lightly greased 12x8x2-inch baking dish. cover and bake at 350° for 30 minutes. Remove cover and bake an additional 15 minutes or until lightly brown. Serves 8-12.

This is a nice side dish for pork chops, too.

Mrs. Jeff Kosoris (Susan)

Susan's Lasagna

Meat Sauce:
1 pound Owen's regular
  sausage
1 clove minced garlic
2 (6-ounce) cans tomato paste
1½ teaspoons basil
1½ teaspoons salt
1½ teaspoons sugar
1 (16-ounce) can tomatoes,
  undrained
½ cup fresh grated
  Parmesan cheese

Cheese Filling:
1 (8-10-ounce) package
  lasagna noodles
2 eggs, beaten
3 cups fresh ricotta cheese
1 teaspoon salt
½ teaspoon pepper
1½ tablespoons parsley
  flakes
½ cup fresh grated Parmesan
  cheese
1 pound grated fresh
  mozzarella cheese

Brown meat slowly. Drain off excess fat. Add next six ingredients. Simmer uncovered 30 minutes, stirring occasionally. Add ½ cup Parmesan cheese. Cook noodles in large amount of boiling salted water until tender. Drain and rinse. Beat eggs, add remaining ingredients except mozzarella. Grate cheese and reserve ½ cup for top layer. Layer half of the noodles in large baking dish. Spread ½ ricotta filling. Add ½ mozzarella and ½ of the meat sauce. Repeat. Sprinkle with reserved mozzarella. Bake at 375° about 30 minutes or until bubbly. Let stand for 10 minutes before cutting. Freezes well.

Mrs. Jeff Kosoris (Susan)

Pizza Quiche

1 (8-ounce) can crescent rolls
4 eggs, beaten
1 pound sausage, browned
2 tablespoons green pepper
¼ teaspoon pepper
1 (8-ounce) shredded
  Monterrey Jack cheese
¾ cup milk
½ teaspoon salt
¼ teaspoon oregano

Preheat oven to 425°. Place sheet of dough in 13x9-inch pan. Press over bottom and ½-inch up sides to form crust. Seal perforations. Place sausage over crust. Sprinkle with cheese. Combine ingredients; pour over cheese. Bake 20-25 minutes until golden brown. Serves 5-6.

This is a wonderful brunch dish or light supper.

Mrs. Ben Boone (Sharon)

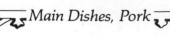

Brunch-Time Bacon Bake

1½ pounds bacon
1 medium onion, finely
   chopped
3 cups cooked rice
¼ cup all-purpose flour
2½ cups milk
½ teaspoon salt
⅛ teaspoon pepper
½ cup grated Parmesan
   cheese
2 small zucchini, coarsely
   shredded
⅓ cup ripe olives, sliced

Cut bacon crosswise into 1-inch pieces. In skillet, cook bacon till crisp; remove. Drain and crumble on paper towel. Reserve drippings. Return 3 tablespoons drippings to skillet; add onion and cook till tender. Spread rice in an 11x7x1½-inch baking dish. Top with half the bacon and onion. Combine flour and remaining drippings in saucepan; mix well. Gradually add milk and cook over medium heat until thickened and bubbly, stirring constantly. Stir in salt, pepper and Parmesan cheese. Pour 1 cup of sauce over bacon and rice. Top with shredded zucchini and sliced olives. Sprinkle with remaining bacon; pour remaining sauce atop. Cover tightly with foil and refrigerate overnight. Remove from refrigerator and let stand at room temperature for 15 minutes. Bake at 375° for 25 minutes. Remove foil and cook for 20 minutes more. Serves 6.

Mrs. M. A. Weedon (Kay)

 When a recipe calls for crumbled bacon, take a package of uncooked bacon and a pair of sharp kitchen shears and snip several times across the entire width of the layers. You will wind up with a lot of "julienne" strips which will fry out into neat little "crumbles."

Sausage Casserole

1½ pounds sausage
2 tablespoons drippings
½ cup chopped onion
1 cup chopped bell pepper
1 cup chopped celery
1 (4-ounce) can mushroom
  pieces
1½ packages Lipton Chicken
  Noodle Soup Mix
3 cups cooked rice
2½ cups water
1 (5-ounce) can water
  chestnuts, drained and
  sliced
⅓ cup slivered almonds

Fry sausage until done. Remove from skillet and sauté onion, pepper, and celery in 2 tablespoons drippings. In large mixing bowl combine all ingredients except almonds. Mix well and turn into 3 quart casserole. Cover and bake 1 hour at 325°. Remove cover, sprinkle with almonds and bake an additional 15 minutes.

This is great for a brunch because it makes a large casserole. You can also put it in 2 smaller casseroles and freeze one. Just thaw, and follow same cooking instructions.

Mrs. David Ballard (Karen)

Pork Chops and Cheddar Rice

6 pork chops
1¼ cups water
1 can cream of mushroom
  soup
1 cup uncooked rice
1 cup shredded cheddar
  cheese
2 tablespoons minced onion
2 tablespoons chopped green
  pepper
1 (4-ounce) can sliced
  mushrooms
1 (2.8-ounce) can Durkee's
  French Fried onions

Preheat oven to 350°. Brown pork chops lightly. Drain and put in a 13x9-inch baking dish. Mix water, soup, rice, ⅔ cup cheese, onion, pepper and mushrooms and pour over pork chops. Cover with foil and bake for 1 hour and 15 minutes. Uncover and top with remaining cheese and French fried onions. Return to oven until cheese melts.

Mrs. Stan Parker (Priscilla)

Apricot Chicken

1 chicken breast, cut in half
½ cup canned apricots
3 tablespoons teriyaki sauce
½ teaspoon ginger
½ teaspoon salt

Place chicken in a dutch oven. Cover with apricots. Add all other ingredients. Cover tightly. Cook on top of stove for 45 minutes. First on medium heat, then turn heat to low and then to simmer. Serve with freshly grated nutmeg on top.

Mrs. Don Nelson (Judy)

Baked Chicken

8 chicken breasts
2 sticks butter
1 cup dry white wine
1 large jar red currant jelly
1 large carton sour cream

In a saucepan, sauté the chicken in the butter until browned. Mix wine, jelly, and sour cream together. Place the chicken in a baking dish and pour the mixture over the chicken. Bake at 350° until chicken is tender—approximately 40-45 minutes.

Mrs. Bill Major (Patsy)

Baked Chicken Breast Supreme

6 boneless chicken breasts, halved
2 cups sour cream
¼ cup lemon juice
4 teaspoons Worcestershire sauce
4 teaspoons celery salt
2 teaspoons paprika
4 teaspoons salt
½ teaspoon pepper
1¾ cups dried bread crumbs
1 cup butter, melted

Wash breasts and dry with cloth. Mix sour cream with lemon juice, Worcestershire, celery salt, paprika, salt and pepper. Add breasts to sour cream mixture, coating each piece well. Cover and refrigerate overnight. Next day, remove breasts from mixture and roll in bread crumbs, coating evenly. Arrange in a single layer in large casserole dish. Melt butter and spoon half over the breasts. Bake uncovered at 350° for 45 minutes. Spoon remainder of butter over breasts and bake 15 minutes longer.

Mrs. Roy Marchbanks (Pam)

Cathy's Chicken Rolls

8 boneless chicken breasts
½ pound shredded ham
½ pound shredded Swiss
   cheese
8 slices bacon
1 (8-ounce) container sour
   cream
1 can cream of mushroom
   soup
1 pound fresh mushrooms,
   sliced
Fresh parsley

With meat mallet, beat chicken breasts to ¼-inch. Place a little ham and cheese in center of each piece. Roll up and wrap each with a slice of bacon, then secure with a toothpick. Place chicken in a 9x13-inch pyrex dish. Mix sour cream, soup and mushrooms and pour over chicken. Cover with foil and bake 2 hours at 300°. Sprinkle with fresh parsley before serving. Serve over wild rice. Serves 8.

Mrs. David Ballard (Karen)

Chicken and Dumplings

1 chicken, boiled & boned
1½ cups sifted flour
½ teaspoon baking powder
1 teaspoon salt
1 egg, beaten
⅓ cup milk
2 tablespoons salad oil or
   melted fat
2 tablespoons minced parsley

Sift flour with baking powder and salt into bowl. Add remaining ingredients, stir until just combined. Roll out on a floured surface. Cut into strips. Cook in chicken broth (boiling) uncovered. Add boned chicken.

Mrs. Joe Grubbs (Jo Beth)

127

Chicken Costa

1 broiler-fryer, cut up
  & skinned
1½ teaspoons Lawry's
  seasoned salt
⅓ cup salad oil
1 medium onion, grated
½ cup chopped celery
½ teaspoon basil
1 package spaghetti sauce
  mix
½ cup sauterne
1½ cups water
4 large carrots, halved and
  quartered
4 medium potatoes, halved
½ teaspoon Lawry's seasoned
  salt
Seasoned pepper to taste
Flour (optional)

Rub chicken with 1½ teaspoons seasoned salt. Heat oil in electric skillet or Dutch oven. Fry chicken until brown. Remove and set aside. Add onion and celery and sauté until tender. Add basil and sauce mix and blend well. Add sauterne and water. Stir. Bring mixture to a boil, then reduce heat. Add chicken, carrots and potatoes. Sprinkle with seasoned salt and pepper. Cover and simmer 45 minutes or until chicken and vegetables are tender. Thicken pan juices with flour if desired.

Mrs. Jeff Kosoris (Susan)

Chicken Divine

2 packages frozen broccoli
  spears
2 cans cream of chicken soup
1 cup mayonnaise
1 teaspoon lemon juice
Salt & pepper to taste
½ cup shredded American
  cheese
2 cups cooked chicken
½ cup bread crumbs
2 teaspoons melted butter

Cook broccoli by directions on package. Prepare sauce by combining chicken soup, mayonnaise, cheese, salt, pepper and lemon juice. Drain broccoli and place in bottom of ungreased 11x7-inch casserole dish. Place bite-sized pieces of chicken over broccoli and pour sauce over both. Combine bread crumbs and butter and sprinkle over top. Bake at 350° for 35 minutes. May be refrigerated 24 hours before baking. Also freezes well. Serves 6.

Mrs. Erling Holey (Susan)

Chicken Elizabeth

4 chicken breasts
1 cup whipping cream
1 cup sour cream
2 tiny wedges roquefort
  cheese
Garlic to taste
Salt & pepper to taste

Roast chicken breasts until golden brown. In saucepan combine remaining ingredients and bring just to a boil. Simmer until sauce thickens. Serve over baked chicken.

Mrs. Mike Hayes (Eva)

Chicken-Ham-Shrimp Dish

6 tablespoons butter
¼ cup chopped onion
6 tablespoons flour
1 teaspoon salt
1½ cups milk
1½ cups chicken broth
1 cup shredded sharp cheese
½ cup chopped green pepper
3 cups chopped cooked
  chicken
1 pound cooked ham, diced
1½ pounds shrimp, cooked
  & cleaned
1 (4-ounce) can mushroom
  slices, drained
2 tablespoons pimiento,
  chopped
Cooked rice

Melt butter in Dutch oven. Sauté onion until tender, but not browned. Stir in flour and salt to make a smooth paste. Add milk and chicken broth gradually, stirring until smooth. Cook and stir until of medium thickness. Add cheese; beat and stir until cheese is melted. Stir in remaining ingredients (except rice) and heat to serve. Serve over rice. Serves 12.

Mrs. Robert M. Cox (Dee)

Chicken Kiev

4 boneless chicken breasts
2 sticks butter
2 eggs
Package crackers, crushed
Bowl water

Pound chicken until flat and thin. Cut into 3x3 pieces. Wrap chicken around slice of butter. Dip in water, then dip in well beaten egg, then dip in crackers. Refrigerate 1 hour. Deep fry about 5 minutes or until golden brown.

Mrs. Ken Box (Dietra)

Chicken Parmesan

1½ cups Italian Progresso
  bread crumbs
1½ cups parmesan cheese
1 tablespoon salt
1 teaspoon pepper
6 chicken breasts or 3 whole
  breasts, deboned
2 sticks butter

Combine bread crumbs, cheese, salt and pepper. Dip the chicken breasts in the melted butter and then in the bread crumbs, being careful to coat the breasts evenly. Place the breasts skin side up in a baking dish and bake in a 350° oven for 35 minutes, uncovered. Do not turn. *This can be prepared the day before and refrigerated, then baked. This freezes well, before or after baking. Especially good served with a savory rice dish.*

Mrs. Joseph S. Smith (Margaret)

Chicken Oyster Casserole

4 boneless chicken breasts,
  skinned
½ cup heavy cream
1 can oysters
½ teaspoon salt
¼ teaspoon pepper
2 tablespoons slivered
  almonds, toasted

Skin and bone chicken. Place in 2 quart casserole. Add ½ cup boiling water. Cover and bake at 350° for 1 hour. Drain off liquid. Add cream, oysters, salt and pepper. Cover and bake 10 minutes longer. Sprinkle with almonds. Serves 4.

Mrs. Pat Sullivan (Gloria)

Lemon Chicken

2 pounds chicken pieces
2 tablespoons shortening
1 cup cream of chicken soup
½ teaspoon salt
2 tablespoons lemon juice
½ teaspoon tarragon leaves, crushed
Dash of pepper
Lemon slices

In skillet, brown chicken, remove from pan, pour off fat and combine remaining ingredients, except lemon slices. Return chicken to skillet, cover, cook over low heat 45 minutes or until tender. Garnish with lemon slices.

Mrs. Galen Kemp (Cindy)

Marinated Chicken Wings

24 chicken wings
1 (16-ounce) frozen orange juice
1 large bottle soy sauce
1 clove garlic, minced

Clean chicken, pat dry. Mix orange juice, soy sauce, and garlic. Marinate chicken in sauce at least five hours. Drain sauce and remove garlic before cooking. Bake at 350° for 45 minutes. Halfway through cooking drain again.

Mrs. Ken Box (Dietra)

Mary Ann's Oven Baked Chicken

1 cut up chicken
Salt
Pepper
1 stick margarine
2 tablespoons Worcestershire sauce
Juice of 1 lemon

Place chicken parts in a large flat pan, and salt and pepper to taste. Melt and mix together the margarine, Worcestershire sauce, and lemon. Pour over the chicken, and bake at 350° for 1 hour.

Mrs. Pat Gardenhire (Susan)

Mimi's Chicken

1 chicken, cut up
Self-rising flour
Vegetable oil
Cracker crumbs
Lawry's seasoning salt

Coat chicken pieces in self-rising flour. Dip in vegetable oil. Coat or shake in cracker crumbs and Lawry's seasoning salt. Bake in shallow pan in oven 1 hour at 350°.

Mrs. Edward Burleson (Nan)

Orange Honey Chicken

⅓ cup peanut oil
¼ cup honey
1 tablespoon grated orange peel
2 teaspoons ground ginger
Dash of salt
1 (3½-pound) fryer, cut up
Orange slices

Arrange chicken pieces in dish. Brush with mixture of other ingredients. Roast uncovered 1 hour at 350°. Garnish with orange slices.

Mrs. Jack Curlin (Nelda)

Oven Fried Chicken with Butter Honey Sauce

1 cup all-purpose flour
2 teaspoons paprika
¼ teaspoon pepper
½ teaspoon salt
4 chicken breast halves, skinned
½ cup butter, melted

Butter Honey Sauce:
¼ cup butter
½ cup honey
¼ cup lemon juice

Butter Honey Sauce: Combine all ingredients and beat well.

Combine flour, paprika, salt, and pepper. Stir well. Dredge chicken in flour mixture. Set aside. Pour melted butter into a 13x9x2-inch baking pan. Place chicken in pan, turning to coat with butter. Cover and bake, meaty side down, at 400° for 30 minutes. Turn chicken pieces and pour Butter Honey Sauce over each piece. Bake uncovered an additional 25-30 minutes or until tender, basting occasionally with sauce.

Mrs. Jeff Kosoris (Susan)

Oriental Pineapple Chicken

6 large chicken breasts,
  skinned and boned (or 12
  halves)
1 tablespoon flour
1½ teaspoons salt
½ teaspoon curry powder
1 teaspoon paprika
1 clove garlic
2 tablespoons butter
1 tablespoon oil
1 cup chicken broth
½ pound fresh mushrooms,
  sliced
3 stalks celery, cut in
  ½-inch diagonal slices
1 large green pepper, cut
  in chunks
8 green onions cut in ½-inch
  diagonal pieces
1 package sweet-sour sauce
  mix
1 (7-ounce) package frozen
  pea pods
1 (1-pound) or (14-ounce)
  can pineapple chunks,
  drained

Roll chicken in mixture of flour, salt, paprika, and curry powder. Rub large cooking vessel with cut clove of garlic—discard garlic. Add butter and oil and melt. Add chicken. Cook over moderate heat until chicken is lightly browned on both sides. Add broth, cover and cook slowly for 20 minutes. Add mushrooms and celery. Cover and cook 2 or 3 minutes. Stir in sweet-sour sauce mix. Add pea pods. Cover and continue cooking until sauce thickens and clears, stirring once or twice (about 4 minutes). Add drained pineapple. Cook 5 minutes. Serve at once. Serves 6-8.

Mrs. Erling Holey (Susan)

Poulet Au Vin

6 boneless chicken breasts
¼ cup butter or margarine
1 can condensed cream of
  mushroom soup
½ cup sherry
Dash of pepper
¼ cup chopped onion

Brown chicken in large skillet. Stir in soup, sherry, and pepper and add onion. Cover, simmer 45 minutes or until chicken is tender. Stir often. Serves 6.

Wonderful served with curried rice!

Mrs. Jim Beller (Linda)

Sherried Almond Chicken

1 cup raw rice
¼ cup melted butter
1 can mushroom soup
1 can cream of chicken soup
1 tablespoon Worcestershire
 sauce
1 skinned chicken (boned
 breasts or 8 pieces with
 bone in)
⅓ cup slivered almonds
1 cup (approximately)
 parmesan cheese
1 cup sherry wine

Mix first 5 ingredients. Put ½ mixture in buttered 9x13-inch pan. Put a layer of chicken and almonds. Cover with a generous amount of parmesan cheese. Spread remainder of rice mixture over chicken. Pour sherry wine over all. Bake 3 hours at 275°. Serves 8.

Mrs. Pat Gardenhire (Susan)

Seven Can Casserole

1 can cheddar cheese soup
1 can cream of mushroom
 soup
1 small can evaporated milk
1 can asparagus tips
1 can French style green
 beans
1 can mushrooms
1 small can/jar chopped
 pimentos
½ cup slivered almonds
1 can Chinese noodles
3 cups bite size chicken
 pieces

Mix all ingredients except Chinese noodles. Bake in a large casserole 30 minutes at 350° or until bubbly. Serve over Chinese noodles. May be frozen. Serves 12.

Mrs. Pleasant Mitchell (Helen)

Special Chicken

1 (10-ounce) package
  broccoli, cooked
2 tablespoons melted butter
1 cup cheese
½ cup sherry
2 cups cooked chicken
1 can cream of chicken
  soup
Salt and pepper to taste

Place broccoli in buttered casserole. Sprinkle with butter, 1 tablespoon cheese, and 1 tablespoon sherry. Spread chicken over broccoli. Sprinkle with 1 tablespoon cheese and balance of sherry. Pour chicken soup, salt and pepper over all. Top with remaining cheese and bake at 350° until hot. Serves 4-6.

Mrs. Jack Price (Betty)

Sweet and Sour Chicken

1 large green pepper,
  chopped
1 or 2 garlic cloves, crushed
  or the equivalent in garlic
  powder
2 tablespoons salad oil
2 cans cream of chicken soup
Juice from canned pineapple
1 (13-ounce) can pineapple
  chunks
2 cups cooked, diced chicken
2 tablespoons soy sauce
1 package sliced almonds
Cooked rice

Sauté pepper and garlic in oil in a large skillet. Add soup and pineapple juice and stir. Add pineapple chunks, chicken and soy sauce. Heat thoroughly on low heat—this burns easily. Top with almonds and serve over rice. Serves 6.

Mrs. Pat Sullivan (Gloria)

Breast of Chicken and Wild Rice

1 can cream of mushroom
   soup
1 soup can milk
1 box Uncle Ben's long grain
   wild rice
1 can mushroom stems and
   pieces
2 chicken breasts, split
   in half

Heat oven to 350°. Blend soup and milk; reserve ½ cup of the mixture. Stir together remaining soup mixture, the rice, and mushrooms (with liquid). Pour into ungreased baking dish, 11x7x2-inch. Arrange chicken breasts on rice mixture. Pour reserved soup mixture over chicken. Cover; bake 1 hour. Uncover; bake 15 minutes longer.

Mrs. Galen Kemp (Cindy)

Chicken Rice with Water Chestnuts

1 chicken, cut up
1 stick oleo or butter
1 onion, finely chopped
½ green (bell) pepper,
   chopped
1 jar chopped pimentos
1½ cups uncooked rice
1 can cream of mushroom
   soup
1 can cream of celery soup
1 can cream of chicken soup
1 can water chestnuts,
   drained and chopped

Salt and pepper chicken pieces. Melt butter with onion and green pepper. Add pimentos, uncooked rice, soups and water chestnuts. Place in a casserole. Place seasoned chicken (skin side down) on top of mixture. Cook 275° for 2½ hours. After one hour, turn chicken pieces and cover.

Mrs. Pete Cunningham (Martha)

Chicken and Rice Casserole

1⅓ cups Minute rice
½ envelope dry onion soup mix
1 can mushroom soup
1 pound chicken breasts
1¼ cups boiling water
¼ cup dry sherry
2 tablespoons chopped pimento
½ cup melted butter
Paprika
Salt and pepper

Combine all ingredients except chicken, butter, and seasoning. Brush chicken with butter and seasonings. Put rice in 1½ quart casserole. Place chicken on top of rice and bake at 350° for 1 hour and 15 minutes. Serves 6.

Mrs. Jack Curlin (Nelda)

Chicken with Curry Glaze

2 fryers, quartered
6 tablespoons flour
1½ teaspoons salt
1 teaspoon ginger
6 tablespoons butter
Hot buttered rice

Curry Glaze:
½ cup onion, chopped
6 slices bacon, finely diced
2 tablespoons flour
1 tablespoon curry powder
1 tablespoon sugar
1 can condensed beef broth
2 tablespoons flaked coconut
2 tablespoons applesauce
2 tablespoons catsup
2 tablespoons lemon juice

Cut away backbones and any small rib bones from chicken. Pull off skin, if desired. Shake chicken pieces in mixture of flour, salt, and ginger in paper bag to coat well. Melt butter in large, shallow baking or roasting pan. Roll chicken in melted butter to coat well, then arrange, skin side up, in single layer in pan. Bake, uncovered at 400° for 20 minutes, or until chicken begins to turn golden. Spoon about half of curry glaze on top of chicken to make a thick coating; bake 20 minutes longer or until tender and richly browned. Arrange chicken around a mound of hot, buttered rice on serving platter. Serves 8.

Curry Glaze: Combine all ingredients in medium-sized saucepan. Heat to boiling, stirring constantly, then simmer 15 minutes, stirring often until thickened. Makes about 2 cups.

Mrs. Mike Leath (Kay)

Curried Chicken & Broccoli

1½ pounds broccoli
4-5 whole chicken breasts or
  1 whole chicken; cooked;
  cut into bite size chunks
2 cans cream of chicken soup
¾ cup mayonnaise
Juice of ½ lemon, scant
½ cup water
1 heaping teaspoon curry
  powder

Cook or steam broccoli until tender. Place in bottom of 2 quart casserole dish. When cool, layer with chicken. Combine remaining ingredients to make sauce. Mix well; pour over broccoli and chicken. Bake uncovered at 350° for 35 minutes or until bubbly. Serves 8-9.

Mrs. Rick Pitts (Becky)

Chicken Enchiladas

1 medium onion, chopped
2 (4-ounce) cans chopped
  green chilies
2-3 tablespoons butter
1 can cream of chicken soup
1 can cream of mushroom
  soup
1½ cups chicken broth
Tortillas
1 (2½-3-pound) chicken,
  cooked and boned
½ pound Longhorn style
  cheddar cheese, shredded
½ pound Monterey Jack
  cheese, shredded

Sauté onion and green chilies in butter until tender. Add soup and broth, blending well; simmer 10-15 minutes. While sauce simmers, soften tortillas by dipping each in simmering mixture a few seconds. Place a small amount of chicken in each tortilla and roll up tightly; place in a lightly greased 13x9x2-inch baking dish. Pour remaining sauce over enchiladas; top with cheeses. Bake 350° for 20-25 minutes. Serves 12.

Mrs. Joe Grubbs (Jo Beth)

Chicken Enchiladas

24 tortillas (heated in skillet)
1 (12-ounce) package
  Monterrey Cheese
1 (12-ounce) package cheddar
  cheese
2 cups chicken, diced
1 onion, chopped and
  sauteéd

Sauce:
1 stick margarine
5 tablespoons flour
¾ cup milk
1 can chicken broth
1 tablespoon hot sauce
1 pint sour cream

Heat tortillas and spread with cheese, chicken, and onion; roll up and place in large casserole dish. Mix sauce ingredients adding sour cream last. Heat ½ minute and pour over enchiladas. Sprinkle with additional cheese if desired. Bake uncovered at 350° for 25 minutes or until bubbly.

Mrs. Mackey Morgan (Margaret)

Chicken Enchiladas

3 chicken breasts, cooked
  and diced
2 cans cream of chicken soup
½ pint sour cream
2 small cans green chilies
1 soup can of water
2 cups cheddar cheese, grated
1 cup onion, chopped
12 tortillas

Boil chicken in seasoned water. Make sauce of soup, sour cream, chilies, and water. Add diced chicken. Combine cheese and onion. Dip tortillas in chicken stock. Stuff with sauce and 1 tablespoon of cheese and onion. Roll up in casserole and cover with remaining sauce. Bake 325° for 30 minutes.

Mrs. Bill Price (Kay)

Chicken Poblano

¾ of small bottle of olive oil
1 medium onion, chopped
1 can chopped chilies, mild
1 pint sour cream
4 boneless chicken breasts
Flour tortillas

Steam chicken in olive oil for 1 hour or until done. Remove from pan. Sauté onion and chopped chilies in juices remaining in pan until soft. Dice chicken and add to onions and chilies; stir in sour cream and heat through. Serve on warm flour tortilla and fold over.

Mrs. Galen Kemp (Cindy)

Green Enchiladas

1 pound ground beef
½ cup onion
½ pound longhorn cheese
1 dozen flour tortillas
½ pound Velveeta
1 (4-ounce) can chopped
  green chilies
1 package green onion dip
  mix

Brown ground beef with onion. Drain well and add longhorn cheese. Spoon mixture into tortillas and roll. Put in 11x7-inch casserole dish. Melt Velveeta, chilies, and dip mix in top of double boiler. Pour over enchiladas and bake at 350° for 25 minutes. (For a softer tortilla, cover while baking. For a crispier tortilla, leave uncovered while baking.)

Mrs. Griggs DeHay (Gay)

King Ranch Chicken

1 chopped onion
1 can Rotel tomatoes
1 can mushrooms
1 can cream of chicken soup
2 cups grated cheddar cheese
1 can chicken broth
2 cups cooked chicken
1 dozen corn tortillas
Chopped green pepper
  (optional)
Chili powder (optional)
Jalapeños (optional)

Sauté onion. Add tomatoes, mushrooms, soup, cheese, broth and chicken. Layer this liquid mixture with tortillas (about 3 layers each). Cook at 350° for one hour. You may add chopped green pepper, chili powder and Jalapeños if desired to make it extra spicy. You may also add a last layer of shredded cheese, if desired. Serves 8-12.

Mrs. Dennis Horak (Barbara)

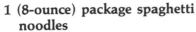

Chicken-Spaghetti Casserole

1 (8-ounce) package spaghetti
   noodles
1 cup chopped celery
3 chicken bouillon cubes,
   dissolved in 4 cups boiling
   water
½ stick margarine
2 (6 ½-ounce) cans chicken
1 can cream of chicken soup
1 (6-ounce) can chopped
   mushrooms
1 small jar pimentos
¼ pound Velveeta cheese cut
   into strips

Cook spaghetti and celery in chicken bouillon. Drain. Mix ingredients, except cheese. Pour into 11x7 or 10x10-inch casserole dish. Submerge strips of cheese into casserole. Bake covered at 350° for 1 hour. (May top with small amount of milk if casserole begins to dry out before 1 hour is completed.)

Mrs. Steve Loftis (Nina)

Chicken Spaghetti

2 chickens, boiled or baked
1 (48-ounce) spaghetti,
   cooked al dente in broth
2 (16-ounce) cans stewed
   tomatoes
2 (4½-ounce) jars sliced
   mushrooms
1 (7-ounce) jar pimentos
6 cans cream of mushroom
   soup (66-ounce)
2 teaspoons worcestershire
   sauce
1 tablespoon tabasco sauce
2 onions, grated
2 stalks celery, grated
1 pound sharp cheese

Cut cooked chicken into bite sized cubes. Reserve 2 cups chicken broth, use as necessary to dilute finished dish. Cook spaghetti in remaining broth plus necessary water. Sauté grated onions and celery. Mix spaghetti, chicken and remaining ingredients. Place in large roaster, top with sharp cheese. Bake 30 minutes at 350°. Serves 35-40.

Mrs. Robert C. Fuller (Madelon)

Chicken Tetrazzini

¼ cup butter or margarine
¼ cup all-purpose flour
½ teaspoon salt
¼ teaspoon pepper
1 cup chicken broth
1 cup whipping cream
2 tablespoons red cooking
  wine
1 (7-ounce) package
  spaghetti, cooked and
  drained
2 cups cubed cooked chicken
  or turkey
1 (3-ounce) can sliced
  mushrooms, drained
½ cup grated Parmesan
  cheese

Heat oven to 350°. Melt butter in large saucepan over low heat. Blend in flour and seasonings. Cook over low heat, stirring until mixture is smooth and bubbly. Remove from heat. Stir in broth and cream. Heat to boiling, stirring constantly. Boil and stir 1 minute. Stir in wine, spaghetti, chicken and mushrooms. Pour into ungreased 2-quart casserole. Sprinkle with cheese. Bake uncovered 30 minutes or until bubbly. To brown, place briefly under broiler.

Mrs. Galen Kemp (Cindy)

Turketti

1¼ cups spaghetti, broken
  into 2-inch pieces
1½-2 cups cooked turkey or
  chicken, cut into bite-sized
  pieces
¼ cup pimentos, diced
¼ cup green pepper,
  chopped
½ cup onion, chopped
1 can cream of mushroom,
  undiluted
½ cup broth or water
½ teaspoon salt
⅛ teaspoon pepper
2 cups sharp cheddar cheese,
  grated

Cook spaghetti and drain. Add all ingredients except ½ cup cheese. Pour into 1½ quart baking dish and top with remaining cheese. Bake at 350° 20 minutes or until bubbly. 6-8 servings.

Mrs. Steve Kelley (Cindy)

Chicken Pot Pie

½ cup butter or margarine, melted
3 tablespoons all-purpose flour
3 cups chicken broth
1 cup milk
3 cups diced, cooked chicken
½ teaspoon salt
¼ teaspoon pepper
1 (16-ounce) can mixed vegetables, drained
1 (16-ounce) can green peas, drained
Pastry for 9-inch pie

Combine butter and flour in saucepan over low heat; gradually add chicken broth and milk, stirring constantly until thick and smooth. Stir in chicken, salt, pepper, and mixed vegetables. Mix well. Pour into 13x9x2-inch baking dish. Roll pastry on lightly floured surface, cut into strips one-inch wide and arrange in lattice design over chicken. Bake at 350° for 30 minutes or until pastry is brown.

Mrs. Brett Thacker (Joyce)

Cornish Hens Casserole

1 tablespoon rosemary leaves
1 cup dry white wine
4 Rock cornish hens, quartered
¼ cup all-purpose flour
1 teaspoon salt
½ teaspoon pepper
1 teaspoon chopped fresh parsley
1 clove garlic, minced
½ cup butter
1 pound fresh mushrooms

Soak rosemary leaves in wine for 30 minutes to 1 hour. Place quarted hens in a paper bag containing flour, salt, pepper and parsley. Shake to coat hens thoroughly. Brown garlic in melted butter in skillet and then remove garlic. Add pieces of hen, browning quickly. Place hen in casserole dish. Sauté mushrooms in butter remaining in skillet and add to casserole. Pour wine mixture over casserole. Bake at 350° for 30-45 minutes.

Mrs. Steve Kelley (Cindy)

Crock-Pot Creamy Chicken Stew

2 cans cream of chicken soup
1 can cream of mushroom
  soup
1 can cheddar cheese soup
½ can water
2 jars whole mushrooms
1 can water chestnuts
12 raw chicken breasts, cut
  up bite size
1 package Stew Starter
  "Swift Homemade" chicken
  flavor

Into crock pot mix all ingredients. Cook all day on high. This fills a large crock-pot. Can be served over rice, or as a stew.

Mrs. Robert C. Fuller (Madelon)

Baked Dove with Rice

10-12 doves
1 cup minute rice
1 can cream of mushroom
  soup
1½ cups water
1 tablespoon Worcestershire
  sauce
1 teaspoon parsley flakes
1 small jar mushroom slices

Grease a 9x13-inch baking dish. Sprinkle rice over the bottom of the pan and place dove on the rice. In a small bowl, mix remaining ingredients and pour over the dove. Cover and bake for 20 minutes at 400°, then lower temperature to 300° and bake one hour longer. Serves 4-6.

Mrs. Pleasant Mitchell (Helen)

Steamed Quail or Dove

4 salted birds
½ cup water
½ cup butter or margarine
2 tablespoons Worcestershire
  sauce
1 cup mushrooms
½ cup sherry
Flour
Paprika

Put 4 salted birds in heavy roaster. Put water and butter with birds and steam on top of stove for 30 minutes. Then pour Worcestershire sauce over birds, add mushrooms and sherry, and dust birds with flour. Sprinkle with paprika and steam until tender, 2-3 hours.

Mrs. Bill Major (Patsy)

Dove, Quail, Pheasant with Rice

8 to 12 pieces of game
Salt
¾ cup butter or margarine
2 tablespoons cooking oil
1 large onion, chopped
2 medium garlic cloves,
    minced
1 can mushrooms
3 tablespoons flour
1 can beef consommé
1 can water
¼ cup white or red wine
1 small bay leaf
1 whole clove
2 teaspoons or cubes of
    beef bouillon seasoning

Wash game, pat dry, and salt lightly. Place butter and oil in skillet. Brown unfloured game. Lift out and place aside. In skillet add the chopped onion, garlic and mushrooms (retain liquid) and brown until golden in color. Add flour and stir well. Then add the can of consommé and can of water, wine, mushroom liquid, bay leaf, clove and bouillon seasoning. Return game to this sauce in skillet, cover and simmer for 1 hour or until tender. No additional salt is needed because of the consommé.

Mrs. Jim Beller (Linda)

Gourmet Venison

½ back strap
2 tablespoons lime juice
⅓ cup oil
½ teaspoon thyme
½ stick oleo
¼ cup red wine vinegar
¼ cup red currant jelly

Cut meat into 1-inch steaks (10-12). Pound flat and marinate 2 hours in juice, oil, and thyme. Drain. Melt oleo in skillet. Salt and pepper steaks and brown 2 minutes on each side. Put in casserole. Add vinegar to marinade and cook 10 minutes. Add jelly and cook till melted. Pour over steaks. Cook 30 minutes at 375°, uncovered. Serves 10-12.

Mrs. Tom Curlin (Betty)

145

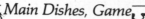

Chicken Fried Venison Steak or Chops

1 venison loin
Garlic salt to taste
Pepper to taste
2 tablespoons meat tenderizer
2 cups buttermilk
Flour

Cut loin into ¾-inch pieces. Trim off all membrane. Beat tenderizer, garlic salt and pepper into each piece. Soak in buttermilk at least 1 hour (overnight is okay). Flour and let set 3 or 4 minutes before frying. I make gravy and serve with hot biscuits, creamed potatoes, green beans, and green salad.

Mrs. Clovis Mitchell (Omajeanne)

This home was built in 1895 on North Rogers Street, just five blocks off the Square. Doctor Simpson had his office in a room at the rear of this corner home early in the twentieth century. During the Depression, the owners enclosed the front porch and rented out cots to people traveling through the area. It has since been restored to its original appearance. The home is built in a modified L-plan. The hip roof ends in two gables on the front of the house, with cresting along the ridge lines of the gables. The box eaves are supported by jig-sawn corner brackets. A restored 7-bay porch with turned wood posts and balusters balances out the pleasing entryway.

EGGS, CHEESE
AND PASTA

Chili Eggs

4 slices bread, cubed
¼ stick oleo, melted
1 cup sharp Cheddar
  cheese, grated
1 can green chilies
4 eggs, beaten
1 tablespoon milk
Salt
Pepper
Dash of hot sauce

Toss bread cubes in oleo and place in the baking dish. Layer cheese, then chilies. Beat eggs with remaining ingredients and pour over the chilies. Chill several hours. (This will keep for 2 days in the refrigerator.) Bake at 350° for 15 minutes or until the center is firm. Serves 4.

Mrs. Mike Leath (Kay)

Monterrey-Green Chili Rice

1 cup raw rice
1½ pints sour cream
2 (4-ounce) cans chopped
  green chilies, drained
1½ teaspoon salt
½ teaspoon white pepper
1 (12-ounce) Monterrey jack
  cheese, grated

Cook rice. Mix with sour cream, chilies, salt, and pepper. In a deep casserole, alternately layer rice mixture and cheese, ending with rice mixture. Top with a layer of the rice mixture. Bake at 305° for 30-40 minutes. Serves 6.

Great side dish for steaks.

Mrs. Craig Curry (Karen)

Add a pat of butter to your water when boiling potatoes to keep the pot from boiling over. This works for spaghetti, too.

Baked Manicotti

1 (8-ounce) box manicotti shells
2 pounds Ricotta cheese
8-ounces grated Mozzarella
⅓ cup grated Parmesan cheese
2 eggs
1 tablespoon chopped parsley
1 teaspoon salt
¼ teaspoon pepper
2 tablespoons grated Parmesan cheese
Large bottle of Prego sauce

Prepare manicotti shells. Set aside. In a large bowl, combine Ricotta, Mozzarella, ⅓ cup Parmesan, eggs, parsley, salt, and pepper with a wooden spoon. Stuff each shell. Spoon some Prego sauce in the bottom of a large baking dish. Layer stuffed shells in dish. Cover with remaining sauce and sprinkle with remaining Parmesan. Bake, uncovered, for 30 minutes at 350°. Serves 8.

You can use your own homemade spicy tomato sauce if you prefer.

Mrs. Joseph S. Smith (Margaret)

To keep your pasta from boiling over, lay a metal spoon on top of the pot. If you are not going to use your pasta with sauce immediately after cooking it, rinse it in cold water and toss in a little olive oil to prevent it from sticking.

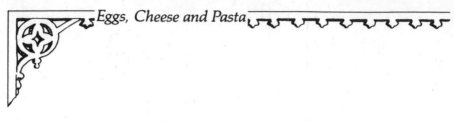

Cheese Soufflé

6 slices thin-sliced, white
  bread
6 tablespoons butter,
  softened
¼ teaspoon dry mustard
⅛ teaspoon cayenne pepper
¼ teaspoon seasoned salt
¾ cup grated Cheddar
  cheese
4 eggs, beaten
½ quart whole milk
Paprika

Trim crust from bread. Mix softened butter with mustard, cayenne, and seasoned salt. Butter one side of bread and layer on the bottom of a 1½ quart greased baking dish. Combine cheese, eggs, and milk and pour over bread. Sprinkle with paprika. Refrigerate several hours or overnight. Bake at 325° for 40-45 minutes or until set and lightly brown. Serve immediately. Serves 6-8.

Great to make ahead for weekend company.

Mrs. Jeff Kosoris (Susan)

Green Chili Cheese Bake

5 eggs, slightly beaten
¼ cup flour
¼ teaspoon baking powder
½ teaspoon salt
1 (10-ounce) carton creamed
  cottage cheese
½ pound Monterrey Jack or
  Cheddar cheese, grated
¼ pound butter, softened
1 (4-ounce) can chopped
  green chilies

Mix all ingredients. Pour into 8-inch square pan or soufflé dish. Bake at 350° for 40-45 minutes. Cut in squares to serve. Serves 6.

Fluffy, light, and easy to make. Delicious served with breakfast.

Mrs. Pleasant Mitchell (Helen)

Three Cheese Casserole

1 pound ground beef
½ cup chopped onion
2 (8-ounce) cans tomato
sauce
1 teaspoon sugar
¾ teaspoon salt
¼ teaspoon garlic salt
¼ teaspoon pepper
4 cups raw noodles
1 cup cream-style cottage
   cheese
8-ounce soft cream cheese
¼ cup sour cream
⅓ cup chopped green
   pepper
¼ cup grated Parmesan
   cheese

In a large skillet, cook meat and onion till meat is lightly browned and onion is tender. Stir in tomato sauce, sugar, salt, garlic salt, and pepper. Remove from heat. Cook and drain noodles. Combine cottage cheese, cream cheese, sour cream, and green pepper. Spread ½ of noodles in a 11x7-inch dish. Top with a small amount of the meat sauce. Cover with the cheese mixture. Layer remaining noodles, then meat sauce. Top with Parmesan. Bake at 350° for 30 minutes. Serves 8-10.

Filling!

Mrs. Joe Grubbs (Jo Beth)

Fettucini

1 pound thin noodles
1 cup cream or half and
   half
½ cup butter
1½ cups grated Parmesan
   cheese

Boil noodles in salted water. Drain. Add cream, butter, and cheese to noodles. Toss and serve. Serves 6-8.

Easy and always a crowd pleaser.

Mrs. Joe Smith (Margaret)

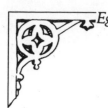

Fettucini Alfredo

1½ sticks butter
Garlic powder (to taste)
Olive oil
1 pound fettucini noodles
1 pint whipping cream
¾ cup Parmesan cheese
¼ cup sour cream

In a saucepan, melt butter with garlic powder. In a large pot, boil water for noodles. Add olive oil to the water to prevent boil-overs. Cook noodles till done. Drain. Return to pot and add butter mixture. With burner on low, slowly add the cream, ½ cup Parmesan, and sour cream, stirring constantly. To serve, pour in serving dish and top with remaining Parmesan. Serves 6-8.

This is an excellent recipe and so easy to make!

Mrs. Jeff Kosoris (Susan)

Garlic Grits

2 cups grits
1½ quarts water
½ cup milk
2 rolls garlic cheese
4 eggs, beaten
1 stick butter
Salt and pepper to taste
Parmesan cheese
Paprika

Combine grits and water and cook till done. Add remaining ingredients and pour into a buttered 9x13-inch pan. Sprinkle with Parmesan cheese and paprika. Bake at 300° for 30 minutes. Serves 12.

This is nice with barbeque or brunch.

Mrs. David Ballard (Karen)

Brunch

2½ cups herbed croutons
2 pounds sausage
2 cups grated Cheddar
  cheese
4 eggs
¼ teaspoon dry mustard
2½ cups milk
1 can mushroom soup
⅓ cup milk
8-ounce can chopped
  mushrooms

Line a 13x9-inch dish with croutons. Brown sausage and layer it over the croutons. Layer cheese on top of sausage. In a separate bowl, mix eggs, mustard, 2½ cups milk. Pour this over cheese. Refrigerate overnight. This next morning, mix mushroom soup, ⅓ cup milk, and mushrooms. Pour over sausage mixture and bake at 300° for 90 minutes. Serve 8.

Mrs. Ken Box (Dietra)

Egg Casserole

6 eggs, beaten
½ cup Cheddar cheese,
  grated
½ cup jack cheese, grated
1 pound sausage
1 teaspoon salt
1 teaspoon pepper
2 slices white bread
2 cups milk

Beat eggs. Combine cheeses. Cook and drain sausage. Combine eggs, ½ of the cheese, sausage, salt, pepper, bread (torn into small pieces), and milk. Pour into a greased casserole. Top with remaining cheese. Bake at 350° for 20 minutes. Serves 6 to 8.

Nice for brunch.

Mrs. Griggs DeHay (Gay)

Crescent Breakfast

1 can Pillsbury Crescent
  Rolls
2 tablespoons melted butter
6 tablespoons mustard
8-ounces Cheddar cheese,
  grated
1 jar sliced mushrooms
1 green pepper, chopped
1 onion, chopped
2 cups cubed ham

Spread rolls out flat in 9x13-inch pan. Mix butter and mustard and spread over rolls. Top this with all the other ingredients. Bake at 400° for 20-25 minutes. Serve 8-10.

A good guest breakfast.

Mrs. Rick Pitts (Becky)

Spana Kopeeta
(Greek Spinach-Cheese Casserole)

3 eggs, beaten
6 tablespoons flour
1 (10-ounce) package
chopped spinach, thawed
1 teaspoon salt
2 cups cottage cheese
2 cups Cheddar, grated
Pepper to taste

Beat the eggs and flour till smooth. Add remaining ingredients and mix well. Bake, uncovered, in a 2 quart casserole for 1 hour at 350°. Let stand 10 minutes before serving. Serves 6.

An unusual side dish.

Mrs. Joseph S. Smith (Margaret)

Crab Quiche

Pastry for 9-inch quiche pan
½ cup mayonnaise
2 tablespoons flour
2 eggs, beaten
½ cup milk
1 (6-ounce) package frozen
crabmeat
2 cups shredded swiss
cheese
⅓ cup chopped green onion

Line a 9-inch quiche pan with pastry. Prick shell and bake at 400° for 12-15 minutes or until lightly browned. Cool. Combine mayonnaise, flour, eggs, and milk. Mix thoroughly. Thaw and drain crabmeat. Stir crabmeat, cheese, and onion into egg mixture. Spoon into quich shell. Bake at 350° for 30 minutes or until firm in center. May substitute shrimp for crab-meat. Serves 4-6.

This is a complete light lunch when served with a tossed salad.

Mrs. Craig Curry (Karen)

Green Chili Quiche

Pastry for 9-inch pan
4 large eggs, beaten
1 tablespoon butter
½ onion, chopped
1 (4-ounce) can chopped
green chilies, drained
2 cups sharp Cheddar,
grated
1 cup sour cream
½ cup milk
½ teaspoon salt
¼ teaspoon pepper

Heat oven to 425°. Line pan with pastry. Prick bottom and sides of crust and bake 14 minutes. Brush crust with egg and bake 2 minutes longer. Remove from oven. Melt butter. Stir in onion and chilies and sauté until soft. Layer onion mixture and cheese in the pie shell. Beat remaining eggs with sour cream, milk, salt and pepper. Pour into shell. Bake at 350° for 30-35 minutes. Serves 4-6.

Good for a family dinner or a ladies' brunch.

Mrs. Jim Beller (Linda)

Hamburger Quiche

1 pound ground beef
2 9-inch pie shells
  (unbaked)
3 cups shredded Cheddar or
  swiss cheese (about 1
  pound)
⅔ cup chopped green
  onions
4 eggs
1 cup mayonnaise
1 cup milk
2 tablespoons cornstarch

Brown beef and drain. Spoon into pie shells. Top with cheese and onion.

In a medium bowl, mix together remaining ingredients. Pour this mixture over the cheese and onion. Bake at 350° for 35-40 minutes or until a knife inserted in center of pie comes out clean. Freezes well. Serves 12-16.

A good, easy recipe that the kids can help make.

Mrs. Joe Grubbs (Jo Beth)

Holiday Quiche

1 unbaked 9-inch pie shell
1½ cups shredded swiss
  cheese
4 tablespoons flour
½ cup diced, cooked ham
3 eggs, beaten
1 cup half and half cream
¼ teaspoon salt
¼ teaspoon dry mustard
Chopped parsley
Chopped pimiento

Prepare pie shell. Combine cheese and flour and layer in pie shell. Layer ham next. Combine eggs, cream, salt, and mustard and beat until smooth. Pour over ham and cheese.

Bake at 325° for 45 minutes or until firm. Cool slightly before cutting. Garnish with parsley and pimiento. Serves 4-6.

Fast and fun to eat!

Mrs. Bill Major (Patsy)

Italian Zucchini Quiche

4 cups thinly sliced, unpeeled zucchini
1 cup coarsely chopped onion
½ cup margarine
½ cup chopped parsley
½ teaspoon salt
½ teaspoon pepper
¼ teaspoon garlic powder
¼ teaspoon sweet basil
¼ teaspoon oregano
3 eggs, well beaten
8-ounces shredded mozzarella
2 teaspoons Dijon mustard
Crust for 9-inch deep dish pan

Heat oven to 375°. Cook zucchini and onions in margarine in a skillet till tender (about 10 minutes). Stir in seasonings.

In a bowl, combine eggs and cheese. Stir vegetable mixture into egg mixture. Spread crust with mustard. Pour vegetable-egg mixture evenly into crust.

Bake at 375° for 18-20 minutes or until knife comes out clean. Let stand 10 minutes before cutting. Serves 6-8.

Mrs. Craig Curry (Karen)

Spinach Quiche

½ pound bacon (or ham)
1 9-inch unbaked, deep dish pie shell
½ cup grated Swiss cheese
1 (10-ounce) package frozen spinach
1 jar mushrooms
1½ cups light cream
3 eggs
Dash salt
Dash pepper
Dash nutmeg

Preheat oven to 350°. Fry bacon till crisp. Drain and crumble into the bottom of a 9-inch deep dish pie shell. Sprinkle with cheese and top with spinach and mushrooms. Beat cream, eggs, and spices together in a separate bowl. Pour over spinach mixture.

Bake 40 minutes at 350° or until it puffs up and looks firm. Let cool 10 minutes before serving. Serves 6.

Easy and a little different from other quiches.

Mrs. Stan Parker (Priscilla)

Fried Rice

3 tablespoons oil
½ cup chopped green
  onions
1 cup sliced celery
1 cup sliced mushrooms
3 cups cooked rice
2 tablespoon soy sauce
1 egg, slightly beaten
½ pound crisp bacon,
  crumbled

Heat oil in a large skillet. Add onions and celery. Cook till tender. Add mushrooms, rice, and soy sauce. Cook for 10 minutes on low heat, stirring occasionally. Stir in egg and cook only until the egg is done. Add bacon and mix well. Serve with extra soy sauce. Serves 6-8.

A tasty dish.

Mrs. Erling Holey (Susan)

Rice Dish

1 cup Uncle Ben's converted
  long grained rice
1 can cream of mushroom
  soup
1 can beef bouillon soup
½ cup chopped green
  pepper
½ cup chopped onion
2 tablespoons Wesson oil
⅓ cup boiling water

Mix all ingredients together in a glass casserole. Bake, covered, for 45 minutes at 350°. Uncover and bake another 15 minutes. Serves 6.

This is a good side dish for chicken or pork.

Mrs. Rick Pitts (Becky)

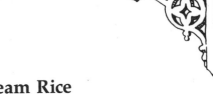

Sour Cream Rice

2 cups raw rice
2 cups sour cream
2 cans green chilies
¾ pound Cheddar cheese

Cook rice. Add sour cream and chilies and mix well. Pour half of mixture into a large casserole. Slice ½ pound of cheese and layer cheese over the rice mixture. Add remaining rice mixture and top with ¼ pound grated cheese. Bake at 350° until heated, about 20 minutes. Serves 8-12.

Easy, tasty, and different. Can be frozen.

Mrs. Roy Marchbanks (Pam)

The Strickland-Sawyer Home was built around the original, smaller home on this site on Oldham Street. Maggie Young Beall, a widow, built her home in 1888 but was unable to pay her bills at the lumber company and lost the house in a sheriff's sale the next year. J. Frank Strickland acquired the home for $1300.00 for his new bride. In 1897 they built the home pictured here over the first one! Mr. Strickland had come to Texas from Alabama in 1878 penniless. He was a man who could foresee great things for Texas and invested wisely to build his fortune. He is perhaps best known as the founder of Texas Power and Light Company and a pioneer in the Interurban Rail Lines which connected the major cities in the state with some of the smaller ones such as Waxahachie. One of the most beautiful features of this Queen Anne home is the corner tower topped by double finials and wrapped around by a second story porch. The imbricated shingles and variety of wood cladding patterns create a composition that is typical of Queen Anne architecture.

VEGETABLES

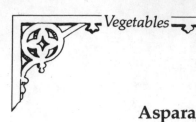

Asparagus Casserole

1 (15-ounce) can asparagus
  (spears or cut)
½-1 cup grated Swiss cheese
2 tablespoons flour
2 tablespoons melted butter
½ tablespoon grated onion
1 teaspoon salt
½ teaspoon pepper
1 teaspoon sugar
1 cup sour cream
½ cup buttered bread
  crumbs
2 teaspoons melted butter

Layer canned asparagus with grated Swiss cheese. Stir flour into melted butter in separate bowl. Add remaining ingredients. Pour mixture over layered asparagus and cheese. Combine bread crumbs and butter and sprinkle over top Bake 30 minutes at 400°. Serves 4-6.

Easy but elegant.

Mrs. James Alderdice (Rosemary)

Rilla's Asparagus Casserole

1 (15-ounce) can asparagus
  spears
2 tablespoons butter
2 tablespoons flour
½ cup milk
½ cup asparagus liquid
Salt and pepper to taste
1 cup grated cheese
½ cup cracker crumbs

Drain asparagus, saving the liquid. Make cheese sauce from butter, flour, milk, asparagus liquid, salt, and pepper. Add cheese, saving some for top of casserole. Butter small square casserole and layer asparagus, crackers, and sauce. Repeat layers and top with cheese. Cook at 350° for 30 minutes. Serves 6.

Double sauce for 2 cans, etc.

Mrs. Tom Curlin (Betty)

Virginia's Asparagus-Pea Casserole

6 tablespoons butter
6 tablespoons flour
3 cups milk
2 (5-ounce) jars Kraft Old
    English Cheese
8-10 Ritz crackers
3 cans cut asparagus,
    drained
1 cup English peas
½ cup chopped almonds

Cook butter, flour and milk until thick. Stir in cheese until melted.

Crumble crackers sparingly over bottom of 9x13-inch casserole. Layer ½ asparagus, ½ peas, ½ almonds. Cover with ½ the cheese sauce. Repeat. Sprinkle top with a little paprika for color. Bake at 350° for 30 minutes. Serves 8-10.

This recipe may be halved and cooked in an 8-inch square pan.

Mrs. Clovis Mitchell (Omajeanne)

Bean Bundles

2 cans vertical packed green
    beans
½ pound bacon
Colored toothpicks

Sauce:
3 tablespoons butter
3 tablespoons tarragon
    vinegar
½ teaspoon salt
1 teaspoon paprika
1 tablespoon fresh chopped
    parsley
1 teaspoon onion juice

Drain beans. Divide into bundles of approximately 5 beans each. Cut 1 slice of bacon in half and wrap around beans and secure with colored toothpick. Broil till bacon is crisp, about 5 minutes.

Sauce: Combine butter, vinegar, salt, paprika, parsley and onion juice. Simmer until hot. Pour over cooked bean bundles and serve.

Beans and sauce may be done ahead of time and refrigerated. Broil bean bundles and reheat sauce at serving time. Serves 8.

Mrs. Joseph S. Smith (Margaret)

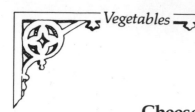

Cheese Baked Beans

1 cup chopped onion
⅔ cup chopped green
 pepper
¼ cup butter
2 (1 pound 2-ounce) jars
 baked beans
1 cup catsup
2½ cups shredded
 Monterrey Jack cheese,
 divided

Preheat oven to 350°. Sauté 1 cup chopped onion, ⅔ cup chopped green pepper in ¼ cup butter. Add baked beans, catsup and 2 cups shredded Monterrey Jack cheese. Bake in 2 quart casserole for approximately 30 minutes until bubbly. Garnish with ½ cup additional shredded cheese. Serves 8.

Mrs. Jeff Kosoris (Susan)

Boston Baked Beans

3 cups whitepea beans,
 soaked overnight in 6
 cups cold water
½ cup brown sugar
3 tablespoons molasses
1½ teaspoons salt
1 teaspoon dry mustard
1 teaspoon ground ginger
1 teaspoon Worcestershire
 sauce
1 pound salt pork
2 small onions, chopped

Drain beans and reserve water drained from them. To beans, add: brown sugar, molasses, salt, mustard, ginger, and Worcestershire sauce, mixing all together well. Cut off ¼ of the salt pork and place it in the bottom of a 2 quart bean pot or casserole. Add onions and pour in beans with their seasonings. Cover with some of the reserved water. Score rind of remaining salt pork and place it on top of beans. Cover pot or casserole, preheat it on top of range (using an asbestos mat over very low heat to prevent cracking bean pot), then cook in a slow oven (225°) for 8 hours. If liquid reduces, add enough reserved water to keep beans moist but not too wet. Serve with steamed Boston Brown Bread. Serves 10.

Mrs. Bill Atkinson(Pam)

Hawaiian-Style Baked Beans

2 (1-pound) cans pork and
  beans
¼ pound cooked ham,
  diced
½ teaspoon dry mustard
¼ cup brown sugar, firmly
  packed
2 tablespoons finely
  chopped onion
1 cup pineapple chunks,
  drained (reserve liquid)
½ cup pineapple juice

Grease a 1½ quart baking dish. Spoon 1 can of pork and beans into the bottom of the dish. Combine ham, mustard, brown sugar, onion, pineapple and pineapple juice. Spoon over layer of beans, and top with remaining can of pork and beans. Cover and bake at 350° for 1 hour. Serves 5-6.

Mrs. Steve Kelley (Cindy)

Company Casserole

2 cans French style green
  beans
1 can mixed Chinese
  vegetables
1 can cream of mushroom
  soup
1 can French-fried onions
Grated cheese

Mix green beans, Chinese vegetables and soup. Bake for 20 minutes at 350°. After 20 minutes crumble onions on top and add enough grated cheese to cover top, then cook an additional 10 minutes. Serves 6-8.

Mrs. Alvis Bynum (Jimmie Faye)

 Never add salt to dry beans that you are cooking until they are already tender or else they will remain hard.

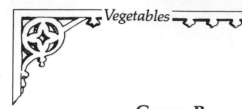

Green Bean Casserole

3 medium cans green beans
Pinch garlic salt (any style)
4 tablespoons butter
4 tablespoons flour
1 can cream of mushroom
  soup
1 tablespoon chili powder
½ pound Velvetta cheese
Crushed corn flakes
Chopped almonds

Boil green bean 20 minutes. Add pinch of garlic salt. Stir, then drain and put in 13x9-inch pyrex dish. Mix next 5 ingredients together and stir over low heat until cheese melts. Pour mixture over green beans. Cover with crushed corn flakes and chopped almonds. (Use own judgement as to amounts.) Bake at 350° for 30 minutes. Serves 8.

A nice way to dress up green beans for guests.

Mrs. Bobby Oliver (Emily)

Mary Elizabeth Smith's Green Beans

2 (16-ounce) cans green
beans
1 thinly sliced onion
1 tablespoon salad oil
1 tablespoon vinegar
Salt and pepper

Sour Cream Dressing:
1 cup sour cream
½ cup Hellman's
  mayonnaise
1 teaspoon lemon juice
¼ teaspoon dry mustard
1 tablespoon prepared
  horseradish
¼ teaspoon onion juice
2 teaspoons chopped chives

Marinate drained green beans and onion in vinegar and oil. Sprinkle with salt and coarse pepper. After 1 hour, drain and cover with sour cream dressing. For dressing, simply mix all ingredients in small bowl. May be made 48 hours in advance. Serves 6.

An interesting salad change.

Mrs. Robert M. Cox (Dee)

String Bean Casserole

1 (8-ounce) can mushrooms, sliced
1 medium onion, chopped
1 stick butter or margarine
¼ cup flour
2 cups warm milk
1 cup light cream
3 teaspoons soy sauce
1 teaspoon MSG
¾ pound sharp Cheddar cheese, grated
5 cans French-style green beans, drained well
1 (5-ounce) can sliced water chestnuts, drained
¾ cup sliced blanched almonds

Sauté mushrooms and onions in butter. Add flour, milk, cream, soy sauce, MSG and cheese. Simmer until cheese melts. Mix green beans with sauce, then add water chestnuts. Pour into casserole dish and top with almonds. Bake 375° for 20 minutes. This recipe may be halved. Serves 13-15.

Mrs. Steve Loftis (Nina)

When mashing potatoes, use water and lots of butter instead of milk — this will make them fluffier and lighter.

Pickled Beets

2 jars small beets, drained
1 scant cup sugar
1 jar Kraft horseradish
4 tablespoons vinegar

Combine sugar, horseradish, and vinegar. Pour sauce over beets and refrigerate 24 hours before serving. Serve chilled.

Mrs. Randall Klein (Louise)

Broccoli Casserole

2 tablespoons vegetable oil
1 package (12 to 16 ounce)
  frozen chopped broccoli
1 small chopped onion or
  equivalent chopped green
  onion
1 cup chopped celery
1 can cream of chicken soup
1 small jar Cheez-Whiz
1 cup canned milk
1 cup uncooked Minute
  Rice
1 small jar sliced
  mushrooms

In oil sauté broccoli, onion, and celery. Stir in remaining ingredients and allow to cook a few minutes. Pour into greased dish and cook covered (325° to 350°) for about 45 minutes or until lightly brown.

Mrs. Rusty Graham (Nelda)

Broccoli-Blue Cheese Casserole

2 tablespoons melted butter
2 tablespoons all purpose
  flour
½ teaspoon salt
1 (3-ounce) package cream
  cheese (softened)
1 ounce blue cheese,
  crumbled (about ¼ cup)
1 cup milk
2 (10-ounce) packages
broccoli (spears or chopped)
  cooked & drained
½ cup crushed Ritz crackers

In a sauce pan, blend butter, flour, salt, and cheese. Add milk all at once. Cook and stir until mixture boils. Stir in cooked broccoli. Pour into 2½ quart casserole dish or 11x7-inch pyrex dish. Add cracker crumbs to top. Bake at 350° for 30 minutes. Serves 8.

Mrs. Craig Curry (Karen)

Broccoli Casserole

1 stick margarine
1 cup chopped onion
1 cup chopped celery
2 cans mushroom soup
1 (8-ounce) Cheeze Whiz
2 (10-ounce) packages
   chopped broccoli
3 cups cooked rice

Sauté in margarine the onion and celery. Add remaining ingredients. Mix all together, place in greased casserole. Bake 45 minutes at 375°. Serves 8.

Mrs. Gary Morrow (Rikki)

Broccoli Medley

2 (10-ounce) packages
   broccoli spears
1 cup chicken broth
½ pound bacon cut into 1
   inch pieces
2 cup sliced mushrooms,
   fresh
½ cup chopped green
   onions and tops
1 (8-ounce) can water
   chestnuts, drained and
   sliced
¼ cup slivered almonds
1 teaspoon salt
⅓ teaspoon pepper
Pimento strips

Cook broccoli in chicken broth till crisp-tender, about 8 minutes. Drain, reserving ⅓ cup liquid. Cut into bite-size pieces. Fry bacon till slightly crisp, about 5 minutes. Add remaining ingredients, except broccoli, liquid, and pimento. Cook and stir till bacon is crisp and mushrooms are tender, about 5 minutes. Just before serving, combine this mixture with the broccoli and liquid. Heat. Arrange on a serving dish. Garnish with pimento. Serves 12.

Mrs. Bill Major (Patsy)

Broccoli and Rice

1 package frozen broccoli
2 eggs, well beaten
½ cup milk
½ cup butter
2½ cups cooked rice
½ cup chopped parsley
½ cup chopped onions
1 can mushroom soup
½ cup grated Cheddar
   cheese

Cook 1 package frozen broccoli as directed. Drain. Mix together in a bowl 2 eggs well beaten, ½ cup milk, and ½ cup softened butter. In another bowl, combine 2½ cups cooked rice, ½ cup chopped parsley, and ½ cup chopped onions. Turn all the above into a casserole dish and cover mixture with 1 can mushroom soup and grated cheese. Bake 30 minutes at 300°.

Mrs. Bill Major (Patsy)

Sweet-Sour Cabbage

1 large head cabbage
1 large onion, chopped
4 tablespoons bacon
   drippings
1 cup sugar syrup
1 teaspoon salt
¼ teaspoon pepper
¼ cup apple cider vinegar

Shread cabbage thin. Sauté onion until soft in bacon drippings in a kettle. Stir in cabbage, salt, pepper, and sugar syrup. Heat slowly to boiling, cover and simmer 25 minutes. Remove from heat, drizzle vinegar over cabbage and toss to mix.

Sugar Syrup: Pour ⅔ cup boiling water over ⅔ cup sugar and cook gently until slightly thick.

Mrs. Jack Hightower (Nancy)

Ginger Candied Carrots

12 carrots
4 tablespoons butter
½ cup brown sugar
1½ teaspoons ground ginger
½ teaspoon caraway seeds

Cook carrots until tender (25 minutes). Melt butter. Add brown sugar, ginger and caraway seeds to butter. Set aside. When carrots are tender, drain and pour butter mixture over them. Cook over low heat for 5 minutes, stirring occasionally. Serves 6.

Mrs. Mike Hayes (Eva)

Sunshine Carrots

7-8 medium sized carrots
1 tablespoon brown sugar
1 teaspoon corn starch
¼ teaspoon ground ginger
¼ teaspoon salt
¼ cup orange juice
2 tablespoons butter

Bias-slice carrots, about ½ inch thick, and cook until tender. Meanwhile combine sugar, cornstarch, ginger and salt. Add orange juice and cook, stirring constantly until thickened and bubbly. Boil 1 minute, remove from heat. Stir in butter. Pour over hot carrots. Serves 6.

Mrs. Erling Holey (Susan)

Keep onions in your refrigerator before you use them to cut down on the tears and strong odor when they are cut.

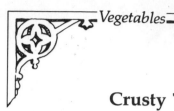

Crusty Topped Cauliflower

1 large head cauliflower
½ cup mayonnaise
2 tablespoons Dijon mustard
½-¾ cup shredded Cheddar
   cheese

Cook whole cauliflower in small amount of salted water for approximately 20 minutes. Place in flat pan. Mix ½ cup mayonnaise, 2 teaspoon Dijon mustard together. Pour over cauliflower. Sprinkle with ½-¾ cup shredded cheese. Bake at 350° about 10 minutes or until cheese melts. Serves 6.

Mrs. Gary Morrow (Rikki)

Becky's Corn Pie

3 large eggs, beaten
1 can whole kernel corn,
   drained
1 small can (8¾-ounce)
   cream style corn
1 stick margarine melted
½ cup yellow corn meal
4 ounces Monterrey Jack
   cheese, grated
4 ounces Cheddar cheese,
   grated
1 (4-ounce) can chopped
   green chilies
Pinch salt
½ teaspoon Worcestershire
   sauce

Mix all ingredients well. Pour into well greased 10-inch pie plate. Bake at 325° for 1 hour, uncovered (or until set). Serves 6-8.

Mrs. David Ballard (Karen)

Jalapeño Corn

2 cans shoe peg corn
(white)
2 (3-ounce) package cream
cheese
½ stick margarine
½ cup milk
Dash of garlic salt
1 (4-ounce) can green chilies
(chopped)
(If you want it hotter add
jalapeños)

Drain corn. Melt cream cheese and margarine in milk. Blend well. Add corn, garlic salt, green chilies. Bake in square casserole dish at 350° for 20 minutes or until bubbly. This can be mixed together one day and cooked the next or frozen. Serves 6.

Mrs. Lonell Wilson (Betty)

Scalloped Corn

1 can whole kernel corn,
drained
1 can cream style corn
1 small onion, chopped
3 tablespoons chopped
pimento
3 tablespoons chopped
green chilies
Salt and pepper
¾ cup milk
1 cup bread crumbs

Mix all ingredients in 1½ quart dish and dot with butter. Bake 30 minutes at 350°. Serves 6.

Mrs. David Ballard (Karen)

Two Corn Casserole

½ cup margarine
¾ cup green pepper,
chopped
⅓ cup onion, chopped
1 (17-ounce) can creamed
corn
1 (17-ounce) can whole
kernel corn, not drained
3 eggs, well-beaten
1¼ cups corn muffin mix
1 cup shredded Cheddar
cheese

In a small skillet, melt margarine and sauté green pepper and onion till crisp-tender. In a large bowl combine both corns, egg, and muffin mix. Blend well. Add onion mixture. Mix well. Pour into a greased casserole. Sprinkle with Cheddar cheese. Bake at 350° for 55 to 65 minutes or until firm and set. Let stand 5 minutes before serving. Serves 6.

Mrs. Ron Johnson (Sharon)

Wyatt's Cafeteria's Baked Eggplant

1 pound eggplant peeled
1 cup dried bread crumbs
½ cup canned evaporated milk
¼ cup whole milk
¼ cup butter, melted
¼ cup finely chopped onion
¼ cup finely chopped green pepper
¼ cup finely chopped celery
2 eggs, slightly beaten
1 tablespoon chopped pimento
2 teaspoons salt
½ teaspoon pepper
¼ teaspoon sage
⅛ teaspoon monosodium glutamate
1½ cups (4-ounces) Cheddar cheese, grated

Cut peeled eggplant into 1 inch cubes and soak in refrigerator overnight, or a minimum of 6 hours. Drain eggplant and place in pan. Cover with water and simmer until tender. Soak bread crumbs in milk. Sauté onions, green pepper and celery in melted butter for about 15 minutes until tender. Combine cooked eggplant, bread crumbs, and sautéed vegetables. Add eggs, pimento, and seasonings. Blend thoroughly. Place in greased baking dish and bake at 350° for 45 minutes. Top with grated cheese and return to oven until cheese melts. (If using an 11x7-inch dish bake about 30 minutes. If using an 1½ quart dish bake about 45 minutes.) Serves 6-8.

Mrs. Harold Dorsey (Wilma)

Scalloped Eggplant

1 large eggplant, diced (4 cups)
⅓ cup milk
1 (10½-ounce) can condensed cream of mushroom soup
1 slightly beaten egg
½ cup chopped onion
¾ cup herb-seasoned stuffing
½ cup herb-seasoned stuffing
2 tablespoons melted butter or margarine
4 ounces (1 cup) sharp American cheese shredded

Cook diced eggplant in boiling water until tender, 6-7 minutes, then drain. Meanwhile gradually stir milk into soup; blend in egg. Add drained eggplant, onion, and ¾ cup stuffing. Toss lightly to mix. Turn into greased 10x6x1½-inch baking dish. Finely crush ½ cup stuffing. Toss with 2 tablespoons melted margarine or butter. Sprinkle over casserole. Top with shredded cheese. Bake at 350° for 20 minutes. Serves 6-8.

Mrs. Ken Box (Dietra)

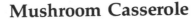

Mushroom Casserole

¼ cup butter
1 pound fresh mushrooms,
  chopped
1 small onion, chopped
1 medium green pepper,
  chopped
1 can cream of mushroom
  soup, undiluted
1 (8-ounce) jar mayonnaise
6 slices bread
¼ cup butter
1½ cups grated Cheddar
  cheese divided into thirds
2 eggs
1 soup can of milk
Buttered bread crumbs

Melt ¼ cup butter in large skillet. Add mushrooms and cook gently for 2 minutes; add onion and pepper. Sauté for 3 minutes. Remove from heat; stir in soup and mayonnaise. Spread bread slices with ¼ cup butter; cut in 1 inch squares. In a 9-inch baking dish, layer half of bread cubes, half of mushroom mixture; add ⅓ of cheese. Repeat. Beat eggs, add milk and pour over casserole. Refrigerate at least 1 hour. Top casserole with buttered crumbs and remaining ⅓ cheese. Bake uncovered at 325° for 1 hour. Serves 6-8.

Nice at the holidays.

Mrs. Randall Klein (Louise)

 Use an egg slicer to slice fresh mushrooms for sautéing.

Sautéed Mushrooms

2 tablespoons butter
1 tablespoon sour cream
4 tablespoons sautérne
1½ teaspoons tarragon
Salt and pepper (to taste)
½ pound fresh whole
  mushrooms, washed
Parmesan cheese

Melt butter, add sour cream, sautérne, tarragon, salt and pepper. Add mushrooms. Cover and simmer until tender. Sprinkle with Parmesan cheese. Serves 2-4.

Mrs. Jeff Kosoris (Susan)

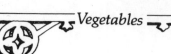

Fried Okra, Potatoes And Onion

1 cup onions, chopped
1 cup potatoes, diced
2 cups okra, sliced
Yellow corn meal
Oil for frying

Take all ingredients and roll in corn meal. Fry until all ingredients are crispy and brown. Serves 4.

Mrs. Gary Morrow (Rikki)

Potato Casserole

1 (2-pound) bag frozen hash brown potatoes
½ cup chopped onion
½ cup melted margarine (save ½ for top)
10 ounces grated Cheddar cheese
1 can cream of chicken soup
1 teaspoon salt
½ teaspoon black pepper
1 cup sour cream
Bread crumbs

Mix all ingredients together except reserved margarine and bread crumbs. Put into well greased large casserole, sprinkle top with crumbs and bake 1 hour and 10 minutes at 350°. For variation, try using 8 ounces of cream cheese instead of Cheddar and corn flakes or Peppridge Farm stuffing mix instead of bread crumbs. A good recipe for large family gatherings. Serves 15.

Mrs. Lonell Wilson (Betty)

Cheese Potato Casserole

6 medium potatoes
1 cup grated Cheddar cheese
½ cup milk
2 tablespoons butter
1 (8-ounce) carton sour cream
¼ cup chopped onion
1 teaspoon salt
¼ teaspoon pepper
Paprika

Cook potatoes in skins until done. Chill. Peel and grate potatoes. Combine cheese, milk and butter, cook over low heat until cheese and butter melt, stirring occasionally. Remove from heat, stir in sour cream, onion, salt, and pepper. Fold cheese mixture into potatoes. Pour into greased 2 quart casserole, dot with butter and sprinkle with paprika. Bake at 350° for 45 minutes. Serves 6.

Mrs. Bill Price (Kay)

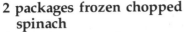

Spinach Casserole

2 packages frozen chopped
   spinach
6 ounces cream cheese
1 can cream of mushroom
   soup
1 can french fried onion
   rings
½ stick margarine
1 cup crushed Ritz crackers

Cook and drain spinach. Set aside. Melt cheese in soup. Stir in spinach and onions. Pour into buttered 9x11-inch casserole. Melt margarine and mix with cracker crumbs. Sprinkle on top of spinach mixture. Bake at 325° for 25-30 minutes. Serves 6-8.

Mrs. Homer Denning (Linda)

Spinach Casserole

1 package frozen chopped
   spinach
1 cup grated cheese
1 cup butter
1 teaspoon grated onion
1 egg, beaten
1 can cream of mushroom
   soup
1¾ cup Pepperidge Farm
   Herb Stuffing
Salt and pepper to taste

Cook and drain spinach. Add cheese, butter, onion, egg, and soup and mix well. Toss in one cup of stuffing. Add salt and pepper to taste. Pour into a buttered one quart casserole. Add ¾ cup stuffing as topping and dot with a little more butter. Bake at 350° for 30 minutes. This can be made ahead and frozen. Serves 6.

Mrs. Craig Curry (Karen)

Spinach Soufflé

2 packages frozen chopped
   spinach
1 can mushroom soup
¼ cup mayonnaise
2 eggs, beaten
1 small onion, minced
Salt and pepper to taste

Thaw spinach, and mix all ingredients together. Pour into 1½ quart casserole and bake 1 hour at 325°. Serves 8.

Mrs. David Ballard (Karen)

Sour Cream Spinach

2 packages frozen chopped
  spinach
1 medium onion, chopped
½ stick butter
1 pint sour cream
1 (1½-ounce) can Parmesan
  cheese
1 (14-ounce) can artichoke
  hearts

Cook and drain spinach according to package directions. Sauté onion in butter. Add sour cream, Parmesan cheese, and onion to spinach. Put in a buttered casserole. Arrange quartered artichoke hearts on top. Bake at 325° for 30 minutes. Serves 8.

A nice company dish-something special.

Mrs. Bill Major (Patsy)

 To keep your potatoes snowy white while boiling them, add a teaspoon of vinegar or fresh lemon juice to the water.

Yellow Squash-Green Chilies Casserole

6 cups chopped yellow
  squash
1 cup chopped onion
½ teaspoon salt
½ teaspoon pepper
¼ teaspoon garlic powder
¼ cup sugar
1 stick melted butter
1 (3-ounce) can peeled,
  chopped green chilies
1 medium jar chopped
  pimento
3 large eggs, well beaten
1½ cups grated Cheddar
  cheese
1 package crushed Keebler
  Townhouse crackers
1 stick melted butter

Cook squash and onion for 10 minutes after it comes to a boil. Drain well. While still hot, add salt, pepper, garlic powder, sugar and butter. Mix well. Add green chilies, pimento and eggs. Pour into casserole dish. Sprinkle cheese over squash mixture. Sprinkle crackers over cheese. Top with melted butter. Bake for 30 minutes at 350°. Serves 6-8.

Mrs. Craig Curry (Karen)

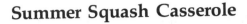

Summer Squash Casserole

2 pounds yellow squash
¼ cup chopped onion
1 can cream of chicken soup
1 cup sour cream
1 cup shredded carrots
1 (8-ounce) package Herb
  Seasoned Stuffing mix
½ cup butter or melted
  margarine

In saucepan, cook sliced squash and chopped onion in boiling salted water for 5 minutes. Drain. Combine cream of chicken soup and sour cream. Stir in shredded carrot. Fold in drained squash and onion. Combine stuffing mix and butter. Spread half of stuffing mixture in bottom of pyrex 13x9-inch dish. Spoon vegetable mixture on top. Sprinkle remaining stuffing over vegetables. Bake 350° for 25-30 minutes or until heated thoroughly. Serves 8.

Mrs. Erling Holey (Susan)

Stuffed Squash

8 medium yellow squash
1 (10-ounce) package frozen
  chopped spinach
2 hard-boiled eggs, chopped
1 teaspoon finely chopped
  onion
4 tablespoons melted butter
10-12 crushed Ritz crackers
½ teaspoon Worcestershire
  sauce
Salt and pepper to taste
¼ cup shredded Cheddar
  cheese

Boil 8 whole squash just barely tender. Remove an oval slice from squash and scoop out contents with a spoon. Cook and drain spinach. Combine all ingredients except cheese. Stuff mixture back into squash. Top with cheese. Bake squash in 9x13-inch pan with ½ inch water in the bottom at 300° for 40 minutes. Serves 8.

A colorful sidedish.

Mrs. Pleasant Mitchell (Helen)

Squash Posh

½ cup chopped onion
1½ pounds fresh squash
1 cup mayonnaise or sour
cream
1 cup Parmesan cheese
2 eggs
¼ teaspoon pepper, salt
1 tablespoon melted butter
½ cup bread crumbs

Cook squash and onion till tender. Drain well. Mash and mix with mayonnaise, cheese, eggs, and seasonings. Pour into greased casserole. Mix butter and crumbs and sprinkle on top. Bake 350° for 30 minutes. Serves 6.

Mrs. Joe Grubbs (Jo Beth)

Squash Casserole

1½ cups cooked squash
1 cup medium sharp cheese,
grated
1 small jar pimento,
chopped
3 tablespoons onion, finely
chopped
3 tablespoons melted
margarine
¼ teaspoon black pepper
2 eggs, well beaten
1 cup cracker crumbs
1 cup milk, scalded

Combine all ingredients, adding hot milk last. Pour into buttered 1 quart baking dish. Bake one hour in 325° oven. Serve hot. Serves 8.

Mrs. James Alderdice (Rosemary)

 Try a little sugar and salt in the juice when cooking canned vegetables to make them taste more homegrown.

Squash Casserole

12 medium yellow squash
1 bunch green onions, sliced
2 tablespoons butter
1 can cream of celery soup
2 whole eggs
⅓ cup bread crumbs
¼ teaspoon garlic powder
Pinch of basil
1 tablespoon Worcestershire
  sauce
1 teaspoon salt
Grated cheese
Bread or cracker crumbs
Butter

Cook squash in salted water until tender. Drain and break up, but do not mash. Brown green onions in butter and stir into the celery soup. Add eggs, bread crumbs and seasonings. Combine the soup mixture with squash. Put into a buttered casserole dish and cover with grated cheese. Add additional bread crumbs. Dot with butter. Cook at 375° for 45 minutes. Serves 8-10.

Mrs. Joseph S. Smith (Margaret)

Mexican Squash Casserole

4 medium yellow squash,
  sliced
½ onion, diced
1 tomato, diced
2 tablespoons melted butter
1 teaspoon garlic salt
¼ cup Picante sauce
1½ cups crushed tortilla
  chips
1½ cups grated Cheddar
  cheese

Simmer squash, onion and tomato until tender and drain. (Easy to cook in microwave.) Mash vegetables. Add butter, garlic salt, picante sauce, tortilla chips, and cheese. Stir. Place mixture in buttered baking dish. Bake at 350° until cheese is melted. Serves 6.

Mrs. Frank A. Blankenbeckler III (Alice)

Colachi

1 medium onion, chopped
1 bell pepper, chopped
2 tablespoons salad oil
3 cups zucchini or yellow
  squash, sliced
2 tomatoes, chopped
2 teaspoons Picante sauce
1 (7-ounce) can whole corn,
  drained
1 cup grated cheese

Sauté onion and pepper in oil. Add squash, tomatoes, and Picante sauce. Cook until tender. Add corn and cheese. Heat till bubbly. Serves 6-8.

Mrs. Roy Marchbanks (Pam)

Tomatoes Stuffed With Broccoli

4 medium tomatoes
1 (10-ounce) package frozen
  chopped broccoli
1 (6-ounce) roll garlic cheese
Salt and pepper to taste

Cut tops off tomatoes and scoop out the pulp being careful not to pierce skin. Cook broccoli according to package directions and drain. Combine cooked broccoli, cheese, salt and pepper in food processor and process to smooth, not runny consistency. Stuff tomatoes with broccoli mixture. Bake at 400° for 10 minutes. Serves 4.

Especially pretty served at Christmas time.

Mrs. Erling Holey (Susan)

Scalloped Sliced Tomatoes

4 medium size tomatoes
4 tablespoons butter
1 cup diced celery
½ cup chopped onion
1 teaspoon salt
1 teaspoon sugar
1 teaspoon basil leaves,
  crushed
⅛ teaspoon pepper
1 cup plain croutons

Preheat oven to 350°. Core tomatoes. (Peel, if desired). Cut into ¼ inch slices. Overlap slices in 2 rows in buttered 13x9x2-inch casserole. Set aside. Melt butter in medium saucepan. Add celery and onion. Sauté about 2 minutes, stir in salt, sugar, basil and pepper. Spoon all but ¼ cup celery mixture over tomatoes. Toss croutons with reserved ¼ cup celery mixture. Spoon down center of casserole between tomatoes. Cover and bake until tomatoes are cooked, about 30 minutes. Serves 8.

Mrs. Griggs DeHay (Gay)

Zingy Zucchini Casserole

1 (20-ounce) package crinkle
  cut zucchini
1½ cups snack crackers,
  crumbled
6 tablespoons margarine,
  melted
2 eggs, beaten
1 cup cottage cheese
½ cup Cheddar cheese,
  grated
¼ cup green onions, minced
Dash of tabasco sauce

Thaw and drain zucchini. Combine crumbs and melted margarine; set aside. Spread drained zucchini in bottom of 9x9-inch baking dish. Sprinkle half of crumbs over zucchini. Combine eggs, cheese, onions, and tabasco; pour over crumb layer. Top with remaining crumbs. Bake in oven at 350° for 25 to 30 minutes. Serves 6.

Mrs. Harold Dorsey (Wilma)

Ratatouille

1 medium eggplant
6 small zucchini
3 small onions
3 green peppers
3 cloves garlic
½ cup olive oil
6 medium tomatoes, quartered
½ teaspoon dried sweet basil
½ teaspoon dried thyme
1 cup chopped parsley
Parmesan cheese

Peel eggplant and slice or cube. Slice unpeeled zucchini. Peel and slice onions. Quarter the green peppers. Cook these vegetables separately in olive oil and one crushed clove of garlic. Place the cooked vegetables in a casserole with tomatoes, herbs and remaining garlic. Cook gently for ½ hour, the last few minutes without the casserole cover so the liquid is reduced. Vegetables should be soft but not puréed. The liquid should be quite thin. Season to taste with salt and pepper. Sprinkle with Parmesan cheese before serving. Serves 6-8.

This may be served well-chilled in the summer.

Mrs. Frank A. Blankenbeckler, II (Neil)

 If you don't need to use a whole onion, peel off what you need, just like you would peel off the skin of an orange. This will keep the remaining onion fresher.

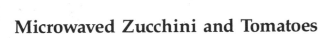

Microwaved Zucchini and Tomatoes

½ cup sliced onion
4 tablespoons olive oil
1 tablespoon chopped
   parsley
1 pound zucchini squash (3
   to 4 small)
2 fresh tomatoes (about ½
   pound)
¼ teaspoon basil
Dry bread crumbs
Grated Parmesan cheese
Paprika

Combine onion and olive oil in a 1 cup glass measure. Cover with plastic wrap and microwave on High 2½ minutes. Add parsley stir and set aside. Slice squash into ¼ inch slices. Place half of slices on bottom of a 1 quart round casserole. Cover with half of onion mixture. Slice one tomato and arrange slices over onion mixture. Sprinkle with half of basil. Repeat layer of squash, onion mixture and sliced tomato. Sprinkle top tomato layer with basil. Top with dry bread crumbs, cheese and paprika. Microwave, uncovered, on High 7 to 8 minutes. Let stand 3 minutes before serving. Serves 6.

A very colorful sidedish with an Italian flavor.

Mrs. Jack Curlin (Nelda)

 To skin a fresh tomato, spear it with a fork and hold it over a gas burner until the skin softens. Then run it under cold water and the skin will come right off.

Apricot Glazed Yams

1 (16-ounce) can yams, drained
1 (17-ounce) can apricot halves
3 tablespoons brown sugar
1 tablespoon cornstarch
¼ teaspoon salt
⅓ cup white raisins
⅛ teaspoon cinnamon
3 tablespoons dry sherry
½ teaspoon grated orange peel

Arrange yams in a 10x16x2-inch baking dish. Drain apricots, reserving liquid. Arrange apricots over yams. Add water to apricot liquid to make 1 cup. In a saucepan, combine brown sugar, cornstarch, salt, cinnamon, apricot liquid, and raisins. Cook over high heat, stirring constantly until it boils. Add sherry and orange peel. Pour over yams and apricots. Bake, uncovered, at 350° for 20 minutes, basting occasionally. Serves 4-6.

Sherry can be omitted.

Mrs. Pleasant Mitchell (Helen)

The Williams-Erwin Home, built in 1893, is one of the finest examples of Queen Anne architecture in the country and is listed in the National Register of Homes. Mr. Edward Williams, a local cotton merchant, built his home on a full city block on West Marvin Street. The lavishness of the home reflects the money and power of the cotton industry in Waxahachie at the turn of the century. Mr. R. K. Erwin, another prominent cotton man and the owner of the cotton seed oil mill, later acquired this home and set out to insure that his home would be a popular gathering place for the citizens of Waxahachie. At one time he had stables, gardens, and a gazebo on the grounds. This 2½ story frame structure has various patterns of beaded board and fancy-cut shingles adding to the texture of the exterior. It is painted in the original pink color.

DESSERTS

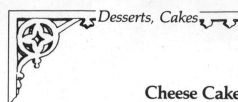

Cheese Cake Dessert

Crust:
1¼ cups graham cracker
   crumbs
½ cup sugar
5 tablespoons melted margarine

Filling:
2 (8-ounce) packages cream
   cheese
1 (3-ounce) package cream
   cheese
1 cup sugar
2 teaspoons grated lemon peel
¼ teaspoon vanilla
3 eggs

Topping:
¼ cup sugar
1 can Comstock cherry pie
   filling
¼ teaspoon almond extract

Mix crust ingredients. Press into bottom of springform pan. Bake at 350° for 5 minutes. Cool completely. Beat cream cheese with other filling ingredients, adding eggs one at a time. Pour into the springform pan and bake at 300° for one hour. Cool completely. Mix together topping ingredients and cook over low heat until thickened. Cool. Spread over the top of the cake. Serves 6-8.

Mrs. Cullen Eubank (Mary Pat)

Easy Cheese Cake

Butter
Fine graham cracker crumbs
4 (8-ounce) packages cream
   cheese
1 cup sugar
4 eggs, at room temperature
½ teaspoon vanilla
1 (21-ounce) can cherry pie
   filling

Butter pan and dust with graham cracker crumbs. Bring cream cheese to room temperature. Cream cheese and sugar well. Add eggs, one at a time, beating well after each. Beat till there are no lumps. Add vanilla. Pour into prepared pan. Bake at 350° for 35-40 minutes or until firm. Cool. Remove from pan. Top with cherry pie filling. Serves 8.

Mrs. Mike Leath (Kay)

Aunt Ottie's Snicker Cake

1 box German chocolate cake
   mix
1 stick margarine
1 (16-ounce) bag caramel candy
⅓ cup milk
½ cup chopped pecans
1 cup chocolate chips

Mix cake mix as directed. Pour half of batter into a 9x13-inch cake pan which has been greased and floured. Bake at 350° for 20 minutes. Melt in a large saucepan over low heat the margarine, caramels, and milk. Pour this over the baked cake. Sprinkle pecans and chocolate chips over the caramel mixture. Pour remaining cake batter over all of this and bake at 225° for 20 minutes, then at 350° for 10 minutes. Cool completely. and cut into squares or bars to serve. Serves 12-16.

Mrs. Robert M. Cox (Dee)

Canadian Chocolate Cake

1 Devil's Food Cake mix
8 ounces cream cheese, softened
1 egg
½ - ¾ cup sugar
1½ cups chocolate chips

Mix cake mix as directed. Pour into a greased 10-inch bundt pan. Mix remaining ingredients to make the topping. Spoon topping evenly over the cake. (It will sink.) Bake at 350° for 50-60 minutes or until a tester comes out clean. Cool 10 minutes before removing from pan. Serves 8-10.

A nice snack cake.

Mrs. Mike Leath (Kay)

Chocolate Chip Cake

1 yellow cake mix
1 small package instant vanilla
  pudding mix
1 cup Wesson oil
1 cup milk
2 eggs
1 small package chocolate chips
1 (8-ounce) bar German
  chocolate, grated
¼ cup powdered sugar

Mix all ingredients except ¼ cup of the grated German chocolate and the powdered sugar. Bake at 350° for 40-50 minutes in a 9x13-inch pan. Combine remaining ¼ cup chocolate with powdered sugar and spinkle over cooled cake. Serves 8-12.

Mrs. Joe Grubbs (Jo Beth)

Chocolate-Cinnamon Cake

Cake:
1 stick butter
½ cup Crisco
4 tablespoons cocoa
1 cup water
2 cups flour
2 cups sugar
2 eggs
½ cup buttermilk
1 teaspoon cinnamon
1 teaspoon soda
½ teaspoon salt
1 teaspoon vanilla

Icing:
1 stick butter
4 tablespoons cocoa
6 tablespoons Pet milk
1 box powdered sugar
1 teaspoon vanilla
1 cup chopped pecans

Bring butter, Crisco, cocoa, and water to a boil. Mix remaining ingredients together and pour warm mixture over them. Stir well. Pour into a greased and floured sheath pan. Bake at 375° for 25-30 minutes. Twenty minutes before cake is done, start the icing. Bring butter, cocoa, and milk to a boil. Add remaining ingredients and stir well. Pour on cake while hot and cover with foil. Serves 12-16.

Mrs. Erling Holey (Susan)

Chocolate Sheath Cake

Cake:
1 stick margarine
½ cup shortening
1 cup water
4 tablespoons cocoa
2 cups sugar
2 cups flour
2 eggs, beaten
½ cup buttermilk
1 teaspoon soda
1 teaspoon cinnamon
1 teaspoon vanilla

Icing:
1 stick margarine
4 tablespoons cocoa
6 tablespoons milk
1 pound powdered sugar

Bring margarine, shortening, water and cocoa to a boil. Let mixture cool a little. Add sugar and flour. Then add eggs, buttermilk, soda, cinnamon, and vanilla.

Bake in a 9x13-inch pan at 350° for 25 minutes.

To make icing, bring margarine, cocoa, and milk to a boil for one minute. Add powdered sugar. Mix well and ice cooled cake. Serves 12-15.

Mrs. Gary Morrow (Rikki)

Code's Chocolate Cake

2 sticks butter
½ cup Crisco
3 cups sugar
5 eggs
3 cups flour
½ teaspoon baking powder
½ cup cocoa
1 cup milk
1 teaspoon vanilla

Cream butter and Crisco with sugar. Add eggs one at a time, beating well after each one. Combine dry ingredients and add alternately with milk to sugar mixture. Add vanilla.

Bake in a well greased and floured tube pan for 90 minutes at 325°. Serves 12-16.

Mrs. Robert M. Cox (Dee)

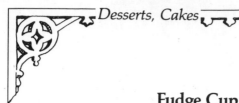

Fudge Cup Cakes

1 stick butter
1 square semi-sweet chocolate
2 eggs
1 cup sugar
¾ cup flour
1 teaspoon vanilla

Melt butter and chocolate on low heat. Beat in eggs, then add sugar, flour, and vanilla. Mix well. Pour into tins and bake 25-30 minutes at 350°. Serves 12.

You can sprinkle chopped nuts on top for variety before baking.

Mrs. Bobby Oliver (Emily)

Fudgies

2 sticks oleo
4 squares semi-sweet chocolate
4 eggs
1¾ cups sugar
1 cup flour
1 teaspoon vanilla

Melt oleo and chocolate in saucepan. In medium bowl, mix eggs, sugar and flour. Add melted chocolate and oleo with egg mixture. Stir with a spoon. Add vanilla. Mix well. Fill cup cake holder ⅔ full. Bake 30 minutes at 350°. Yields 18-24 cupcakes.

Mrs. Jim Beller (Linda)

Hershey Bar Cake

½ pound butter
2 cups sugar
4 eggs
2 teaspoons vanilla
½ teaspoon salt
8 plain Hershey bars
2½ cups sifted flour
¼ teaspoon baking soda
1 cup buttermilk
½ cup chopped nuts
Powdered sugar

Cream butter and sugar. Add eggs one at a time, beating well after each. Add vanilla and salt. Melt Hershey bars with 2 tablespoons of water. Add to batter. Mix flour and soda together and add to batter, alternately with buttermilk. Fold in nuts. Pour into a greased bundt pan.

Bake in a pre-heated 325° oven for one hour and 45 minutes. Remove from pan after 15 minutes. Dust with powdered sugar. Serves 12.

Mrs. Rick Pitts (Becky)

Hot Fudge Sundae Cake

1 cup flour
¾ cup sugar
2 tablespoons cocoa
2 teaspoons baking powder
¼ teaspoon salt
½ cup milk
2 tablespoons salad oil
1 teaspoon vanilla
1 cup chopped nuts
1 cup brown sugar
¼ cup cocoa
1¾ cup hot tap water

Preheat oven to 350°. In an ungreased 9x9x2-inch pan, stir flour, sugar, 2 tablespoons cocoa, baking powder, and salt together. Mix in milk, oil, and vanilla, stirring with a fork till smooth. Stir in nuts. Spread out evenly in pan. Sprinkle with brown sugar and ¼ cup cocoa. Pour hot tap water over batter—do not mix. Bake 40 minutes. Spoon into dessert dishes. Serves 9.

A good cake to serve with ice cream.

Mrs. Erling Holey (Susan)

Milky Way Cake

Cake:
6 Milky Way bars
2 sticks oleo
2 cups sugar
4 eggs
2½ cups flour
½ teaspoon soda
1¼ cups buttermilk
1 cup chopped nuts

Icing:
2½ cups sugar
1 cup evaporated milk
6 ounces semi-sweet chocolate
    chips
1 cup marshmallow cream
1 stick oleo

For cake, melt the candy bars and 1 stick oleo. Set aside. Cream sugar with 1 stick oleo. Add eggs and then flour and soda alternately with buttermilk. Add the melted candy and nuts to the batter. Grease and flour 3 layer pans. Pour batter into pans and bake at 325° for 15-20 minutes. Cool.

For icing, cook sugar and milk to soft ball stage. Add remaining ingredients and stir till melted. Ice cake. Serves 8-10.

Mrs. Pat Sullivan (Gloria)

Red Earth Cake

Cake:
1 stick oleo
1½ cups sugar
2 eggs
2 cups flour less 2 tablespoons
¼ teaspoon salt
3 tablespoons cocoa
1 cup buttermilk
1 teaspoon soda
3 tablespoons hot coffee
1 tablespoon red food coloring
1 teaspoon vanilla

Icing:
1 box powdered sugar
1 stick oleo
3 tablespoons cocoa
3 tablespoons hot coffee
1 teaspoon vanilla
1 teaspoon red food coloring

For cake, mix oleo, sugar, and eggs. Sift dry ingredients and add to batter. Add remaining ingredients. Mix well. Bake at 350° for 25-30 minutes in 2 layer pans. Mix all icing ingredients together and frost cooled cake. Serves 8-10.

Mrs. Tommy Nelson (Nancy)

Turtle Cake

1 German chocolate cake mix
14 ounces caramels (about 48)
¾ cup melted margarine
½ cup evaported milk
1 cup chocolate chips
1 cup pecan pieces

Mix cake as directed on box. Bake ½ of batter in a 9x13-inch pan at 325° for 15 minutes. Remove from oven.

Melt caramels, margarine, and milk in a double boiler. Pour over cake. Sprinkle chocolate chips and ½ of the pecans over cake. Add remaining batter. Sprinkle remaining pecans over the cake. Bake 20 minutes at 325°. Serves 9-12.

This cake needs no icing. Serve it with ice cream or whipped cream.

Mrs. Pleasant Mitchell (Helen)

Tunnel of Fudge Cake

1½ cups margarine
6 eggs
1½ cups sugar
2 cups flour
(12½-ounce) package of
    creamy Double Dutch
    frosting mix
2 cups chopped pecans

Cream margarine in a large bowl. Add eggs one at a time, beating well after each. Add sugar, beating at high speed till light and fluffy. Stir in flour and frosting mix with nuts, by hand. Pour batter into a greased and floured bundt pan. Bake at 350° for 60-65 minutes. Cool 2 hours before removing. Cake will have a wet center, the tunnel of fudge! Serves 10-12.

Mrs. Jim Jenkins (Pam)

Bohemian Coffee Cake

Cake:
2½ cups flour
1 teaspoon salt
1 teaspoon cinnamon
1 teaspoon nutmeg
1 cup brown sugar
1 cup white sugar
2 eggs
1 cup Wesson oil
1 cup buttermilk
1 teaspoon soda
1 teaspoon vanilla
1 cup coconut
1 cup chopped pecans

Icing:
8 ounces soft cream cheese
½ stick softened margarine
1 box powdered sugar
1 cup chopped pecans
1 cup coconut
2 teaspoons vanilla
2 tablespoons milk

Sift flour with salt and spices. Set aside. Cream sugars, eggs, and oil. Beat buttermilk with soda, well, by hand. Add to creamed mixture. Gradually add dry ingredients. Stir in vanilla, coconut, and pecans. Bake at 350° for 50 minutes in a tube pan for 40 minutes in layer pans or a 9x13-inch pan. Mix all icing ingredients and ice cooled cake. Serves 8-12.

Very rich — good for brunch or coffees.

Mrs. Dennis Horak (Barbara Sue)

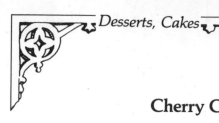

Cherry Coffee Cake

1 cup oleo
1¾ cups sugar
4 eggs
1 teaspoon vanilla
1½ teaspoons baking powder
3 cups sifted flour
1 can cherry pie filling
Powdered sugar
½ teaspoon almond extract

Beat together oleo and sugar. Add eggs one at a time, beating after each addition. Add vanilla, baking powder, and flour. Mix well. Spread ⅔ of the batter on a greased cookie sheet. Spread pie filling over batter. Drop remaining batter over fruit by spoonfuls here and there. Bake at 350° for 35 minutes. While cooling, mix powdered sugar, almond extract, and just enough water to make a light drizzle glaze. Drizzle icing over warm cake and serve. Serves 8-12.

You can change this by substituting strawberry or peach pie filling.

Mrs. Tommy Nelson (Nancy)

Coffee Cake

2 cups Bisquick
4 eggs
1 pound brown sugar
Chopped nuts (optional)
Chopped maraschino cherries
1 cup powdered sugar

Mix Bisquick, eggs, brown sugar, and nuts. Batter will be thick. Spoon into greased 7x11-inch pyrex baking dish. Bake at 325° for 30-35 minutes or until lightly browned. When cool, top with nuts and cherries. Drizzle a thin glaze made from the powdered sugar and water. Serves 10.

This is also known as sad cake, because it falls when you take it out of the oven.

Mrs. B.D. Cope (Charlene)

Sour Cream Coffee Cake

⅓ cup brown sugar
1¼ cups sugar
1 tablespoon cinnamon
1 cup pecan pieces
1 cup butter, softened
2 eggs
1 teaspoon vanilla
2 cups flour
1 teaspoon baking powder
1 teaspoon soda
½ teaspoon salt
1 cup sour cream
¾ cup powdered sugar
Water

Combine brown sugar, ¼ cup sugar, cinnamon, and pecans. Set aside. Cream butter and 1 cup sugar. Add eggs, one at a time, beating well after each. Stir in vanilla. Combine dry ingredients and add to creamed mixture alternately with sour cream. Pour half of batter into a greased and floured 9x13 inch pan. Sprinkle half of nut mixture on batter. Top with remaining batter and nut mixture.

Bake at 350° for 35 minutes. Cool. Drizzle with glaze made from powdered sugar and a little water. Serves 12-15.

Mrs. Pete Cunningham (Martha)

Carrot Cake

Cake:
1½ cups Wesson oil
2 cups sugar
4 eggs
2 cups grated carrots
1 small can crushed pineapple
& juice
1 cup nut pieces
2½ cups flour
1 teaspoon soda
2 teaspoons cinnamon
½ teaspoon salt

Icing:
8 ounces cream cheese
1 stick butter
1 box powdered sugar
2 teaspoons vanilla

Blend together oil, sugar, and eggs. Add carrots, pineapple, and nuts. Fold in dry ingredients. Bake in a greased and floured bundt pan at 350° for 40-50 minutes. Blend cream cheese and butter for icing. Add powdered sugar and vanilla. Ice cake when cool. Serves 8-12.

This is a versatile cake — can be baked in layers, sheath pans, tube pan, etc.

Mrs. Joe Grubbs (Jo Beth)

197

Cherry Nut Cake

Cake:
1½ cups sugar
½ cup shortening
¾ cup sweet milk
¼ cup cherry juice
2½ cups flour
3½ teaspoons baking powder
1 teaspoon salt
1 teaspoon vanilla
2 teaspoons almond extract
½ cup chopped cherries
1 cup coconut
½ cup pecans
4 egg whites

Icing:
2 boxes powdered sugar
½ cup chopped cherries
½ cup nuts
½ cup coconut

Cream sugar and shortening. Add milk and cherry juice. Sift together dry ingredients and add to first mixture. Mix well. Add remaining ingredients (except egg whites). Beat egg whites well and fold into cake batter. Pour into 3 round cake pans. Bake at 375° for 30 minutes or till done. Combine icing ingredients with enough cherry juice to make a good spreading consistency. Ice cooled cake between layers and on top. Serves 8-12.

A good old-fashioned cake.

Mrs. Pat Sullivan (Gloria)

Ferol's Fiesta Lemon Cake

1 (3-ounce) package lemon Jello
¾ cup boiling water
1 package yellow cake mix
4 eggs
¾ cup oil
2 teaspoons lemon extract
2 cups powdered sugar
Juice of 2 lemons

Mix Jello and boiling water and set aside to cool. Mix cake mix, eggs (one at a time), oil, and lemon extract at medium speed. Add Jello. Pour into a well-greased bundt pan and bake at 350° for 35-40 minutes. Remove from pan after cooling 10 minutes. Ice with a glaze made from powdered sugar and lemon juice while cake is still warm. Serves 9-12.

Any flavor of Jello can be used in this recipe with a similar flavor in the icing.

Mrs. Pat Gardenhire (Susan)

Date Cake

Cake:
½ cup butter
1½ cups sugar
2 eggs, well beaten
1 cup boiling water
1 teaspoon soda
½ box dates, diced
1 cup pecans
1 teaspoon vanilla
2 cups flour

Icing:
1 cup milk
2 cups sugar
½ box dates, diced
1 cup pecans
2 tablespoons butter
1 teaspoon vanilla
Pinch of salt

Cream butter and sugar. Add eggs. Set aside. Combine boiling water, soda, and dates. Let sit a few minutes. Add to sugar mixture, with remaining ingredients. Mix well. Cook at 350° for 30-35 minutes.

For icing, cook milk and sugar till thick. Add dates and stir till dates melt. Remove from heat and add remaining ingredients. Ice cooled cake. Serves 8-12.

A very moist cake.

Mrs. Ron Johnson (Sharon)

Fresh Blackberry Cake

1 cup butter
2 cups sugar
3 eggs
3 cups flour
2 teaspoons baking soda
1 teaspoon cinnamon
1 teaspoon ground cloves
2 cups fresh frozen
    blackberries, thawed
    and drained

Preheat oven to 350°. Grease and flour pan. Cream butter and sugar; add eggs. Combine dry ingredients and add to creamed mixture. Blend in berries. Pour into pan and bake 25-30 minutes. Serve warm with whipped cream. Serves 9-12.

Nice for Breakfast, too!

Mrs. James Fanning (Valanne)

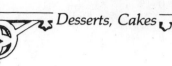

Hummingbird Cake

Cake:
3 cups flour
2 cups sugar
1 teaspoon salt
1 teaspoon soda
1 teaspoon cinnamon
3 eggs, beaten
1½ cups salad oil
1½ teaspoons vanilla
1 (8-ounce) can crushed
   pineapple
1 cup chopped pecans
2 cups bananas, sliced

Icing:
2 (8-ounce) packages cream
   cheese
1 cup butter
1 teaspoon vanilla
1 box powdered sugar
1 cup chopped pecans

Combine dry ingredients in a large bowl. Add eggs and oil. Stir till just moistened. Add vanilla, undrained pineapple, nuts, and bananas. Stir. Spoon batter into pan which has been greased and floured. Bake at 350° for 25-30 minutes or till cake tests done. Cool in pan 10 minutes, then remove cake and cool completely while making icing. Cream softened cream cheese and butter. Add vanilla and powdered sugar. Ice cake and sprinkle with 1 cup nuts. Serves 8-12.

Mrs. Michael Leath (Kay)

Magic Fruit Cake

2 tall cans Eagle Brand milk
2 pounds chopped dates
1 pound coconut
2 cups chopped pecans

Mix together all ingredients. Pour into a greased tube pan. Bake at 325° for 60 minutes. Cool before removing from pan. Serves 8-12.

An easy alternative to traditional fruit cake.

Mrs. Mike Hayes (Eva)

Italian Cream Cake

Cake batter:
½ cup Crisco
1 stick oleo
2 cups sugar
5 eggs, separated
1 teaspoon soda
½ teaspoon salt
2 cups flour
1 cup buttermilk
1 teaspoon vanilla
2 cups coconut
2 cups pecans

Icing:
1 stick oleo
1 pound powdered sugar
1 cup pecans
8-ounces cream cheese
1 teaspoon vanilla

For cake, cream Crisco, oleo, and sugar. Add egg yolks, one at a time. Combine dry ingredients and add to sugar mixture alternately with buttermilk. Stir in vanilla, coconut, and pecans. Beat egg whites till stiff. Fold egg whites into batter. Bake in 3 layer pans which have been greased and floured for 30 minutes at 350°.

Cream icing ingredients together and ice when cake has cooled. Serves 10-12.

Mrs. Joe Grubbs (Jo Beth)

Orange Pineapple Cake

Cake:
1 box yellow or white cake mix
1 large can mandarin oranges, undrained
1 cup salad oil
4 eggs

Icing:
1 large can crushed pineapple in heavy syrup
1 (3-ounce) package instant pudding mix
1 (8-ounce) carton Cool Whip

Mix cake ingredients together. Bake in 3 9-inch round greased and floured cake pans at 325° for 20 minutes. Cool. While cake is cooling, mix pineapple in syrup with pudding mix. Refrigerate. When pudding is semi-set, mix in Cool Whip. Refrigerate till firm. Ice cake. Serves 8-10.

Very moist and rich.

Mrs. Elmer Nooner (Margaret)

Pina Colada Cake

¼ cup cooking oil
1 box cake mix, yellow or white
1½ cups water
2 eggs, beaten
1 (14-ounce) package coconut
1 (12-ounce) carton Cool Whip
1 (12-ounce) can cream of
   coconut

Grease 9x13-inch pan with oil. Dump into pan the cake mix, water, eggs, and half the coconut. Mix together. It will be runny and lumpy. Bake at 350° for 30-35 minutes. While cake is baking, mix remaining coconut and Cool Whip to make icing. When cake comes out of the oven, punch holes in top and pour the cream of coconut over it. Let cake cool completely. Ice with Cool Whip mixture. Store in refrigerator. Serves 12-15.

Mrs. Dennis Horak (Barbara Sue)

Pineapple Cake

Cake:
2 cups flour
2 cups sugar
2 teaspoons soda
1 (20-ounce) can crushed
   pineapple, undrained
2 eggs
2 cups pecans (optional)

Icing:
1 (8-ounce) package cream
   cheese
½ cup butter
2 cups powdered sugar
4 teaspoons vanilla

Mix all cake ingredients together. Pour into a greased and floured 9x13-inch pan. Bake at 350° for 30-40 minutes. Beat icing ingredients until creamy. Spread on cooled cake. Serves 12-16.

Mrs. Pete Cunningham (Martha)

Pineapple Upside-Down Cake

½ cup butter
1 cup brown sugar
1 #2 can sliced pineapple
10-12 pecan halves
1 cup flour
1 teaspoon baking powder
⅛ teaspoon salt
3 eggs, separated
1 cup granulated sugar
5 tablespoons pineapple juice

Melt butter in 9x9-inch pan or 9″ iron skillet. Spread brown sugar evenly in pan and arrange pineapple slices on top. Fill in spaces with pecan halves. In another bowl, sift together flour, baking powder, and salt. Set aside. Beat egg yolks till light and gradually add sugar. Add pineapple juice and flour mixture. Fold in stiffly beaten egg whites. Pour batter over pineapple. Bake at 375° for 30-35 minutes. Turn upside down on cake plate to serve. Serve with whipped cream if so desired. Serves 6-8.

Mrs. Steve Kelley (Cindy)

Pineapple Upside-Down Cake

Cake:
2 cups sugar
1 cup butter
1 cup milk
2 teaspoons baking powder
3 cups flour
1 teaspoon vanilla
5 eggs, beaten

Icing:
1½ cups sugar
1 cup milk
1½ teaspoons flour
1 can crushed pineapple

Cake: Blend butter and sugar. Add eggs and vanilla. Blend in flour, baking powder and milk. Cook at 350° until springs back when touched.

Icing: Mix and let boil until thick. Spread on cake after cake is cooled.

Mrs. Randy Owens (Liz)

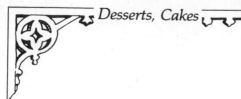

Pistachio Almond Cake

1 yellow cake mix
1 small box pistachio pudding
   mix
1¼ cups water
4 eggs
¼ cup cooking oil
7 drops green food coloring
4 drops almond extract

Mix all together and pour into a greased and floured bundt pan. Bake 50-55 minutes at 350°. Serves 12.

Mrs. Mike Hayes (Eva)

Pumpkin Cake

Cake:
2 cups sugar
1½ cups oil
4 eggs
2 cups flour
1 teaspoon salt
2 teaspoons soda
3 teaspoons cinnamon
1½ cups pumpkin

Icing:
8-ounces cream cheese
1 stick butter
1 teaspoon vanilla
1 box powdered sugar
1 cup chopped pecans

Beat sugar, oils and eggs. Sift dry ingredients together and add to sugar mixture alternately with pumpkin. Bake 50-60 minutes at 350° in a greased and floured tube pan. To make icing, mix all ingredients together. Ice cooled cake. Serves 10-12.

Mrs. Griggs DeHay (Gay)

Sour Cream Banana Cake

½ cup margarine
2 cups sugar
4 eggs, separated
1 cup sour cream
1 cup mashed bananas
2½ cups sifted flour
1 teaspoon soda
1 teaspoon baking powder
1 teaspoon vanilla

Cream margarine and sugar. Add egg yolks, beating well after each one. Add sour cream and bananas and beat well. Sift dry ingredients and stir into batter. Add vanilla. Beat egg whites until stiff and fold into batter. Pour into a greased and floured 10-inch tube pan. Bake at 325° for 50-60 minutes. Serves 10-12.

A cake that is not too sweet.

Mrs. Bill Price (Kay)

Aunt Iva's Gingerbread

1 cup butter, softened
1 cup sugar
2 eggs, well beaten
2 cups flour
1 teaspoon cinnamon
1 teaspoon ground cloves
1 teaspoon ginger
1 cup dark molasses
1 teaspoon soda
1 cup boiling water
Powdered sugar

Cream butter and sugar. Add eggs, flour, and seasonings and molasses. Mix thoroughly. Dissolve soda in boiling water. Add to batter and mix well. Pour into a greased 9x13-inch pan. Bake at 375° for 30 minutes. Cool. Dust with powdered sugar. Serves 12.

Easy to do — the kids can help do most of the mixing.

Mrs. Dennis Horak (Barbara Sue)

Apricot Pound Cake

1¼ cups cooking oil
1 small package orange Jello
6 eggs
2 packages Gladiola pound
   cake mix
1 teaspoon lemon extract
1½ cups apricot nectar

Add oil and jello to slightly beaten eggs. Alternately add mix, extract, and nectar to egg mixture. Pour into a large loaf pan and bake at 300° for 1½ hours. Serves 8-10.

Mrs. Joe Grubbs (Jo Beth)

 Try baking a prepared cake mix with ¼ cup vegetable oil added to the batter in six empty one-pound coffee cans. This makes a nice size cake for one or two people who might let a larger cake ruin. The extra cakes are easy to freeze for later.

Chocolate Pound Cake

1 cup butter
½ cup Crisco
3 cups sugar
5 eggs
3 cups sifted flour
½ teaspoon baking powder
½ teaspoon salt
4 tablespoons cocoa
1 cup milk
1 tablespoon vanilla

Cream together butter, Crisco, and sugar. Add eggs one at a time, beating well after each. Sift together flour, baking powder, salt and cocoa. Add dry ingredients alternately with milk. Add vanilla. Pour into a greased and floured tube pan or bundt pan. Bake at 300° for 1 hour, 20 minutes or until it tests done. This makes a very large cake, so don't cook it too fast. Serves 12-16.

A moist, mild chocolate cake—good with ice cream.

Mrs. David Ballard (Karen)

Cinnamon Pound Cake

3 cups sugar
3 sticks oleo
1 teaspoon vanilla
5 eggs
3 cups cake flour
1 cup milk
¼ teaspoon baking powder
4 tablespoons brown sugar
1 tablespoon cinnamon
1 cup powdered sugar
1 teaspoon vanilla
2 tablespoons milk

Cream sugar and oleo. Add 1 teaspoon vanilla. Add 5 eggs one at a time, beating well after each one. Mix cake flour and baking powder and add to egg mixture alternately with 1 cup of milk. Mix brown sugar and cinnamon in a small bowl. Grease and flour pans. Layer batter and sugar mixture in a tube pan in 4 layers. Bake 1 hour, 15 minutes at 350°. Mix powdered sugar, 1 teaspoon vanilla, and 2 tablespoons of milk to form a glaze. Dribble glaze over cooled cake. Serves 9-12.

A nice holiday brunch cake.

Mrs. Roy Marchbanks (Pam)

Lemon Pound Cake

3 cups flour
3 cups sugar
1 cup butter
1 cup buttermilk
6 eggs (whites can be beaten and folded into cake mixture)
1½ teaspoons salt
¼ teaspoon soda
2 teaspoons lemon flavoring

Lemon Glaze:
1½ cups powdered sugar, sifted
4 tablespoons lemon juice
1 teaspoon lemon extract

Blend sugar and butter in mixing bowl. Add eggs one at a time, blend after each. Sift dry ingredients together alternately with buttermilk. (Put soda in buttermilk). Add egg white if beaten. Pour batter into 10-inch tube pan and bake at 350°. Grease and flour tube pan first. Bake 1 hour 10 minutes.

Beat lemon glaze ingredients together while cake is baking and let stand. Pour over warm cake.

Mrs. Jack Hightower (Nancy)

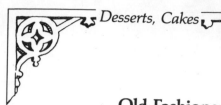

Old-Fashioned Pound Cake

1 cup butter, softened
½ cup solid shortening
3 cups sugar
5 eggs
3 cups flour
1 teaspoon baking powder
1 cup milk
1 teaspoon vanilla extract
1 teaspoon lemon extract

Cream butter and shortening. Add sugar, beating till fluffy. Add eggs one at a time, beating well after each one. In a bowl, combine flour and baking powder. Add to creamed mixture, alternating with milk. Mix well. Stir in vanilla and lemon extracts. Pour into a greased and floured 10-inch tube pan and cake at 350° for 1 hour and 15 minutes or till cake tests done with toothpick. Cool in pan 10-15 minutes. Remove from pan and cool completely. Serves 12-15.

This is a good cake that goes a long way.

Mrs. Rick Pitts (Becky)

Philadelphia Cream Cheese Pound Cake

2 sticks oleo
1 stick butter
8 ounces cream cheese
6 eggs
3 cups sugar
1 teaspoon vanilla
3 cups flour

Cream oleo, butter, and cream cheese in a large mixing bowl. Gradually add 2 eggs and sugar and vanilla. Add flour and remaining eggs (one at a time) alternately, ending with flour. Blend thoroughly. Pour into a well greased and floured bundt pan. Bake at 300° for 1½ hours. Serves 12.

An easy to make, moist cake.

Mrs. Kirk Brown (Ellen)

Poppy Seed Cake

1 yellow cake mix (not pudding
   type)
¾ cup oil
½ cup sugar
8 ounces sour cream
2 tablespoons poppy seeds
4 eggs

Mix all ingredients, beating well after each egg is added. Pour into a greased and sugared bundt pan. Bake at 350° for one hour. Remove from pan immediately. Serves 12.

A very easy cake to handle.

Mrs. Pete Cunningham (Martha)

Sour Cream Butter Pound Cake

Butter recipe cake mix
   (or yellow cake mix with
   2 teaspoons of butter
   flavoring added)
4 eggs
¾ cup oil
½ cup sugar
2 teaspoons almond extract
8 ounces sour cream

Mix all ingredients except sour cream. Fold in sour cream. Bake in a well-greased bundt pan at 350° for 50-60 minutes. Serves 8-12.

Mrs. Roy Marchbanks (Pam)

Baker's Icing

5 tablespoons flour
1 cup milk
1 cup sugar
1 stick margarine (not butter)
½ cup vegetable shortening
1 teaspoon flavoring

Mix flour and milk in a saucepan and cook till thick. Cool to room temperature. Add sugar, margarine, and shortening and whip 8 minutes. Add flavoring and mix well. Makes 2 cups of icing.

Will stay fresh a long time.

Mrs. Stan Parker (Priscilla)

Nut Caramel Icing

1 tablespoon flour
1½ cups sugar
½ cup butter
½ cup milk
½ teaspoon vanilla
2 tablespoons sugar
1 cup nuts

Mix flour with 1½ cups sugar. Add butter, milk, and vanilla. Mix well. Brown 2 tablespoons of sugar in a skillet. Add to other mixture in a sauce pan. Bring to a boil until it forms soft balls. Beat well and add nuts.

A good icing on spice cake.

Mrs. Roy Marchbanks (Pam)

One-Minute Chocolate Frosting

1 cup sugar
¼ cup (scant) cocoa
¼ cup butter
¼ cup milk
1 teaspoon vanilla
Nuts, if desired

Mix sugar, cocoa, butter, and milk. Bring to a full rolling boil for one minute. Remove from heat. Add vanilla. Beat until mixture begins to thicken. Ice cake and sprinkle with nuts. Yield: frosting for a 9x9-inch loaf cake.

Very easy — very good!

Mrs. Gary Morrow (Rikki)

Pineapple Frosting

1 cup crushed pineapple
½ cup sugar
1 egg yolk
Grated rind of one lemon
Pinch of salt
2 tablespoons corn starch

Mix all and cook over medium heat for 5-10 minutes or until thick. Stir continuously. Cool and frost a white cake. Yield: 1½ cups.

This is a good recipe to have when you need something quick to take to church or to a party.

Mrs. Steve Loftis (Nina)

Buttermilk Pie

1 stick butter
3 cups sugar
6 eggs, beaten
2½ tablespoons flour
1⅓ cups buttermilk
1 teaspoon vanilla
1 teaspoon lemon extract
2 unbaked pie shells

Cream together butter and sugar. Add beaten eggs, flour, buttermilk, vanilla, and lemon extract. Pour into pie shells. Bake at 350° for 50-60 minutes. This is the pie that your southern grandmother used to make. Serves 12.

Mrs. Joseph S. Smith (Margaret)

Caramel Pie

1 can Eagle Brand milk
½ stick oleo
Graham cracker crust

Boil Eagle Brand milk (still in the can) in a large pan of water for 3 hours. [Do not let it boil dry-add water as needed during this time.] Remove from can and add oleo. Whip until creamy with electric mixer. Pour into graham cracker crust. Chill and serve. Serves 6-8.

Mrs. Randy Owens (Liz)

Chess Pie

¾ stick oleo
2 cups sugar
1 tablespoon flour
1 tablespoon meal
4 eggs
1 cup milk
1 tablespoon vanilla
1 unbaked pie shell

Cream oleo, sugar, flour and meal. Add 4 eggs and beat well. Stir until smooth. Add milk and vanilla. Bake in 9-inch unbaked pie shell at 350° about 45 minutes or until firm. Serves 6.

Mrs. Roy Marchbanks (Pam)

Pineapple Chess Pie

1½ cups sugar
¾ stick butter or margarine
1 tablespoon cornmeal
3 tablespoons flour
Pinch of salt
2 eggs
1 (8-ounce) can crushed
  pineapple
1 unbaked pastry shell

Combine sugar, butter, cornmeal, flour and salt with a pastry blender or fork. Add eggs one at a time. Beat well after each addition. Add pineapple. Pour into unbaked pastry shell and bake at 350° for 45 minutes. Serves 6-8.

Mrs. Steve Kelley (Cindy)

French Coconut Pie

1 stick oleo
1½ cups sugar
1 tablespoon vinegar
1 teaspoon vanilla
3 eggs
1 small can coconut
1 unbaked pie shell

Melt oleo in saucepan. Add sugar, vinegar, and vanilla. Beat eggs and add to above. Add coconut. Pour into unbaked pie shell. Bake 400° for 10 minutes. Reduce to 300° and bake until firm in center. Serves 6.

Mrs. Roy Marchbanks (Pam)

French Pecan Pie

3 egg whites, stiffly beaten
1 cup sugar
1 teaspoon vanilla
22 Ritz crackers, rolled fine
1 cup chopped pecans
1 cup whipped cream

Beat egg whites, add sugar slowly, then add vanilla, crackers and nuts. Pour into well buttered pie pan. Top with whipped cream. (May sprinkle German chocolate shavings over the cream.)

This can be made using muffin tins instead of a pie pan for ready-made individual servings. Serves 6-8.

Mrs. Gary Morrow (Rikki)

Oatmeal Pecan Pie

¼ pound butter
2 cups sugar
4 eggs, well beaten
1½ cups white Karo syrup
1 (7-ounce) can Angel Flake coconut
1½ cups oatmeal
1 teaspoon vanilla
½ cup pecans, chopped fine
2 unbaked pie shells (9-inch)

Melt butter; add sugar, eggs and syrup. Mix well. Fold in oatmeal and coconut. Stir in vanilla. Pour into unbaked pie shells and sprinkle nuts over top. Bake at 375° for 10 minutes. Then reduce temperature to 325° and continue baking until done, about 25-45 minutes. Makes 2 pies. Freezes well. Serves 12-16.

Mrs. Daryl Schliep (Gerrie)

Baba's Chocolate Pie

3 eggs
1¼ cups sugar
2 tablespoons cocoa
2 tablespoons flour
2 cups milk
⅛ teaspoon salt
1 teaspoon vanilla
⅛ teaspoon cream of tartar
4 tablespoons sugar
1 pie crust, (9-inch)

Beat until stiff 1 whole egg and 2 egg yolks. Set aside egg whites for meringue. Combine sugar, cocoa, flour, and salt. Add to egg mixture. Add milk to mixture. Cook over medium heat, stirring constantly, for approximately 15 minutes until thickened. Pour into pre-cooked pie crust. Top with meringue. (Beat until stiff 2 egg whites, 4 tablespoons sugar, and cream of tartar). Bake in 350° oven for 12 minutes. Cool 2 hours.

Mrs. Gary Morrow (Rikki)

 Use ice water instead of tap water in your pie crust to make it lighter.

Chart House Mud Pie

½ package Nabisco chocolate
wafers
½ cup melted butter
1 quart coffee ice cream
1½ cup fudge sauce
1 cup whipped cream
½ cup slivered almonds

Crush wafers and add butter. Mix well. Press into pie plate. Cover with soft coffee ice cream. Put into freezer until ice cream is firm. Top with cold fudge sauce. Store in freezer approximately 10 hours. Top with whipped cream and slivered almonds to serve. Serves 8.

A rich, no-cook pie.

Mrs. Pat Gardenhire (Susan)

Daiquiri Pie

1 (3-ounce) package lemon
flavored pie mix
1 (3-ounce) package lime
flavored gelatin
⅓ cup sugar
2½ cups water, divided
2 eggs, slightly beaten
½ cup light rum
2 cups Cool Whip
1 baked (9-inch) pie shell
(regular or graham
cracker)

Mix pie mix, gelatin and sugar in saucepan; stir in ½ cup water and eggs. Blend well. Add remaining water. Cook and stir over medium heat until mixture comes to a full boil. Remove from heat and stir in rum. Chill about 1 and ½ hours. Blend Cool Whip into chilled mixture. Spoon into pie crust and chill till firm. Serves 6-8.

Mrs. Ron Johnson (Sharon)

 To make graham cracker crumbs, put the crackers in a zip-lock type bag and roll the bag with a rolling pin.

Fudge Macaroon Pie

3 squares unsweetened
  chocolate
½ cup butter
3 eggs, slightly beaten
¾ cup sugar
½ cup flour
1 teaspoon vanilla
⅔ cup Eagle Brand milk
2⅔ cups coconut

Melt chocolate and butter in a saucepan over low heat. Stir in eggs, sugar, flour and vanilla. Pour into greased 9-inch pie plate. Combine milk and coconut. Spoon over chocolate mixture, leaving ½ to 1-inch border. Bake at 350° for 30 minutes. Cool and serve. Serves 6-8.

Mrs. Griggs DeHay (Gay)

German Chocolate Pie

1 stick oleo
9 squares or ½ package
  German chocolate
1 cup sugar
½ cup flour
3 beaten eggs
1 teaspoon vanilla
1 cup pecans

Combine and melt together oleo and chocolate. Mix sugar and flour; add eggs and chocolate mixture. Add vanilla and pecans last. Grease pie pan and bake 25 minutes at 350°. Serve with whipped cream. Serves 6-8.

Mrs. Griggs DeHay (Gay)

Prize Peach Cobbler

¾ cup flour
Less than ⅛ teaspoon salt
2 teaspoons baking powder
1 cup sugar
¾ cup milk
½ cup oleo
2 cups fresh sliced peaches
  (or 1 large can)
¾-1 cup more sugar for
  fresh peaches

Sift flour, salt and baking powder. Mix with one cup sugar, slowly stir in milk to make batter. Melt butter in pan-pour batter over butter. DO NOT STIR! Carefully spoon over this the combined peaches and sugar. Bake 1 hour at 350°. Good hot or cold. Serve with cream if desired.

Mrs. Tommy Nelson (Nancy)

Peach Cobbler

Crust:
½ teaspoon baking powder
½ teaspoon salt
4 cups flour
1½ cups Butter Flavor Crisco
½ cup ice water

Filling:
3 pounds peaches (fresh or
   frozen) peeled and sliced
1 teaspoon cinnamon
1½ cups sugar
½ cup butter

Crust: Mix baking powder, salt, and flour. Cut shortening into flour mixture. Blend in water until smooth. Form into ball. Divide dough into half. Roll half of dough in a rectangle to fit a 9x13 inch baking dish. Line the dish with the dough and pierce bottom and sides with fork. Bake at 350° for 10 minutes. Cool.

Filling: Heat peaches in heavy saucepan to a simmer; do *not* add water. Add sugar, cinnamon, and butter. Pour this mixture into crust. Use the remaining dough to make lattice crust on top. Sprinkle sugar over the top and bake at 375° for 30 minutes or until golden brown. Serves 10-12.

Great with ice cream.

Mrs. David Ballard (Karen)

Peanut Butter Pie

10-12 Oreo cookies, crushed
¼ cup melted butter
1 (8-ounce) cream cheese,
   softened
½ cup sugar
½ cup smooth peanut butter
1 (4½-ounce) Cool Whip,
   thawed

Toss crushed Oreo's with melted butter. Press mixture into a 9-inch pie pan to form crust. Mix cream cheese, sugar, and peanut butter till smooth. Blend in thawed Cool Whip. Spoon into crust. Garnish with chocolate chips or cool whip. Chill one hour to set. Serves 6.

Mrs. Pleasant Mitchell (Helen)

Cherry Blossoms

2 (8-ounce) packages cream
    cheese, soft
¾ cup sugar
2 eggs
1 tablespoon lemon juice
1 teaspoon vanilla
24 vanilla wafers
1 (21-ounce) can cherry pie
    filling

Beat cream cheese, sugar, eggs, lemon juice and vanilla till light and fluffy. Line small size muffin pans with paper cups and place a vanilla wafer in bottom of each cup. Fill the cups two-thirds full with cream cheese mixture. Bake in 375° oven for 15-20 minutes or till set. Top each with about one tablespoon pie filling. Serves 12.

Mrs. Pete Cunningham (Martha)

Lemon Ice Box Pie

1 (8-ounce) Philadelphia
    cream cheese
1 cup Eagle Brand milk
⅓ cup fresh lemon juice &
    grated rind
1¼ cups graham cracker
    crumbs
¼ cup sugar
¼ cup butter, softened

Beat first 3 ingredients with electric mixer. Set aside. Make crust from remaining ingredients and bake until golden brown. Add filling and refrigerate. Serves 6-8.

Mrs. Jack Curlin (Nelda)

Mamaw's Quick Pies

1 can Eagle Brand milk
1 (13½-ounce) carton Cool
    Whip
3 tablespoons lemon juice
2 small cans crushed
    pineapple, drained
2 graham cracker crusts

Combine ingredients and pour into crusts and chill two hours. Makes 2 pies! Serves 16.

So Easy!

Mrs. Jim Jenkins (Pam)

No Cook Strawberry Pie

1½ cups fine vanilla wafer
  crumbs
⅓ cup melted butter
½ cup butter
1½ cups sifted powdered
  sugar
2 eggs, beaten
1 teaspoon vanilla
1½ cups drained, sweetened
  strawberry slices (fresh
  or frozen)
1-2 cups heavy cream,
  whipped

Mix all but 2 tablespoons crumbs with melted butter; press into buttered 9-inch pie pan; chill until firm. Cream butter and powdered sugar; add beaten eggs and vanilla, beat until fluffy. Spoon into chilled crust. Fold strawberries into whipped cream and spread over mixture in crust. Sprinkle with remaining crumbs. Refrigerate until firm; about 8 hours. Serves 6-8.

Mrs. Joe Smith (Margaret)

Strawberry Pie

1 box vanilla pudding mix
  (not instant)
1 (3-ounce) strawberry jello
2 cups water
1 teaspoon lemon juice
1 medium (8-ounce) cool
  whip
1-2 cups sliced fresh
  strawberries
1 (9½-inch) pie crust, baked

Cook pudding mix, strawberry jello, water, and lemon juice, stirring until it boils. Chill until thickened. Fold in cool whip and strawberries. Pour into prepared (baked) pie crust. Chill. Serves 6-8.

This is good in a graham cracker crust, also.

Mrs. Alvin Bynum (Jimmie Faye)

 To make substitute whipped topping, add a sliced banana to an egg white and beat till stiff. Then add sugar to taste.

Sweet Potato Pie

4 cups sugar
1½ cups boiled sweet
  potatoes
1 teaspoon nutmeg
4 eggs
2 cups milk
¾ cup melted butter
3 (9-inch) pie shells

Mix sugar, potatoes, and nutmeg until creamy. Add eggs and mix lightly. Add sweet milk and mix well. Add butter and mix well. Place in crust in 400° oven for 15 minutes or until filling is golden brown; lower temperature to 300° and bake 60 minutes. Makes 3 pies.

Mrs. Lonell Wilson (Betty)

Fool Proof Crust

4 cups flour
1¾ cups Crisco
1 tablespoon sugar
2 teaspoons salt
½ cup cold water
1 egg
1 tablespoon vinegar

Mix together first 4 ingredients in large mixing bowl. Beat together last 3 ingredients in a separate bowl, then add to flour mixture. Put dough in the refrigerator for 15 minutes before using. Roll out dough. Bake at 350° for about 15 minutes when a cooked crust is needed. Makes 4-6 crusts.

This may be stored in refrigerator for 2 weeks before using or frozen for months.

Mrs. Bobby Oliver (Emily)

Foolproof Pie Crust

1 egg
1 tablespoon vinegar
Water
5 cups flour
2 teaspoons salt
2 cups shortening

Break the egg in a cup size container. Beat the egg, then add the vinegar and water enough to fill the cup size container. Sift the flour with the salt. Cut the shortening into the flour until it forms pea size particles, then add the liquid and continue blending. Roll out pie crust to desired sizes. Makes 4 or 5 crusts.

Mrs. Kirk Brown (Ellen)

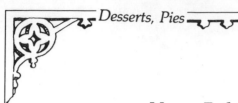

Never Fail Pastry

1 cup flour
½ cup shortening
½-1 teaspoon salt
¼ cup ice water

Cut shortening into flour and salt mixture until pieces are the size of small peas. Add ice water all at once. Stir till moistened and dough is pliable. Recipe may be doubled or halved. This makes one single crust.

Chinese Chews

3 egg whites
½ cup flour
2 teaspoons vanilla
1⅓ box dates
2 cups pecans
⅔ cup sugar
Dash salt

Beat egg whites until very stiff. Fold in flour and sugar. Mix pecans and dates with ¼ cup flour. Add to egg white mixture. Add vanilla and salt. Drop on cookie sheet by teaspoons. Bake 350° for 15 to 18 minutes.

Mrs. Robert C. Fuller (Madelon)

Chocolate Crinkle Clusters

2 cups sugar
2 ounces (2 squares) unsweetened chocolate
⅔ cup milk
2 tablespoons light corn syrup
2 tablespoons butter or margarine
1 teaspoon vanilla
1½ cups crushed Quaker Life Cereal
1 cup flaked or shredded coconut

Combine sugar, chocolate, milk, syrup, and butter in medium sized sauce pan. Heat to boiling point, stirring constantly. Cook without stirring to 236°, or until a soft ball forms when dropped into cold water. Add vanilla. Cool 5 minutes without stirring. Add life cereal and coconut, stirring until well combined. Keep candy over hot water while dropping by teaspoons onto waxed paper. Makes 4 dozen pieces.

Mrs. Tommy Nelson (Nancy)

Divinity

2 cups sugar
½ cup white Karo syrup
½ cup water
¼ teaspoon salt
2 egg whites, stiffly beaten
1 tablespoon vanilla
1 cup pecans, chopped

Combine sugar, Karo syrup, water and salt in a saucepan and bring to a boil. Cook until mixture reaches hard ball stage on a candy thermometer. Pour syrup mixture over egg whites in a slow stream, beating constantly. Beat until mixture loses its gloss and is not sticky. Add vanilla and pecans and drop by spoonfuls onto waxed paper.

Mrs. Gary Morrow (Rikki)

Easy Fudge

1 (12-ounce) package semi-sweet chocolate morsels
1 can Eagle Brand milk
1 cup chopped pecans
½ teaspoon vanilla

Melt ingredients in double boiler and pour into buttered dish. Cool and cut into tiny squares.

Mrs. Jim Jenkins (Pam)

Fabulous Fudge

1 (7-ounce) jar marshmallow creme
1½ pounds milk chocolate kisses
5 cups sugar
1 (13-ounce) can evaporated milk
½ cup butter or margarine
6 cups pecans or walnuts, coarsely chopped

Place marshmallow creme and kisses in large bowl; set aside. Combine sugar, milk, and butter in a pan. Bring mixture to a rolling boil, then cook for 7-8 minutes. Pour hot mixture over kisses and creme. Mix well with wooden spoon. Stir in nuts. Pour into 2 well buttered 9x13-inch pans. Let cool completely and then cut into squares.

If your children don't like nuts, you can use rice krispies.

Mrs. David Ballard (Karen)

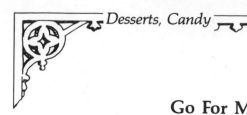

Go For Mores

1 cup sugar
⅔ cup white syrup
1 cup peanut butter
½ stick margarine
1 teaspoon vanilla
6 cups corn flakes

Bring sugar and syrup to a boil. Add peanut butter, margarine, and vanilla. Cook until all is melted. Pour hot mixture over corn flakes. Mix well and spoon out onto wax paper.

Easy, do ahead recipe!

Mrs. Ron Johnson (Sharon)

Haystacks

2 (6-ounce) packages
  butterscotch chips
1 tablespoon peanut butter
1 cup roasted Spanish
  peanuts
1¼ cups shoestring potatoes

Melt chips and peanut butter in double boiler. Remove from heat. Then add peanuts and shoestring potatoes. Mix well and drop on wax paper. Let cool.

Mrs. Ron Johnson (Sharon)

Martha Washington Candy

2 boxes confectioners' sugar,
  sifted
1 stick oleo, melted
1 can Eagle Brand milk
1 teaspoon vanilla
4 cups chopped pecans
1 tall can angel flake coconut
1 package (½-pound)
  German Sweet Chocolate
1 block gulfwax paraffin

Cream ingredients, add nuts. Chill in refrigerator, then roll into small balls. Melt chocolate and paraffin over low heat. Dip balls (stuck on a toothpick) into chocolate mixture, one at a time. Drop onto wax paper.

This candy is moist on the inside and has a hard chocolate coating. Stays fresh 2 or 3 weeks, if it lasts.

Mrs. Robert C. Fuller (Madelon)

Mexican Cream Candy

½ pound oleo or butter,
melted
4 cups sugar
1 large can Pet milk
3 tablespoons white Karo
½-1 cup pecans, chopped
2 teaspoons vanilla

Mix butter, sugar, milk and Karo in a large pan. Cook until mixture forms a soft ball in cool water. Cook over medium heat, stirring constantly. This takes approximately 45-60 minutes. Add chopped pecans and vanilla and remove from heat. Beat until creamy. You may set the pan in a bowl of ice water while beating to speed up the cooling process. Drop onto wax paper or pour into a well greased 9x13-inch pan and cut when hardened.

Mrs. Tommy Nelson (Nancy)

 Smooth skinned lemons with the least points on the ends are better tasting than the long, rough-skinned ones.

Orange Balls

1 (6-ounce) can frozen orange
juice
1 (12-ounce) box vanilla
wafers
1 stick margarine, melted
1 (1-pound) box powdered
sugar

Thaw orange juice but do not dilute. Finely crush cookies. Reserve 1 cup crumbs. Mix orange juice, melted margarine, powdered sugar, and vanilla wafer crumbs. Form into 1-inch balls. Roll in remaining crumbs. Refrigerate at least one hour before serving. Yields 5 dozen.

Variation: *Add finely chopped coconut or nuts to taste.*

Mrs. Pleasant Mitchell (Helen)

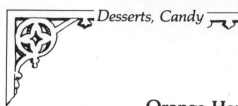

Orange Haystacks

1 pound candy orange slices,
   chopped
2 cups coconut
1 cup pecans, chopped
1 can Eagle Brand milk
2 cups powdered sugar

Place first 4 ingredients in a pyrex or Corningware dish. Cook in 350° oven 10-15 minutes until bubbly. Add 2 cups powdered sugar. Mix well and drop by teaspoons on waxed paper.

Mrs. Bill Price (Kay)

Granny Dee's Peanut Brittle

3 cups sugar
1 cup white corn syrup
½ cup water
3 cups raw peanuts
1 tablespoon butter
1 teaspoon salt
1 teaspoon soda

Boil sugar, corn syrup, and water to soft ball (240°) in large pan. Add peanuts and stir continuously to hard crack stage (300°). Remove from heat and add remaining ingredients. Stir until evenly blended. Pour immediately onto greased cookie sheet. Cool and break in desired size pieces with knife handle.

Mrs. Gary Morrow (Rikki)

Peanut Butter Fudge

2 cups sugar
¾ cup milk
1 cup marshmallow creme
1 cup peanut butter

Cook sugar and milk until mixture forms a soft ball, 232°. Remove from heat; add marshmallow creme and peanut butter. Mix thoroughly; pour into 9x13-inch pan. Cool, cut into pieces. Makes 20 servings.

Mrs. Gary Morrow (Rikki)

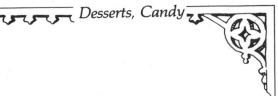

Peanut Butter Fudge

2 cups sugar
1/8 teaspoon salt
3/4 cup milk
2 tablespoons light corn
  syrup
4 tablespoons peanut butter
1 teaspoon vanilla

Combine in saucepan first 4 ingredients. Cook over medium heat, stirring frequently till mixture reaches soft ball stage. Remove from heat and let cool a few minutes. Stir in peanut butter and vanilla. Beat till creamy. Pour into buttered 8x8-inch pan. When thoroughly cooled, cut into small squares.

Mrs. Rusty Marchman (Diann)

Peanut Clusters

1 (6-ounce) package
  chocolate chips
1 (6-ounce) package
  butterscotch chips
2 tablespoons peanut butter
1½ cups peanuts

Melt chips and peanut butter together in double boiler over low heat. Take off burner immediately after melted. Add peanuts. Drop by teaspoonfuls onto waxed paper. Refrigerate 15 minutes to harden.

Microwave method: Melt chips on high. Add peanut butter and melt. Add peanuts and follow above instructions.

Mrs. Ken Box (Dietra)

Peanut Patties

3 cups sugar
½ cup water
3 cups raw peanuts
1 cup white Karo syrup
1 stick butter
1 tablespoon vanilla
Dash salt
Red food coloring

Put sugar, peanuts, water and Karo in a pan and bring to a boil, stirring constantly. Boil 5 minutes. Add remaining ingredients. Beat until smooth and chalky in appearance. Drop by spoonfuls onto foil.

Mrs. Stan Parker (Priscilla)

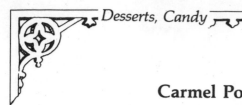

Carmel Popcorn

6 quarts popcorn (popped)
2 sticks butter
2 cups brown sugar
½ cup Karo
½ teaspoon salt
1 teaspoon vanilla
½ teaspoon baking soda

Mix butter, brown sugar, Karo, and salt. Bring to a boil. Remove from heat. Add vanilla and baking soda. Pour mixture over popcorn. Bake at 250° for 30 minutes. Stir after 15 minutes.

Mrs. Bobby Oliver (Emily)

Popcorn Balls

½ cup popcorn
¾ cup granulated sugar
¼ cup brown sugar
½ cup light corn syrup
½ cup water
1 teaspoon white vinegar
¼ teaspoon salt
¼ cup butter or margarine

Pop corn and put in large bowl. Combine in saucepan sugars, syrup, water, vinegar, and salt. Heat over medium-high heat, stirring frequently. Cook until candy thermometer reaches 260° or syrup forms a ball when dropped into cold water. Reduce heat, add butter and stir until melted. Pour syrup in a thin stream over the corn. Stir until corn is well coated. Cool slightly. Butter hands and shape into 3-inch balls. Cool on wax paper.

Mrs. Gary Morrow (Rikki)

Rocky Road

2 (8-ounce) or 12
  (1⅜-ounce) milk chocolate
  bars
3 cups tiny marshmallows
¾ cup coarsely broken
  walnuts

In medium saucepan, slowly melt chocolate over low heat, stirring constantly. Remove from heat; beat smooth. Stir in marshmallows and nuts. Spread in a buttered 8x8x2-inch pyrex pan. Cut into squares. Makes 1½ pounds.

Mrs. Craig Curry (Karen)

226

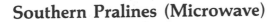

Southern Pralines (Microwave)

1½ cups firmly packed light
  brown sugar
⅔ cup half and half
½ teaspoon salt
2 tablespoons butter or
  margarine
1½ cups pecan halves

Combine sugar, half and half, and salt in a deep 3 quart casserole; mix well. Stir in butter; microwave on High for 7 to 9½ minutes or until mixture reaches soft ball stage (235°) stirring once. Stir in pecans and cool about one minute. Beat by hand until mixture is creamy and begins to thicken (about 3 minutes). Drop by tablespoons onto waxed paper. Let stand until firm. Makes 2 dozen.

Mrs. Jim Beller (Linda)

Candied Pecans

1 cup sugar
½ cup water
1 teaspoon vanilla
1 teaspoon cinnamon
1 pound pecans (halves)

Mix sugar, water, vanilla, and cinnamon in a 10-inch skillet. Boil 5 minutes or until mixture strings from spoon. Remove from heat and add pecans, coat, and spread on wax paper to cool.

Mrs. Gary Morrow (Rikki)

Spiced Pecans

1 egg white
1 teaspoon water
1 pound pecan halves
½ cup sugar
¼ teaspoon salt
½ teaspoon cinnamon

Beat egg white and water until frothy. Add the pecan halves and mix lightly. Combine sugar, salt, and cinnamon in a large bowl. Add the pecans and toss lightly until well covered. Spread evenly on a buttered cookie sheet. Bake at 225° for one hour, stirring every 15 minutes.

Mrs. Michael Leath (Kay)

Turtles

1 package caramels
2 tablespoons water
3 cups pecans
1 large Hershey bar
⅓ cake paraffin

Melt caramels and water in double boiler. Add nuts and drop by teaspoonfuls onto wax paper. Melt hershey bar and paraffin in double boiler. Dip pecan clusters in chocolate when they are cooled. Place on waxed paper until cooled again.

The caramel and water mixture may be melted in microwave. Watch and stir often until melted. Add nuts and proceed as before.

Mrs. Ken Box (Dietra)

Fruit Bars

Step 1:
1 cup flour
½ cup oleo
1 tablespoon milk
1 egg
1 teaspoon baking powder
¾ cup favorite preserves

Step 2:
1 egg
¼ cup oleo
1 cup brown sugar
1 cup coconut
1 cup oatmeal
1 teaspoon vanilla

Mix ingredients of step one and pat in bottom of 8x10-inch greased pan. Cover with favorite preserves. Mix ingredients in step 2 and spread on top of preserves layer. Bake at 350° for 30 minutes. When cool cut into bars. Serves 12.

Good served warm with vanilla ice cream on top.

Mrs. Tommy Nelson (Nancy)

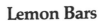

Lemon Bars

Crust:
1 cup flour
½ cup butter
¼ cup sifted confectioners
   sugar

Filling:
3 eggs, beaten
1 cup sugar
2 teaspoons lemon juice
2 teaspoons flour
½ teaspoon vanilla

Lemon Cream Cheese Frosting:
1 (3-ounce) package cream
   cheese, softened
1 teaspoon lemon juice
1½ cups confectioners sugar
½ teaspoon grated lemon rind

Combine crust ingredients and pat into bottom of 8-inch square pan. Bake at 350° for 15-20 minutes. Cool. Combine filling ingredients and pour over cooled crust. Bake at 350° for 25 minutes. Cool.

Combine all ingredients and beat until smooth. Spread directly on cooled filling. Cut into finger-sized bars.

Mrs. Mackey Morgan (Margaret)

Nell's Apricot Bars

1 Duncan Hines (only) yellow
   butter recipe cake mix
1 cup flour mixed with cake
   mix
1½ sticks margarine (softened)
1 cup coconut
1 cup chopped pecans
1 (10-12 ounce) jar apricot
   preserves

Cut butter into cake mix and flour. Add nuts and coconut. Mix well. Pat ⅔ mixture into 9x13-inch ungreased pan. Spread apricot preserves over mixture. Crumble remaining mixture over preserves. Bake 1 hour at 325°.

Mrs. Lonell Wilson (Betty)

Orange Cookies

1½ cups brown sugar
¾ cup butter
2 eggs, beaten
1 teaspoon vanilla
2½ cups flour
½ teaspoon soda
½ teaspoon salt
½ cup buttermilk
1½ teaspoons orange rind
1 cup chopped pecans

Cream sugar and butter. Add beaten eggs and vanilla. Sift flour, soda, and salt together. Add to cream mixture alternately with buttermilk. Add orange rind and pecans. Mix together thoroughly. Drop on greased cookie sheet and bake at 350° for 12 minutes.

Glaze:
½ cup orange juice
1 cup white syrup

Mix together and cook on low heat until warm. Spoon over cookies while still warm.

Mrs. Cullen Eubank (Mary Pat)

Orange Slice Cookies

1 cup granulated sugar
1 cup packed brown sugar
1 cup shortening
2 eggs
1 teaspoon vanilla
2 cups all-purpose flour
1 teaspoon baking powder
1 teaspoon baking soda
½ teaspoon salt
2 cups quick cooking rolled oats
2 cups (12-ounce) orange slices, snipped
1 cup flaked coconut

Mix sugars and shortening and beat until fluffy. Add eggs and vanilla; beat well. Mix together flour, baking powder, baking soda and salt; add to sugar mixture. Add oats, candy and coconut. Roll into 1 inch balls. Place on greased cookie sheet. Bake 350° for 10-12 minutes or until lightly browned.

Mrs. B. D. Cope (Charlene)

Nana's Molasses Sugar Cookies

¾ cup shortening
1 cup sugar
¼ cup molasses
1 egg
2 teaspoons baking soda
2 cups flour
½ teaspoon cloves
½ teaspoon ginger
1 teaspoon cinnamon

Melt shortening; cool. Add sugar, molasses, and egg. Beat well. Sift dry ingredients and add to first mixture. Mix well. Form into 1 inch balls and roll in sugar. Bake at 325° for 6-8 minutes. Watch carefully, these are dark cookies and they will burn quickly. Yields 3 dozen.

Mrs. David Ballard (Karen)

Nutmeg Sugar Cookies

2 tablespoons sugar
½ teaspoon nutmeg, divided
1½ cups flour
¾ cup sugar
1 teaspoon cream of tartar
½ teaspoon baking soda
⅛ teaspoon salt
½ cup butter, softened
1 egg
½ teaspoon vanilla

Combine sugar and ¼ teaspoon nutmeg in a small bowl. Set aside. Combine dry ingredients (including remaining nutmeg) in a large bowl. Add butter, egg, and vanilla. Beat on low, 3 minutes. Roll dough into 1 inch balls. Roll balls in nutmeg-sugar mixture. Bake on ungreased cookie sheet, 2 inches apart, at 400° for 10-12 minutes. These cookies freeze well up to 3 months. Yields 40 cookies.

Mrs. Pleasant Mitchell (Helen)

Dee's Brownies

¾ cup sifted flour
1 cup sugar
5 tablespoons cocoa
½ teaspoon salt
½ cup shortening
2 eggs
1 teaspoon vanilla
½ cup chopped pecans

Have all ingredients at room temperature and place altogether in large mixing bowl. Beat for three minutes until well mixed. Grease and flour 8-inch square pan. Pour brownie mixture into pan and bake at 350° for 30 minutes.

Mrs. Robert M. Cox (Dee)

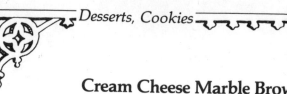

Cream Cheese Marble Brownies

Brownie mixture:
2 ounces unsweetened
  chocolate
½ cup sweet butter
1 cup sugar
2 eggs
½ cup flour
Pinch of salt
½ teaspoon vanilla

Filling:
3 ounces cream cheese
2 tablespoons softened butter
1 egg
1 tablespoon flour
¼ cup sugar
¾ teaspoon vanilla

Preheat oven to 350°. Grease an 8-inch square pan. Melt chocolate in top of double boiler and set aside. In large mixing bowl, cream butter until soft. Gradually add sugar, beating until mixture is light and fluffy. Add eggs, one at a time, beating to incorporate each. Sift or whisk flour and salt and stir into mixture. Stir in melted chocolate and vanilla.

For filling, beat together cream cheese, butter, egg, flour, sugar and vanilla. Spread thin layer of basic brownie batter in prepared pan. Spoon cheese filling over batter. Spoon remaining batter over filling. Swirl with knife to marblize. Bake for 35-40 minutes.

Mrs. Joe Grubbs (Jo Beth)

Betty's Best Brownies

2 cups sugar
½ cup cocoa
1 cup Crisco
Pinch of salt
1 teaspoon vanilla
1 cup chopped nuts
4 eggs
½ cup evaporated milk
1 cup flour

Cream first four ingredients. Add remaining ingredients and mix well. Bake in greased and floured pan (11x17-inch) or 2 smaller pans. Bake at 350° for 25 minutes.

Mrs. Lonell Wilson (Betty)

Brownie Icing

1 box powdered sugar
Pinch salt
3 tablespoons cocoa
¾ stick margarine
6 tablespoons milk
1 teaspoon vanilla

Melt butter, milk, salt and vanilla in saucepan. Add to cocoa and powdered sugar. Beat well. Pour over hot brownies.

Mrs. Lonell Wilson (Betty)

Coconut Cookies

¾ cup sugar
½ cup shortening (Crisco)
1 egg
½ teaspoon vanilla
1 cup plus 2 tablespoons sifted
   flour
1 teaspoon baking powder
¼ teaspoon salt
1 cup coconut

Cream together sugar, shortening, egg, and vanilla until light and fluffy. Sift flour, baking powder and salt together, then blend into sugar mixture. Add coconut and mix well. Drop by teaspoonsful on greased baking sheet. Bake at 350° for 8-10 minutes.

Mrs. Steve Loftis (Nina)

Quick Macaroons

1 (14-ounce) bag coconut
1 (14-ounce) can Eagle Brand
   milk
2 teaspoons vanilla

Combine all ingredients and mix well. Drop onto well greased baking sheets, 1 inch apart. Bake at 350° for 10-12 minutes or until light brown. Remove immediately. Makes 5 dozen.

Variations: *Add red or green food coloring at Christmas; add 1 cup mini-chocolate chips; add 1 cup raisins; add 1 cup chopped nuts; add 4 squares of melted semi-sweet chocolate; decorate with cherry halves or sugar crystals.*

Mrs. Pleasant Mitchell (Helen)

An easy way to send iced cupcakes to school in the lunch box is to split cupcakes in half and put the icing in the middle. This makes them a lot easier and cleaner to pack, and the kids think they're great.

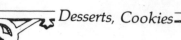

Buffalo Chip Cookies

2 cups Post Toasties
2 cups oatmeal
1 cup coconut
1 cup chopped pecans
1 (6-ounce) package chocolate
chips
1 cup margarine
1 cup Crisco
2 cups brown sugar
2 cups white sugar
4 eggs
2 teaspoons vanilla
4 cups flour
2 teaspoons soda
2 teaspoons baking powder
½ teaspoon salt

In large bowl mix Post Toasties, oatmeal, coconut, pecans and chocolate chips. In mixer cream together margarine, Crisco, brown sugar, and white sugar. Add to the above eggs, vanilla, flour, baking powder, soda and salt. Mix well. Empty batter into large bowl and mix all ingredients together. Use ¼ measuring cup of batter for each cookie (6 to cookie sheet). Bake at 325° about 15 minutes or until light brown.

Mrs. Alvis Bynum (Jimmie Faye)

Oatmeal Cookies

½ cup sifted flour
¼ teaspoon soda
½ teaspoon salt
¼ teaspoon cinnamon
¼ cup brown sugar
2 tablespoons granulated sugar
¼ cup shortening
1 egg, beaten
1 tablespoon milk
1 cup rolled oats
½ cup raisins or nuts

Preheat oven to 375°. Grease cookie sheets. Sift flour, soda, salt and cinnamon in a mixing bowl. Add brown sugar, granulated sugar, shortening, beaten egg and milk. Beat vigorously by hand for 50 strokes. Stir in oats, raisins (or nuts). Drop by teaspoonfuls, about 2 inches apart on cookie sheet. Bake 12-15 minutes or until golden brown, at 375°. Yields 3-4 dozen.

Mrs. Steve Loftis (Nina)

Mrs. Herman Cook's Cookies

1 (6-ounce) package semi-sweet
   chocolate bits
2 tablespoons margarine
1 can (14-ounce) sweetened
   condensed milk
1 cup plus 1 tablespoon flour
1 teaspoon vanilla
1 cup chopped pecans

Melt over boiling water the chocolate bits and margarine. Add milk. Stir together. Add flour slowly, stirring constantly over hot water. Add vanilla. Take off water and add pecans. Drop in small amount (teaspoonfuls) on teflon or greased and floured cookie sheet. Bake 7-8 minutes at 350°. Yields 4 dozen.

Can freeze after cooling.

Mrs. Randy Owens (Liz)

Pierre's

2 eggs
⅔ cup sugar
1 cup chocolate chips
1 teaspoon vanilla
⅔ cup flour
½ teaspoon baking powder
½ teaspoon salt
¼ cup melted butter
Powdered sugar

Beat eggs. Add sugar and cream together. Add remaining ingredients. Bake 350° about 30 minutes in 8x8-inch pan. Sprinkle with powdered sugar. Be sure to serve warm.

Mrs. Erling Holey (Susan)

Butter Cookies

1½ cups butter or (3 sticks
   margarine)
1 cup sugar
3 egg yolks
1 teaspoon vanilla
4 cups flour

Cream butter and sugar. Add egg yolks and vanilla. Work flour in. Shape into small balls (a heaping teaspoon of dough), make a thumb print depression in each and fill with tart jelly. Bake on ungreased cookie sheet for 12-15 minutes at 375°. Makes about 5 to 6 dozen.

Mrs. Randy Owens (Liz)

California Blondies

1¼ cups sifted all-purpose
 flour
1¼ teaspoons baking powder
½ teaspoon salt
⅔ cup butter, softened
½ cup granulated sugar
⅔ cup firmly packed light
 brown sugar
1 teaspoon vanilla
2 teaspoons grated orange rind
1 teaspoon grated lemon rind
2 eggs
2 teaspoons milk
1 cup slivered, blanched
 almonds (4-ounces)

Combine the flour, baking powder, and salt in small bowl; stir to mix well. Set bowl aside. Beat together butter and granulated sugar in medium-size bowl until light and fluffy. Beat in brown sugar until well blended. Add vanilla and orange and lemon rinds; mix well. Beat in eggs, one at a time, beating well after each addition. Blend in milk. Fold in reserved flour mixture and almonds. Spread evenly in prepared pan. Bake in preheated oven (350°) for 30 to 35 minutes or until wooden pick inserted in the center comes out barely moist. Cool completely in pan on wire rack. Cover with aluminum foil; let stand 8 hours or overnight. Cut into 20 blondies. Garnish each with dab Orange Glaze, whole blanched almond and thin strip orange rind, if desired.

Orange glaze: Combine 2 tablespoons softened butter, ½ cup sifted confectioners sugar, 2 teaspoons frozen orange juice concentrate, thawed, and 1 tablespoon milk in small bowl. Beat until smooth and creamy and a good spreading consistency.

Mrs. Rick Pitts (Becky)

To marble an angel food cake, drop a few drops of food coloring on top of the batter after you have put it in the pan and run a knife through the batter. Then bake. When you slice your cake, the color effect will be nice.

Congo Bars

1 pound box brown sugar
²⁄₃ cup corn oil
3 eggs (beat well after each)
2¾ cups flour
½ teaspoon salt
2½ teaspoons baking powder
1 teaspoon vanilla
1 cup chopped nuts
1 cup chocolate chips

Cream brown sugar, oil and eggs. Sift together remaining ingredients and combine with creamed mixture. The dough will be very heavy. Bake at 350° for 35 minutes in greased 13x9-inch pan. Cut in squares when partly cool.

Mrs. Griggs DeHay (Gay)

Date Cookie Roll-Ups

1 (8-ounce) package dates
  (chopped)
1 cup sugar
1 cup water
1 cup chopped pecans
1 cup oleo
2 cups brown sugar
2 eggs
1 teaspoon vanilla
4 cups flour (sifted)
½ teaspoon soda
½ teaspoon salt

In saucepan, cook first 3 items until "a little thick." Then add pecans and let cool. In large mixing bowl, add remaining ingredients to make dough mixture. Divide mixture into five parts. Roll out one part of mixture on wax paper to ⅛ inch thick and spread with small (1/5) part of date mixture. Roll up cookies using wax paper to help roll (long roll). Slice cookies ½ inch thick and bake at 375° for 10 to 12 minutes. Fix remaining cookie mixture and dough mixture in same way. Can store cookie logs in freezer till you need. Slice log while chilled or frozen for better results. Yields 6 dozen.

Mrs. Kirk Brown (Ellen)

237

Dream Bars

First part:
½ cup butter
1 cup flour
½ cup brown sugar
1 teaspoon vanilla
½ teaspoon baking powder
2 teaspoons flour
1½ cups coconut grated
1 cup chopped nuts

Second part:
1 cup brown sugar
2 eggs beaten

First part:
Mix butter, brown sugar, and flour into regular cake pan (12x8-inch). Cook slowly for 20 to 30 minutes. Be careful not to burn.

Second part:
Mix brown sugar, eggs, vanilla, baking powder, flour, coconut, and nuts. Spread on top of crust and cook approximately 15 minutes until it carmelizes.

Mrs. Louise Barclay

Greek Clove Crescents

1 cup butter, softened
1½ cups powdered sugar
1 egg
1 teaspoon vanilla
2½ cups flour
1 teaspoon brandy flavoring
6 dozen cloves (whole)

Mix butter, sugar, egg and vanilla well. Blend in flour. Mix in brandy flavoring. Shape into balls and then to crescent shapes (about 1 teaspoon dough). Press a whole clove into center of each. Bake on ungreased cookie sheet 10-12 minutes or until set but not brown at 375°. Cool and dust with confectioner's sugar.

Mrs. Rusty Marchman (Diann)

 Add a pinch of baking powder to powdered sugar icing to keep it from hardening and cracking.

Quick Peanut Brittle Cookies

1 stick prepared pie crust
¾ cup brown sugar
1 beaten egg
½ teaspoon vanilla
¾ cup chopped cocktail
   peanuts

Mix pie crust according to directions on package but do not roll out. Cut in brown sugar until like coarse corn meal. Add egg, vanilla and ¼ cup peanuts. Spread into greased and floured 13x9-inch pan. Press remaining peanuts into top of dough. Bake at 350° for 15-20 minutes. Loosen edges at once but cool on sheet before cutting into 2 inch squares.

Mrs. Lynn Lasswell (Mae Evelyn)

Refrigerator Cookies

1 cup shortening
½ cup sugar
½ cup brown sugar
2 eggs
2¾ cups sifted flour
½ teaspoon soda
1 teaspoon salt
1½ teaspoons vanilla
½ cup pecans

Cream together shortening, sugars, and eggs. Add dry ingredients slowly with vanilla and pecans. Roll mixture into a log, wrap in waxed paper, and refrigerate. Slice and bake cookies at 350° for eight minutes.

Mrs. Griggs DeHay (Gay)

Pecan Puffs

½ cup butter
2 tablespoons sugar
1 teaspoon vanilla
1 cup chopped pecans
1 cup cake flour
Powdered sugar

Beat the butter by hand until soft. Add the sugar and beat until creamy. Add vanilla, then add the chopped pecans and flour and mix together thoroughly. Shape into balls. Place on a greased cookie sheet and bake at 300° for 25-35 minutes until brown. Roll in powdered sugar while they are hot and again when they are cool.

Mrs. Cullen Eubank (Mary Pat)

Sand Tarts

2 sticks margarine
½ cup powdered sugar
2 cups plus 2 tablespoons sifted
  flour
1 teaspoon vanilla
½ cup chopped pecans

Cream together margarine and powdered sugar. Add flour, vanilla, and pecans. Roll into small sized ball or crescent shape and place on dry cookie sheet. Bake at 350° for 15 minutes until slightly browned. (Roll in powdered sugar while still warm for added sweetness.)

Mrs. Steve Loftis (Nina)

Toffee Squares

2 sticks oleo
1 cup brown sugar
1 teaspoon vanilla
1 egg yolk
2 cups sifted flour
Pinch of salt
1 giant Hershey Chocolate Bar
1 cup finely chopped nuts or
  coconut

Mix first 4 ingredients. Add flour and salt. Spread dough on large cookie sheet. Bake at 350° for 15-20 minutes. Put giant Hershey bar on warm dough. Place back in oven until chocolate can be spread over dough. (Do not overcook chocolate) Cut in squares while warm. Sprinkle nuts or coconut over top.

Mrs. Roy Marchbanks (Pam)

Banana Daiquiri Ice Cream

2 eggs
½ cup sugar
Dash salt
1 cup mashed ripe bananas
  (about 3 medium)
1 cup half & half or light cream
2 tablespoons rum
1 tablespoon lime juice

In medium bowl beat eggs until thick. Gradually beat in sugar and salt. Stir in remaining ingredients. Turn into can of 1-quart ice cream maker. Freeze according to manufacturer's directions. Turn into freeze container, and let ripen for about 2 hours in freezer. Makes 1 quart.

Mrs. Lynn Lasswell (Mae Evelyn)

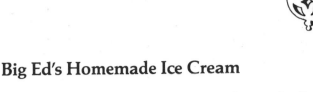

Big Ed's Homemade Ice Cream

5 eggs, beaten
1 cup sugar
1 (14-ounce) can Eagle Brand
   milk
2 (12-ounce) cans Pet milk
1 tablespoon vanilla
Whole milk
Fruit (optional)

Mix eggs, sugar, Eagle Brand milk, Pet milk and vanilla. Pour into freezer cylinder. Add whole milk to "fill line" on cylinder. Add fruit if you prefer. Makes 4 quarts.

Mrs. Jim Jenkins (Pam)

Creamy Peach Ice Cream

4 cups peaches, peeled and
   mashed
3½ cups sugar
Juice of 2 lemons
2 cups heavy cream
Half and Half

Mix peaches, sugar, and juice. Pour into freezer can and add cream. Stir. Fill can up to ¾ full with Half and Half. Freeze and enjoy. Yields 1 gallon.

Mrs. Mike Owens (Suzy)

Fruited Ice Cream

4 eggs, beaten
2 cups sugar
2 ripe bananas, mashed
1 pint strawberries
1 small carton whipping cream
1 can Eagle Brand milk
3 oranges (pulp, juice & ⅛ cup
   rind)
2 lemons (pulp, juice & ⅛ cup
   rind)

Add mixture to freezer container of any size and fill with whole milk to fill line on container and mix. Yields 1 gallon.

Mrs. Kirk Brown (Ellen)

Homemade Chocolate Ice Cream

1 large carton Cool Whip
2 cans Eagle Brand milk
2 quarts chocolate milk

Mix all ingredients together until completely blended. Pour mixture into ice cream freezer and freeze. Makes a gallon of cream.

Mrs. Kirk Brown (Ellen)

Banana Pudding

4 eggs, separated
6 heaping tablespoons cornstarch
2 cups milk
¼ teaspoon salt
2 cups sugar
2 tablespoons butter or oleo
2 teaspoons vanilla
3 large bananas
Vanilla wafers

Combine egg yolks with cornstarch mixed with milk. Add salt, sugar, and butter. Cook in double boiler until thick. Remove from heat. Add vanilla. Layer in oven-proof dish starting with vanilla wafers, pudding, bananas, and ending with egg whites beaten for meringue. Brown meringue in hot oven for a few minutes.

Mrs. Gary Morrow (Rikki)

Strawberry Mousse

2 egg whites, room temperature
¼ teaspoon cream of tartar
Pinch of salt
2 cups whipping cream
1¼ cups powdered sugar, sifted
2 cups strawberries, pureed and chilled
Whipped cream (garnish)

Beat egg whites, cream of tartar and salt in small bowl until stiff and glossy. Whip 2 cups cream with sugar in medium bowl until stiff. Whisk strawberry puree into cream until mixture is very thick. Gently fold in egg whites, blending well. Spoon mousse into champagne glasses. Refrigerate at least 1 hour. Garnish each with whipped cream just before serving. Serves 10.

Can be prepared one day ahead.

Mrs. Jack Curlin (Nelda)

Chocolate Almond Delight

30 oreos
6 tablespoons melted butter
3 eggs
3 sticks *real* butter
2½ cups powdered sugar
½ teaspoon almond extract
1½ cups whipping cream
1 teaspoon vanilla
⅓ cup sugar
1 package roasted slivered
    almonds

Crush oreos into melted butter and press into 9x13-inch dish. Beat on high for 10 minutes the eggs, butter, powdered sugar and almond extract. Whip cream, add vanilla and sugar, and spread on top of filling. Top with roasted almonds.

Mrs. Homer Denning (Linda)

Frozen Chocolate Dessert

½ cup melted butter
1¼ cups graham cracker
    crumbs
⅔ cup butter
2 cups powdered sugar
3 egg yolks, slightly beaten
2 squares melted unsweetened
    chocolate
Pinch of salt
1 teaspoon vanilla
½ cup chopped pecans
3 egg whites, beaten well
1 quart vanilla ice cream

Crust: Combine melted butter and graham cracker crumbs. Pat crumb mixture on bottom of 9x13-inch pan for crust.

Filling: Cream butter and powdered sugar together. Add egg yolks, chocolate, salt, vanilla and nuts. Fold in egg whites. Pour filling on crumbs. Freeze for 2 hours. After 2 hours, soften the vanilla ice cream. When it can be spread, put it on top of the frozen filling. Sprinkle with graham cracker crumbs for decoration and return to the freezer.

Mrs. Erling Holey (Susan)

Fruit Delight

1¾ cups milk
1 pound diced marshmallows
1 cup crushed pineapple,
  drained
2 bananas, diced
1 cup whipped cream
½ cup chopped nuts
½ cup maraschino cherries,
  chopped
Vanilla wafer crumbs
  (approx. 30)

Bring milk to boiling point and pour over marshmallows. Stir until melted—then add pineapple. When mixture is cool fold in bananas, cream, nuts and cherries. Line 8x8 baking dish with vanilla wafer crumbs. Save some crumbs to place on top. Pour fruit mixture in crumb lined pan. Top with vanilla wafer crumbs. Refrigerate until ready to serve.

Mrs. Bill Price (Kay)

Fruit Pizza

1 package Pillsbury refrigerated
  sugar cookies
1 (8-ounce) package cream
  cheese
½ cup sugar
1 teaspoon vanilla
Fresh, canned, or frozen fruit

Cut sugar cookies as directed on package. Rool into ⅛ inch slices and place on round pizza pan slightly overlapping. Bake 12 minutes at 375°. Beat cream cheese, sugar, and vanilla, then spread on cooled cookie crust. Top with fresh, canned, or frozen fruit. Bananas, pineapples, mandarin oranges, strawberries and blueberries are good!

Mrs. Bill Major (Patsy)

Hot Spiced Baked Apple With Double Cream

8 firm red apples
3 tablespoons sugar
1½ teaspoons cinnamon
2⅔ cups heavy cream
1 tablespoon vanilla
8 tablespoons sugar

Wash, dry, and core eight apples, then place in a shallow baking dish side by side. Sprinkle with sugar and cinnamon, and bake in a preheated 400° oven for 50-60 minutes. Remove from the oven, and place in heated bowls. Mix heavy cream, vanilla, and sugar, and pour ½ cup of mixture over each portion before serving. Serves 8.

Mrs. William H. Atkinson (Pam)

Lemon Fluff

1 (14½-ounce) can Pet Milk
(1¾ cups)
1 (4-ounce) package lemon jello
1¾ cups hot water
¼ cup lemon juice
1 cup sugar
2½ cups vanilla wafer crumbs
(crushed)

Chill milk in ice tray for 2-3 hours. Dissolve gelatin and chill until partially set. Whip gelatin until light and fluffy. Add lemon juice and sugar (slowly) and beat again. Now whip the chilled milk and fold into jello mixture. Line a large pan with crushed vanilla wafer crumbs and then pour in the above mixture. Chill in freezer until firm. Cut in squares to serve and add a lemon twist on top if desired.

Mrs. Tommy Nelson (Nancy)

Strawberries (or Grapes) In French Cream

1 cup heavy cream
⅓ cup powdered sugar
½ cup sour cream
½ teaspoon grated orange rind
2 pints strawberries (or grapes)

Beat cream until stiff. Fold in rest. Don't do too far in advance as may become runny.

Mrs. Tom Curlin (Betty)

Penny's Strawberry Bruleé

1 (8-ounce) package cream
  cheese
1½ cups sour cream
6 tablespoons sugar
2 pints fresh sliced strawberries
1 cup brown sugar

Beat cream cheese and sour cream until fluffy. Add sugar. In 9x13-inch dish layer strawberries and pour cream cheese mixture over them. Sprinkle brown sugar on top and put on bottom shelf of oven. Broil until bubbly.

Mrs. Jim Jenkins (Pam)

Strawberry Crêpes

3 egg yolks
¼ teaspoon vanilla
3 tablespoons melted butter
  or margarine
½ cup all-purpose flour
¼ cup sugar
½ cup milk
3 egg whites
Oil to brush pan
1 cup slivered almonds
1 cup brown sugar
8 small cartons frozen sliced
  strawberries

In a small bowl, beat together egg yolks and vanilla, stir in butter. Stir together all-purpose flour and sugar, add to egg yolk mixture alternately with milk, beating after each addition. In a large bowl, beat egg whites until stiff peaks form—gently fold batter mixture into egg whites. Brush a 6-inch skillet with oil. Spoon a rounded tablespoon batter into skillet—tilt skillet until batter runs to edges. Cook over medium high heat until underside is browned, maybe 45 seconds. Loosen edge and invert onto a paper towel. Continue cooking one crêpe at a time. Before cooking crêpes, whip one quart whipping cream. Make an assembly line with slivered almonds (approx. 1 cup), brown sugar, and defrosted sliced strawberries. As you finish each crêpe, open onto a plate, add about a tablespoon of strawberries and fold crêpe over. Add more strawberries on top, followed by generous amount of whipping cream and brown sugar. Top with slivered almonds.

Mrs. Jim Jenkins (Pam)

Wendy's Apple Kutchen

½ cup margarine or butter, softened
1 box Betty Crocker yellow cake mix
½ cup flaked coconut
1 can (21-ounce) pie sliced apples, well drained, or 2½ cups sliced pared baking apples
½ cup sugar
1 teaspoon cinnamon
1 cup dairy sour cream
2 egg yolks or 1 egg

Heat oven to 350°. Cut butter into dry cake mix until crumbly. Stir in coconut. Mix lightly together with fork in ungreased oblong pan, 13x9x2-inch. Bake 10 minutes. Arrange apple slices on warm crust. Mix sugar and cinnamon; sprinkle on apples. Blend sour cream and egg yolks; drizzle on apples. (Topping will not completely cover apples) Bake 25 minutes or until edges are light brown. Do not overbake. Serve warm. Serves 16.

Mrs. Gary Morrow (Rikki)

Sopapillas

4 cups flour
1 teaspoon salt
4 teaspoons baking powder
2 tablespoons shortening
1½ cups water
Shortening for frying

Sift flour with salt and baking powder. Work shortening into flour until well blended. Add enough water to make a soft dough, just slightly sticky. Knead well and let stand about 30 minutes before forming into round balls which are in turn rolled ⅛ inch thick. Fry the saucer-sized dough in deep hot fat (365°) until brown, dropping each sopapilla into the hottest part of the fat. Turn once. Drain.

Can roll in cinnamon and sugar while hot.

Mrs. Gary Morrow (Rikki)

This horseshoe-arch is a detail of the front porch of the Williams-Erwin Home which graces the cover of our book. The ball and spindle frieze is quite unusual. Below the horseshoe are turned wood posts joined by modified arches. We have chosen various features of this porch to decorate the pages of our cookbook — the symbol by the cooking hints we have interspersed in the pages of the book comes from the decoration along the top of the porch, and the corners and running head on each page of our book is the trim just below this on the side of the porch. Every opportunity for embellishment has been taken advantage of on this horseshoe-arch. It is easy to see why this style of architecture has come to be known as Gingerbread.

..."AND ALL THE TRIMMINGS"

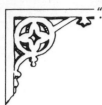

Hot Dill Pickles

Cucumbers
1 head and stem of dried
    dill/jar
1 clove garlic/jar
1 pepper pod/jar
1 cup salt
1 quart vinegar
3 quarts water

Pack cucumbers into hot jars. Add dill, garlic, and pepper to each jar. Combine salt, vinegar and water in saucepan. Bring to a boil over high heat. Cover cucumbers with boiling hot liquid, leaving ½-inch head-space. Seal jars and process in hot water bath for 20 minutes.

Mrs. John Stroope (Susan)

Sweet Green Tomato Pickles

7 pounds green tomatoes
    (about 28 medium sized),
    sliced thick
2½ cups pickling lime
2 gallons water
4 pounds sugar
1½ quarts vinegar
½ quart water
1 tablespoon salt
1 teaspoon celery seed
1½ teaspoons whole cloves
1½ tablespoons pickling
    spice
2 teaspoons crushed red
    pepper
2 teaspoons whole pepper
    corns

Soak tomatoes in solution of pickling lime in 2 gallons of water for 24 hours. (Must use enameled pan). Rinse well—each piece by hand—and soak again for 3 hours in clear water. Rinse again and soak over-night in mixture of sugar, vinegar, ½ quart of water salt, celery seed, whole cloves, pickling spices, red pepper, and pepper corns. Bring to boil and cook 35 minutes or until tomatoes are clear looking. Pack in hot jars and seal. Makes 12 quarts.

Hint: *Start around 3 or 4 in the after-noon to make your time come out right. Stir very little as they are brittle.*

Mrs. Rusty Marchman (Diann)

Squash Pickles

8 cups small squash, sliced
  thin
2 cups onion, sliced very thin
4 bell peppers, sliced
  (may use 1 red for color)
2 cups vinegar
3 cups sugar
2 teaspoons mustard seed
2 teaspoons celery seed
1 teaspoon turmeric

Combine squash, onions, and bell peppers in large bowl or pan. Salt lightly and let stand for 1 hour. Drain. Heat vinegar, sugar, and seasonings to a boil. Add raw vegetables and bring to a boil. Boil for about 5 minutes, remove from heat and pack, hot, into hot sterile jars, leaving ¼-inch head space. Adjust caps. Process 15 minutes in boiling water bath canner. Yield 4 pints.

Mrs. Kirk Brown (Ellen)

Cranberry-Orange Chutney

1 cup fresh orange sections
¼ cup orange juice
4 cups cranberries
2 cups sugar
1 cup chopped, unpeeled
  apple
½ cup raisins
¼ cup chopped walnuts
1 tablespoon vinegar
½ teaspoon ginger
½ teaspoon cinnamon
2 cups water

Combine all ingredients in a large saucepan and bring to a boil. Reduce heat and simmer 5 minutes or until berries begin to burst. Chill. Yield: 5½ cups.

Mrs. Bill Major (Patsy)

Peach Preserves

6 cups peaches, chopped
   or sliced
6 cups sugar
Juice of ½ lemon
2 cups liquid

Combine in a large pot. Cook over medium heat until boiling. Stir constantly. Boil until consistency you want, approximately 30 minutes. Pour into jars and seal.

Mrs. Pat Sullivan (Gloria)

Strawberry Preserves

2 quarts strawberries
5 cups sugar
½ cup lemon juice

Mix strawberries and sugar. Let stand 4 hours. Put on to boil. When full rolling boil is reached, continue boiling for 8 minutes. Add lemon juice and boil 2 minutes more. Pour into jars and seal.

Mrs. Pat Sullivan (Gloria)

Homemade Maple Syrup

½ cup sugar
1 cup Karo
1 cup water
Maple flavoring

Boil sugar, Karo and water together slowly until desired consistency and until sugar is dissolved. Add maple flavoring to taste.

This is handy to know when you run out of store-bought syrup, and it's fun, too.

Mrs. Mike Hayes (Eva)

Apple Glaze

½ cup sugar
Heaping tablespoon flour
Heaping tablespoon vinegar
½ cup water
Dash of salt

Cook ingredients until thick and transparent. Then add 1 tablespoon butter. Pour over chopped (peeled) apples (about 6-8 medium size) while mixture is still warm.

Mrs. Kirk Brown (Ellen)

Peach Sauce

1 can peaches, undrained
Dash of cinnamon
Dash of nutmeg
4 tablespoons sherry

Mix ingredients together and let set overnight in a sealed jar. Delicious over ice cream.

Mrs. Dwight Esselman (Ann)

Cranberry Sauce

2 cups frozen or fresh
   cranberries
1 cup water
½ cup granulated sugar
½ cup brown sugar
2 teaspoons cinnamon
1 teaspoon cloves
1 cup pecan halves

Combine berries, water, and granulated sugar in saucepan. Boil till berries pop. Stir in brown sugar, spices, and pecan halves. Cool. Yields 3 cups.

Mrs. Pleasant Mitchell (Helen)

Romanoff Sauce

1 quart sour cream
2 cups light brown sugar
⅛ teaspoon nutmeg
⅛ teaspoon cinnamon
1 tablespoon light rum or
   brandy

Mix all ingredients thoroughly and chill. Serve over fresh strawberries, or your favorite fresh fruit!

Mrs. David Ballard (Karen)

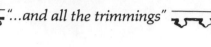

Praline Sauce

1 cup brown sugar
¼ cup Karo syrup
2 tablespoons butter
½ cup half and half
1 teaspoon vanilla
⅛ teaspoon salt
1 cup pecans, toasted

Put brown sugar, Karo, and butter in sauce pan over low heat. Once this is melted, add half and half and remaining ingredients. A favorite of the family when served over Blue Bell ice cream. Serves 4.

Mrs. Jack Price (Betty)

Microwave Hot Fudge Sauce

½ cup sugar
3 tablespoons cocoa
1½ tablespoons cornstarch
Dash of salt
½ cup water, room
  temperature
2 tablespoons butter
1 teaspoon vanilla

Mix together dry ingredients in a 1 quart casserole or a 2 cup glass measuring cup. Stir in water. Cook in microwave on HIGH, or full power, for 1½ minutes. Stir halfway through cooking time. Blend in butter. Cook on HIGH for 30 seconds, or until butter is melted. Stir halfway through cooking time. Blend in vanilla. Stir thoroughly. May be heated 15 to 30 seconds longer if a thicker sauce is desired. Yields 1 cup.

Mrs. Erling Holey (Susan)

Shrimp Sauce

2 parts catsup
1 part horseradish
Dash Worcestershire sauce
Dash lemon juice
Dash garlic salt

Mix all ingredients together, chill, and serve.

Mrs. Bobby Oliver (Emily)

Spicy Venison Sauce

1 cup margarine
½ cup fresh lemon juice
1 teaspoon salt
1 teaspoon pepper
2 tablespoons
  Worcestershire sauce
2 jalapeños, diced with seeds

Bring all ingredients to a boil and simmer 10 minutes.

Can be used as:
(1) An overnight basting sauce
(2) A basting sauce while cooking
(3) Use to reheat venison in foil—pour over and put in oven till warm.

Mrs. Kirk Brown (Ellen)

Pesto Sauce

2 cups packed fresh
  basil leaves
½ cup fresh parmesan cheese
½ teaspoon salt
2 cloves garlic, mashed
½ cup good olive oil

Combine all ingredients in a food processor. Will freeze. Use this to spice up meat dishes such as spaghetti, meatloaf, soup, stew, etc. May also use a small amount on fresh tomatoes.

Mrs. Jack Curlin (Nelda)

Bar-B-Que Sauce

¼ pound butter
½ cup vinegar
1 cup catsup
2 tablespoons Worcestershire
  sauce
¼ teaspoon hot sauce
4 tablespoons lemon juice
Salt and pepper to taste
½ cup brown sugar
1 chopped onion

Mix together and boil slowly for 5 minutes. Use over meat on grill for basting.

Mrs. Daryl Schliep (Gerrie)

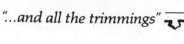

Remoulade Sauce

½ cup Crisco oil
¼ cup lemon juice
1 teaspoon chives
4 teaspoons horseradish
1 teaspoon paprika
1 teaspoon black pepper
1 teaspoon salt
3 tablespoons prepared
  mustard
1 teaspoon tabasco
1 teaspoon Worchestershire
  sauce
1½ cups chili sauce
½ cup chopped celery
2 green onions, including
  tops, chopped
3 cloves garlic, minced
1 tablespoon chopped dill
  pickle
1 tablespoon parsley
½ cup mayonnaise
1 tablespoon vinegar
1 cup olive oil
1½ tablespoons sugar

Add all ingredients together. Mix well. Add this to creole mustard. Use with shrimp.

Creole Mustard

¼ cup dry mustard
¼ teaspoon salt
½ teaspoon sugar
1/8 teaspoon white pepper
¼ teaspoon tabasco sauce
2 tablespoons mayonnaise
¼ teaspoon thyme
¼ teaspoon horseradish
1 teaspoon flour

Mix all together and add sufficient boiling water to make a thick paste. Mix well until smooth, pour in jar and cover. Mix creole mustard with Remoulade to make shrimp sauce.

Mrs Bill Major (Patsy)

Hot Pepper Jelly

1½ cups cider vinegar
5½ cups sugar
¾ cup green pepper
¾ cup hot pepper
1 plastic bag certo

Mix vinegar and sugar, set aside. In a blender chop green pepper and hot pepper (remove seeds first). Add to sugar mixture. Bring to rolling boil over high heat and boil for 15 minutes. Stir constantly. Add the certo, bring back to a full rolling boil and boil 1 minute. Remove from heat and set aside for 15 minutes. Pour into hot jars and seal. Makes 3 pints.

Hint: *wear rubber gloves when handling hot peppers.*

Mrs. Alvin Bynum (Jimmie Faye)

Creole Seasoning

1 (26-ounce) free flowing
   salt
½ (1½-ounce) can black
   pepper (optional)
1 (2-ounce) red pepper
1 (1-ounce) bottle pure garlic
   powder
1 (1-ounce) chili powder
1 (1-ounce) Accent
1 teaspoon powder thyme
1 teaspoon bay leaf
1 teaspoon sweet basil

Mix first six ingredients and use like salt. For seafood use half of mixture and add remaining 3 ingredients.

Mrs. Bill Major (Patsy)

Cathy's Shish-Kabobs Marinade

1 envelope Lipton's dry onion
  soup mix
2 tablespoons sugar
½ cup catsup
½ cup water
⅓ cup vinegar
⅓ cup salad oil
2-3 tablespoons dry mustard
1-2 teaspoon lemon juice

Mix all ingredients together in sauce pan and bring to a boil. Simmer 20 minutes. Cool completely. Add chunks of meat to be used in kabobs and cover tightly. Refrigerate at least six hours. Make your kabobs with whatever your family likes: onion, green pepper, mushrooms, cherry tomatoes, pineapple chunks, etc. Grill to desired doneness. Serves 6-8.

Mrs. Jim Jenkins (Pam)

 When packing a picnic lunch, put your catsup and mustard, pickles and olives, etc, in the cups of a muffin tin to make them easier to carry. This way you won't have to worry about carrying a lot of small jars and clean-up will be easier, too.

Waxahachie Junior Service League
P.O. Box 294
Waxahachie, Texas 75165

Send me _____ copies of **"GINGERBREAD...and all the trimmings"** at $13.95
per copy plus $2.00 postage and handling.
Enclosed is my check or money order for $ _____ .

Name _____

Street_____

City _____ State _____ Zip _____

Make check payable to Waxahachie Junior Service League.

Waxahachie Junior Service League
P.O. Box 294
Waxahachie, Texas 75165

Send me _____ copies of **"GINGERBREAD...and all the trimmings"** at $13.95
per copy plus $2.00 postage and handling.
Enclosed is my check or money order for $ _____ .

Name _____

Street_____

City _____ State _____ Zip _____

Make check payable to Waxahachie Junior Service League.

Waxahachie Junior Service League
P.O. Box 294
Waxahachie, Texas 75165

Send me _____ copies of **"GINGERBREAD...and all the trimmings"** at $13.95
per copy plus $2.00 postage and handling.
Enclosed is my check or money order for $ _____ .

Name _____

Street_____

City _____ State _____ Zip _____

Make check payable to Waxahachie Junior Service League.

Reorder Additional Copies